T0315147

Praise for *Mediation*

"In today's world we are called to be mediators in almost everything we do: mediation has become an essential aspect of true leadership and success. This book is a must read, not just for experts and practitioners, but also for whoever wants to foster inclusiveness and reciprocal understanding."

Enrico Letta, Dean of the Paris School of International Affairs and
former Prime Minister of Italy

"As evidenced in this book, mediation benefits all spheres of society. A prominent example is the use of mediation by patrol police officers, which infuses them with both problem-solving and attention to dignity. It promotes nonviolent positive interactions between citizens and police."

Christopher C. Cooper, Attorney, Mediator,
former Washington D.C. Police Officer & U.S. Marine Sergeant

"I always recommend this book to students, because the authors' complementary profiles and lenses account with talent and acuity for the peaceful and democratic uses of mediation."

Jacques Faget, Professor of Law and Sociology, University of Bordeaux

"Military chiefs have a duty to master the art of war, but also of mediation. Hundreds of officers from 120 countries benefitted from this book's principles and used them afterwards in operations."

Loïc Finaz, Vice-Admiral (Ret.), War College (France)

"For anyone interested in mediation or as a reference for experienced practitioners, this book is an accessible and complete resource written by seasoned and world-class mediators. Many EU diplomats and advisers have already benefited from its substance for more than a decade."

Antje Herrberg, Mediator, European External Action Service,
and founder of MediatEUr

"This thought-provoking book is an asset for those who are keen on achieving desired results in diplomatic mediation. It will guide a reader to success, even when the chances look remote."

Oleg Ivanov, Diplomatic Academy, Ministry of Foreign Affairs (Russia)

"Our mission is to support the capacity of Israelis, Palestinians and other regional actors to negotiate more effectively. We need to leverage the mediation methods of this book every day."

Ihab Khatib & Lior Frankiensztajn, Executive Directors, Negotiation Strategies Institute,
Jerusalem-based NGO

"If you love French cuisine, Escoffier's *Guide to Modern Cookery* has been a reference for 100 years. If you are more into mediation, from now on, you can turn to *Mediation*. It is an outstanding collection of everything practical you need to know: from scanning the landscape, preparing the grounds, deciding on principles, to leading through the ups and downs of mediation, preventing mistakes and getting your value systems right."

Peter Maurer, President of the International Committee of the Red Cross

"How might mediators facilitate the resolution of conflict by empowering the parties themselves to negotiate more effectively? Both academics and practitioners need this book: after surveying existing mediation practices and outlining relevant principles it provides thoughtful advice on how best to structure the mediation process and promote the parties' better understanding of their conflict and develop and assess alternative solutions."

Robert Mnookin, Mediator and Law Professor,
Harvard Law School and Program on Negotiation

"This book is essential for mediators and staff working in humanitarian, development, peace and security contexts. Having spent over 30 years with the United Nations in emergencies in Somalia, Rwanda, Burundi, Gaza, Iraq, and Syria, I have witnessed the consequences of conflicts. Today's world needs mediation both for prevention and conflict resolution. My one take-away from the book is that mediation is an art, a skill that one needs to practice and can learn. I highly recommend this book."

Panos Moumtzis, United Nations Assistant Secretary General;
Executive Director, Global Executive Leadership Initiative, and
former Humanitarian Coordinator for the Syria crisis

"As a negotiation adviser, I have often observed the critical importance of responsible mediation. This brilliant book offers the secret keys to delivering success for all sides."

Kalypso Nicolaïdis, Professor of International Relations,
Oxford University and European University Institute

"Without appropriate knowledge and preparation, mediation efforts often fail. The authors optimize the whole mediation process."

Tetsushi Okumura, Professor of Management, Toyo University (Tokyo)

"The very subtitle of this wise and comprehensive guide—*Mediation: Negotiation by Other Means*—reveals a deep and unusual understanding of the intimate relationship of two important processes that are normally treated as wholly separate. Drawing on significant research and extensive experience across multiple continents, this distinguished international group of co-authors will valuably enlighten readers who seek to employ this powerful third-party method of conflict resolution and management."

James K. Sebenius, Professor at Harvard Business School and Director,
Harvard Negotiation Project

"With rising conflicts in today's world, mediation is needed more than ever. Here is a lucid and insightful book on the contemporary practice of mediation, highly practical and usefully illustrated with a range of good examples. It is a genuine pleasure to recommend this excellent book to students, professional mediators, and indeed anyone who practices mediation informally, in other words, most of us."

William Ury, co-author, Getting to Yes, and author, The Third Side

MEDIATION

MEDIATION

NEGOTIATION BY OTHER MOVES

ALAIN LEMPEREUR

JACQUES SALZER

AURÉLIEN COLSON

MICHELE PEKAR

EUGENE B. KOGAN

WILEY

This edition first published 2021.

© 2021 by Alain Lempereur, Jacques Salzer, Aurélien Colson, Michele Pekar, and Eugene B. Kogan

Registered office
John Wiley & Sons Ltd, The Atrium, Southern Gate, Chichester, West Sussex, PO19 8SQ, United Kingdom

For details of our global editorial offices, for customer services and for information about how to apply for permission to reuse the copyright material in this book please see our website at www.wiley.com.

Wiley publishes in a variety of print and electronic formats and by print-on-demand. Some material included with standard print versions of this book may not be included in e-books or in print-on-demand. If this book refers to media such as a CD or DVD that is not included in the version you purchased, you may download this material at http://booksupport.wiley.com. For more information about Wiley products, visit www.wiley.com.

Designations used by companies to distinguish their products are often claimed as trademarks. All brand names and product names used in this book are trade names, service marks, trademarks or registered trademarks of their respective owners. The publisher is not associated with any product or vendor mentioned in this book.

Limit of Liability/Disclaimer of Warranty: While the publisher and author have used their best efforts in preparing this book, they make no representations or warranties with respect to the accuracy or completeness of the contents of this book and specifically disclaim any implied warranties of merchantability or fitness for a particular purpose. It is sold on the understanding that the publisher is not engaged in rendering professional services and neither the publisher nor the author shall be liable for damages arising herefrom. If professional advice or other expert assistance is required, the services of a competent professional should be sought.

Library of Congress Cataloging-in-Publication Data

Names: Lempereur, Alain, author. | Salzer, Jacques, author. | Colson,
    Aurélien, author. | Pekar, Michele, author. | Kogan, Eugene B., author.
Title: Mediation : negotiation by other moves / Alain Lempereur, Jacques
    Salzer, Aurélien Colson, Michele Pekar, Eugene B. Kogan.
Description: Chichester, West Sussex, United Kingdom : Wiley, 2021. |
    Includes bibliographical references and index.
Identifiers: LCCN 2021008530 (print) | LCCN 2021008531 (ebook) | ISBN
    9781119768425 (cloth) | ISBN 9781119805366 (adobe pdf) | ISBN
    9781119805359 (epub)
Subjects: LCSH: Mediation.
Classification: LCC K2390 .L46 2021 (print) | LCC K2390 (ebook) | DDC
    303.6/9—dc23
LC record available at https://lccn.loc.gov/2021008530
LC ebook record available at https://lccn.loc.gov/2021008531

Cover Design: Wiley

Set in 11/14pt MinionPro by SPi Global, Chennai, India

Printed and bound by CPI Group (UK) Ltd, Croydon, CR0 4YY

C9781119768425_240321

I say nothing to one that I cannot say to the other, at the right time, with only a slight difference in emphasis and I report only the things that are indifferent, or known, or serve both in common. There is no reason for which I would permit myself to lie to them.

Michel de Montaigne, *The Essays*, 794B

CONTENTS

ACKNOWLEDGMENTS

We thank all the women and men who have contributed to the theory and practice of mediation all over the world: mentors, colleagues, friends, researchers, and thousands of mediators and participants in seminars who influenced the content of this book.

We are indebted to our mentors and the pioneers: Graham Allison, Michel Barnier, Béatrice Blohorn-Brenneur, Jean-Pierre Bonafe-Schmitt, Jeanne Brett, Guy Canivet, Hervé Cassan, Pierre Drai, Jacques Faget, Roger Fisher, Thomas Fiutak, Steve Goldberg, AJR Groom, Michèle Guillaume-Hofnung, Serge Guinchard, Charles Jarrosson, Hans Kelman, Etienne Le Roy, Jean-Claude Magendie, Peter Maurer, Michel Meyer, Bob Mnookin, Christopher Moore, Jacqueline Morineau, Mirko Nikolic, Bruno Oppetit, Gérard Pluyette, Simone Rozes, Frank Sander, Jim Sebenius, Jean-François Six, Alan and Ari Slifka, Howard Stevenson, Larry Susskind, Sid Topol, Hubert Touzard, Bill Ury, Keith Webb, Andy Williams, Howard Wolpe, and Yvan Zakine.

This book would not have seen the light of day but for our colleagues and friends: the members of the Harvard Program on Negotiation, IRENE at ESSEC, the Kellogg Dispute Resolution Research Center, the Oxford Programme on Negotiation, including Liliane de Andrade, Myriam Bacqué, Stephen Bensimon, Christian Blanc, Linda Benraïs, Jean-Michel Blanquer, Bob Bordone, Claude Bruderlein, Nicholas Burns, Tessa Byer, Paola Cecchi-Dimeglio, Erica Chenoweth, Alain Christnacht, Christopher Cooper, Tim Cullen, Jared Curhan, Jocelyn Dahan, Owen Darbishire, Florrie Darwin, Pierre Debaty, Laurence de Carlo, Jacques Dercourt, Bruno Dupré, Martin Euwema, Luc Fauconnet, Lorraine Fillion, Pamina Firchow, Paul Fisher, Mari Fitzduff, Lior Frankiensztajn, Gary Friedman,

ACKNOWLEDGMENTS

Bruno-André Giraudon, Don Greenstein, Jean-Édouard Grésy, Jérôme Grimaud, Eric Guérin, Susan Hackley, Sheila Heen, Sophie Henry, Antje Herberg, Jocelyne Hervé, Jack Himmelstein, David Hoffman, Sergio Jaramillo Caro, Isabella Jean, Alan Jenkins, Ted Johnson, Sandra Jones, Peter Kamminga, Michel Noureddine Kassa, James Kerwin, Ihab Khatib, Marc Kiredjian, Anne Landois, Enrico Letta, Justin Lêvecque, Maria Madison, Joseph Maïla, Patricia Malbosc, Francesco Marchi, Liz McClintock, Gerry McHugh, Oliver McTernan, Philip Milburn, Jordan Morgan, Nicolas Mottis, Anaide Nahikian, Kalypso Nicolaïdis, Eugene Nindorera, Fabien Nsengimana, Charlotte Pailleux, Ricardo Perez Nuckel, Gabrielle Planes, Bill Rapp, Jim Reiman, Herve Remaud, Tina Robiolle, Monique Sassier, Veronique Schneider, Dan Shapiro, Linda Singer, Marianne Souquet, Guhan Subramanian, Arnaud Stimec, Christian Thuderoz, Joëlle Timmermans-Delwart, Emmanuel Tronc, Michael VanRooyen, David Weil, and Andreas Wenger.

We thank Fiona P. Noonan for her contribution to the translation and to our researchers and assistants: Julianna Brill, Lara Cazemajou, Jacee Cox, Katherine DeCourcy, Michael Dumont, Autumn Galindo, Sarah LaMorey, Cécile Seguineaud, and Elise Willer.

Finally, we thank our colleagues, participants, and mediators in various institutions: Brandeis University, College of Europe, ENA, Ecole Polytechnique, Essec Business School, European Commission, European Institute of Peace, European Peacebuilding Liaison Office, European University Institute, United States Institute of Peace, Alliance for Peacebuilding, International Association for Conflict Management, Harvard University, Sciences Po-Paris, French Ministry of Foreign Affairs, Saïd Business School – Oxford University, UNITAR, various universities, and mediation associations.

INTRODUCTION
Why Do We Need Mediation Methods?

Mediation includes four key concepts that will form the basis of this book: *conflict*, *authority*, *the other*, and *methods*. Let us explore these terms and how they interconnect with the purpose of this book.

Conflict

Conflict is an inevitable dimension of life. First, we all experience inner conflicts between antagonistic aspirations of different parts of our identity. Second, when we bring together groups of individuals, tensions may arise for many reasons: clashes of values and norms, resource allocation, definition or interpretation of rules, reward and sanction mechanisms, etc. Many causes trigger a conflict, which can deepen over time.

On the positive side, *conflict is creative*; it helps reveal how obsolete or unfair certain social arrangements might be. It expresses frustration in the face of perceived or experienced injustice, prolonged oppression, and denial of identity. Conflict provokes new questioning, shakes up established routines, inefficient returns, and can spur innovation. American civil rights activist Septima Poinsette Clark (1898–1987) has remarked: "I have great belief in the fact that whenever there is chaos, it creates wonderful thinking. I consider chaos a gift." Conflict is the engine at the heart of "creative destruction" theorized by economist Joseph Schumpeter (1942). This is the bright side of conflict.

But, on the other hand, *conflict is also destructive*. Waged among groups – countries, organizations, businesses – and individuals, conflict endangers solidarity, cooperation, and mutual exchange; and thrives on selfishness, competition, and self-righteousness. Conflict often generates aggression and inflicts suffering. It has a built-in escalation dynamic – whoever is blamed first is provoked to retaliate, feeding a new assault of greater intensity that causes an even more massive counterattack, and so forth. Each side often looks to dominate and crush the other, while imposing their solution. As damages and victims accumulate, relationships shatter, identities are denied, time is lost, and resources are squandered. Conflict takes a deep emotional toll (e.g. sadness, anger, suffering) and inflicts significant material damages (e.g. wasted resources, property destruction). In the sphere of armed conflict, an even more detrimental result of conflict is the violation of human integrity and dignity (e.g. injuries, rape, death, massacre, and genocide).

This ambivalent reality of conflict – a powerful engine of change, but also an agent of destruction – creates concerns that all human societies address: how to manage conflicts? How to prevent them, mitigate them, resolve them, and even transform them? And who should intervene? This brings us to our next point.

Authority

Conflict resolution systems are often founded on authority. In private life, parents have the authority over their children and over the rules to address familial conflict. In organizations, the upper level has "formal" authority – drawing on the official title or position in the hierarchy – to settle conflicts at the lower levels. In society, overall, the law, in distinguishing between what is legal or not, makes each person part of a system of conflict prevention and regulation. If, despite everything, two parties are in conflict about the interpretation of a legal norm, the judge is there to decide with all the authority conferred upon them by the law. In each case above, authorities are entrusted with the role of ending the conflict.

But authority shows its limits in contemporary society, owing to a combination of factors, including the rise of individualism; the erosion of moral, or religious, norms; the decline, renewal, or rejection of traditional authority figures – the father, instructor, professor, priest, police officer, etc.; the growing influence of liberalism and its deregulation; the democratization of societies and decision-making systems; an increased transparency and questioning of hierarchy in organizations (i.e. "flat organization"); the decline of Fordist business as a bureaucratic organization; the contestation of legitimacies – scholarly, scientific, technical, legal, administrative – and biases – patriarchy, gender, race, ethnicity, sexual orientation – and, in return, the rise of participative mechanisms of consultation, dialogue, and negotiation.

The First Move: A Negotiator's Companion (Lempereur and Colson, ed. by Pekar 2010) summarized the tendency of this vast sociological movement: "impose less and propose more." In conflict management, whatever the context, the involved parties hardly accept a solution imposed on them by an outside authority. There is, everywhere, a growing desire to stay in control of one's life, plans, and trajectory – including one's conflict and its settlement.

The rise of negotiation as a mode of joint decision-making aligns with this shift away from unilateral, top-down diktat. But what happens when negotiation fails and the parties are unable to define an agreement that satisfies both of them? One possibility is to fall back on an authority – a boss or a judge. Another is to invite a third party – neutral, impartial, and benevolent – to reignite negotiations, facilitate the exchanges, and empower the parties to explore the conflict, bring their essential needs to the surface, imagine possible solutions, evaluate them, and finally choose those to which they freely and mutually commit. This is, in a few words, what mediation stands for: it offers a *pursuit of negotiation by other moves*. It reinforces a trend where *the law is first the law of the people* (Lempereur 2011a, 2011c).

A mediator is *not* an authority per se. They do not have the power to make decisions. They do not coerce, choose favorites, and very rarely impose limits. On the contrary, they always seek to empower the parties. They facilitate, encourage, and motivate. Theirs is a strange art: the parties accept their presence at the negotiating table precisely because they have no formal authority over them. This is why, when mediation succeeds, the parties are more likely to recognize the agreement that they themselves produced – with the mediator's support – and discover the strength of this process of third party's facilitated negotiation, and its profound legitimacy.

The Other

Faced with conflict and rejecting the presence of an external authority does not necessarily mean that individually each party has full power to shape the outcome. The parties need to work together, and their cooperation constitutes an inescapable variable in the equation: as much as the parties are part of the problem, they are also part of the solution. Each party cannot ignore the other, just as the other cannot ignore them. Each owns a part of the story, likely contributed to what happened, and is therefore asked to feel responsible for overcoming the conflict.

This is why "the other" constitutes a fundamental theme in this book. In fact, putting the other at the heart of the exchange is essential for

- *each of the parties in conflict*, who can develop empathy toward the other, i.e. put themselves in the other's shoes, so that both sides engage back and forth in a double move toward mutual understanding, where (i) each understands the other better and (ii) each is better understood by the other;

- *the mediator*, who, instead of seizing ownership of the conflict, preserves both parties' control of their conflict and its resolution, through reciprocal recognition of the "two others" and hopefully by each other.

The mediator plays an intermediary role between the two "others." The centrality of the other is evoked in the

- *past*, a time of conflict, ignorance, or condemnation of the other, with different perceptions and opposing visions of "this" radically different other, separation and alienation from the other, creation of negative otherness;

- *present*, a time of mediation, which facilitates a dialogue between the two estranged others, allowing them to analyze the similarities and differences between them in their narratives, in order to foster a mutual recognition of identities and needs, where each "other" might come back in renewed proximity with one another, and where this possible restored link builds some readiness to explore solutions;

- *future*, which may still be uncertain but which can be built together by creating a common ground for a renewed relationship, one where the other is not simply *present* with me, but where the other sees themselves as having a *future* with me in it.

Integrating the other happens through deepening understanding, which requires active perceiving, i.e. a methodical use of listening and looking, and probing – which everyone thinks they practice well, but which can often be improved. The mediator's display of skilled understanding of the two parties is often the platform that enables both of them to understand each other.

Methods

Everyone can improvise and play the role of a mediator, and some perform it well: between one's brothers and sisters, between one's parents and relatives in a dispute, and between classmates, or friends, or colleagues at work. Chapter 2 addresses the question of "informal mediators."

The fact remains that, except for limited cases, effective mediation is rarely well founded on *instinct only*. There is no doubt that some people are more gifted at empathy than others. They might be seen as naturals in benevolent listening. However, they may not employ some fundamental tools of inquiry and probing, or restating that the mediator needs to master before running a session. Learning such tools on the job or by trial and error can be a slow process, and, worst of all, sometimes the consequence of avoidable failure. Mediation is therefore a matter of *methods*: principles and good practices exist, tools are available, techniques are checked, traps are identified – all forming a practical body that everyone can acquire and implement (Lempereur, Salzer, and Colson 2007). As mediation experience grows, such methods need to be tested, refined, and adjusted in an ongoing circle of learning.

Our book integrates both methods and experience. As academics and mediators in the field, including in high-stress/-stakes/-impact environments, we combine knowledge and know-how, as we have practiced and refined them over decades through a worldwide practice for international organizations, governments, NGOs, and corporations. As a result, the models, tools, and examples this book proposes develop several possible methods for mediation. We hope this book will be

- *helpful*, whether you are a potential or a professional mediator, an involved party, a lawyer, an adviser, or a stakeholder;

- *practical* (but not simplistic), as it offers operational principles; it raises real problems, and proposes concrete solutions;

- *subtle* (but not abstruse), as it invites self-awareness, persistent reflection, a capacity to review actions, and change course;

- *comprehensive*, as it approaches *mediation in general, as a process,* in what is applicable to most types of mediation – diplomatic, family, criminal, consumer, labor, corporate, etc. – even if each domain has its specificities (Lempereur 1999b, 1999d);

- *specific*, because it is a book that opens to every reader the possibility of choosing the moves and tools adapted to their needs, experience, and context – to build their own mediation path.

Writing this book is also a part of a broader objective that transcends the dimensions of a single book. It is about helping to reverse a paradoxical trend: Why is mediation still so little practiced around the world while its potential is so great? Although many organizations utilize third-party facilitators, mediation remains a relatively little-used mechanism compared with the plethora of cases in court. Maybe there is not yet, despite the advocacy efforts, enough accessible information on what, concretely, mediation offers: how is a decision made, what are its advantages and limits, how it unfolds, what are its phases, what is a mediator's role, what can the parties expect, etc.?

This is what this book proposes to share with the reader, so that more people, according to their circumstances, consider mediation a useful approach to overcome a conflict or even wish to become mediators themselves.

An Overview of the Book

Chapter 1—*The Perimeter* gives you an overview of existing mediation practices. What is the scope of mediation today? Whether they are informal, temporary, or institutional, or whatever their areas of action, mediators develop an increasing space in many sectors of life: personal, social, economic, administrative, and political. We paint a landscape of these activities, illustrating a wide variety of practices and models. This chapter highlights some variables of differentiation – before and during mediation – along with some guidelines for practice.

Faced with this diverse reality, **Chapter 2** explores the *Pertinence* of mediation. What are its advantages and limits? In what situations should one choose mediation as a mode of action to resolve a conflict? Besides mediation, we present seven third-party approaches that offer complementary wisdoms in the face of conflict. We also analyze two series of criteria that favor mediation: the first lists blockages that freeze the present; the second turns toward the potential of mediation for a renewed future among the parties.

What are some fundamental guidelines that mediators need to keep in mind to guarantee the quality of the process? **Chapter 3** examines seven *Principles* of mediation: independence, neutrality, impartiality, fairness, confidentiality, respect for the law, and self-determination of the parties. As we clarify these essential principles for practice, we also underscore possible tensions among them and how to address them. For example, how do we remain neutral while supporting the fairness of an agreement? How do we combine confidentiality and respect for the law?

Chapter 4 considers the *Preparation* of mediation sessions, beginning with pre-mediation. Whether one is a mediator, involved party, or adviser, we prepare the essential elements before mediation. How to propose, refuse, accept, or, if necessary, impose a mediation? How to choose mediators? What does a "contract to mediate" ahead of a session look like? Whom to convene for a mediation? How, concretely, to prepare as a party or as a mediator? What modes of intervention to choose? And how to arrange the place where mediation happens? There are many questions – strategic, operational, or simply practical – to prepare for.

As we contemplate a mediation session, **Chapter 5** lays out what we call the *PORTAL*, i.e. the introductory six initial moves to connect and to structure the mediation process:

- *Presentation:* Establish contact between the parties and mediator.

- *Objectives* of mediation: Clarify what mediation is and is not; what the mediator's role will be, and what the mediator expects from the parties.

- *Rules:* Explain the guiding *principles* for the process, and obtain the agreement of the parties on them.

- *Time & Steps:* Verify the availability of the parties, the calendar, and the completion date, and also outline the successive next phases in the mediation process.

- *Agreement:* Check one last time that the parties have agreed to proceed as outlined.

- *Launch:* Start the work on the conflict, the substance of the mediation.

The book then devotes two chapters to the methods that apply to the next phases in mediation. The first one concerns understanding the problems of the past, while the second seeks workable solutions for the future.

Problem-solving in **Chapter 6** explores the **Past Toward the Present.** Before venturing to resolve a conflict, we need to explore its background. Inquiring, probing, and restating, as well as managing emotions, become indispensable tools to explore. This stage of the process involves three successive moves, which sometimes overlap:

1. *Identify the Problems*: Invite each party to tell their story of the conflict and raise their key requests.
2. *Deepen Our Understanding of the Problems:* Through deep probing and understanding of the respective narratives and positions, try to spot the underlying needs, motivations, or interests that are essential to each party.
3. *Mutual Understanding:* Work on reciprocal recognition of the causes of the conflict and of the current needs of the parties.

Problem-solving in **Chapter 7** leads from the **Present Toward the Future**. Once mutual understanding of the root causes of the problems and of each other's needs has been reached, the mediation then focuses on how to build solutions and scenarios in the future to meet the needs identified in the present. Here, three successive moves are useful:

1. *Invent Solutions:* Brainstorm as many solutions as possible. How to come up with solutions for oneself and for the other in terms of quantity and quality? Here, the techniques of value creation and creativity will be presented, as well as possibilities for the mediator to suggest ideas.
2. *Evaluate Solutions:* Formulate justification criteria to filter solutions that might work for both parties.
3. *Decide:* If possible, summarize and formalize a reciprocal commitment, for which the next move is to ensure follow-up.

The end of every mediation session focuses on the process of the next steps, and on the appreciation of people's engagement, whether they have reached agreement or not. US President Barack Obama used to say, "hard things are hard." Successful mediation is no exception, and there will likely be numerous obstacles on the way. How to foresee and fix – or, at least, manage – them?

The final chapter, **Chapter 8**, explores potential *Pitfalls,* traps that the mediator needs to manage no matter how they emerged. Some mediators may have good intentions, but their instinctive behaviors can have negative, unintended consequences. We present probable causes of such behaviors and their risks, while suggesting practical approaches to avoid them. Other problems stem from the behaviors of one or both parties. Again, some of their moves, they believe, will serve their interests, but actually end up damaging the very process of mediation. Other challenges arise in spite of the parties' efforts. This chapter proposes methods for the mediator to overcome these critical moments in the interaction with the parties.

Our **Conclusion** illustrates the close links between questioning and ethics in the mediator's role. It suggests more than just a technique, but rather a philosophy for oneself and the other, for the mediator and the parties.

A final point on the book's format concerning examples:

Examples

Throughout the book, whenever we offer examples – either inspired from documented events or from the authors' experiences – to illustrate a point, we will use this indented stylistic layout.

○ **We also add under this format practical suggestions or formulations that serve as an inspiration to help mediators develop their own methods.**

May this book help mediators, parties, stakeholders, and everyone else facilitate the peaceful, constructive, and productive resolution of conflicts. Happy and impactful reading!

CHAPTER 1
THE PERIMETER
Explore Existing Mediation Practices *Before* Seeking Methods

Before proposing a mediation method, it seems important to offer an inventory of existing practices, which will give us the opportunity to explore the breadth and richness of mediation. After a brief tour of the origins of the word, this chapter will examine the multiple instances – informal, ad hoc, or institutional – which contribute to the current mediation culture. Examining numerous mediation examples, this chapter argues that a great diversity of practices can inspire us in the service of the peaceful resolution of conflicts.

The Origins of a Practice and Its Words

Ancient Sources

Historical texts enlighten us on the ancient use of mediation practices. Research (Cardinet 1997) shows that the written history of mediation started around 500 BCE. Notably, the word *mesites* written on papyrus refers to Mitra, half-god and half-man, thus creating a link between humanity and the divine. Further, in his *Constitution for Athens,* Aristotle notes that Solon is a reconciler between two camps. In the second century CE, *mesites* was translated into Latin as "mediator." Human beings, as individuals or belonging to groups of varying social organizations, needed to determine who would "intermediate" among them, and between them, God, and the universe.

1

This is how Christian theology offers one of the first uses of the term, with Jesus as "mediator between God and mankind" (I Timothy 2:5). In 1265, the word *mediateur* first appears in French in Jean de Meung's *Le Roman de la Rose*. In 1382, borrowed from the Latin word *immediatus*, appears the word *immédiat* meaning "direct and without intermediary"; in 1478, the word *médiat*, from the Latin *mediatus*, is used to refer to an indirect action. With the meaning of "intermediary intended to reconcile persons or parties," the French use of the word *mediateur* dates to the sixteenth century. The word *mediation* recalls Old English *midd* for "middle." In 1540, it meant "divide in two equal parts." By the middle of the seventeenth century, the meaning was "occupy a middle place or position." The "act as a mediator, intervene for the purpose of reconciliation" likely hails from 1610, while "settle by mediation, harmonize, reconcile" is probably from the mid-1500s (Online Etymology Dictionary 2020). In 1694, the term *mediation* appears in the dictionary of the French Academy. It is then used widely, even in literature such as in La Fontaine's fable "Vultures and Pigeons": "*They tried their hand at mediation / To reconcile the foes, or part*" (La Fontaine 1668, Fable VIII, 7th book).

Wicquefort or the old and difficult *"status of mediator"*

A diplomat born in Holland, Abraham de Wicquefort (1606–1682) closely observed seventeenth century diplomacy during the 1648 Congress of Westphalia. In 1680–1681, he published *The Ambassador and His Functions*, a scholarly analysis of this profession, which was then in full expansion. Illustrating how established was the practice of mediation between sovereign powers, section XI of volume 2 is entitled *"Of mediation and ambassadors-mediators."* Wicquefort already saw the difficulty of the task: "*The status of mediator is one of the most difficult for the ambassador to bear, and mediation is one of his most unpleasant tasks.*"

More recently, the Convention for the Pacific Settlement of International Disputes, signed at The Hague in 1907, had for its main objective in

Part I: *"The Maintenance of General Peace."* The path to be preferred for this purpose was specified in Part II: *"Good Offices and Mediation."*

Mediation has been a research topic for a long time already. In France, research on mediation dates from the beginning of the twentieth century. A bibliography on the period 1945–1959 contains some 572 references of books and articles (Meynaud and Schroeder 1961). These writings and works relate mainly to mediation in labor relations and collective conflicts, but also in international relations.

The Meaning of a Word

Mediation, in the etymological sense, is constituted by a space, a time, an object, a language, or an intermediary person who opposes the dangers of immediacy – which might lead to overreaction and spiraling confrontation. Historically, mediation holds two distinct meanings, the second of which forms the subject of this book:

- *An intercession, or intervention in favor of another whom we represent.* This is the case, for instance, when a single real estate agency acts as the mediator between the seller of a home and potential buyers. The word retains the meaning of a "reciprocal" intercession for all parties.

- *An impartial external intervention, offered to (and/or requested by) conflicting parties, to organize exchanges with a view to building mutually acceptable solutions.*

Mediators, moderators, facilitators, neutrals, go-betweens, third parties, ombuds: there are many terms, but they refer to the same situation: the presence of an intermediary – a person or a group of people – who intervenes between two or more parties in conflict, seeking to facilitate negotiation between them with a view to arriving at a peaceful solution agreed by them. For Wicquefort, *"the word mediator fairly well expresses [the] function: it consists properly in putting oneself in the middle to bring together the parts that have moved away."* To designate the act of mediation

3

itself, the verb "to mediate" is commonplace in English, while the French modern equivalent – *médier* – remains seldom used.

Mediators: An Overview of Current Practices

As a starting point, let us list key variables for the diversity of mediation practices:

- *Time:* Mediation can be preventive, post-conflict, or even post-litigation (for example, to support the implementation of the judge's decision in family or criminal matters – also called post-sentencing).

- *Areas:* This refers to areas where the existence of mediation is identified and named, from family to schools, from neighborhood to work, from corporate to environmental or international.

- *Objectives:* Relational, facilitative, restorative, and curative. There are even decision-making objectives that move away from the creation of agreements by the parties themselves, in order, above all, to reach a decision: evaluative mediation (with the objective of evaluation in the light of the law; Fruchter 2019) and mediation-arbitration, or "Med-Arb" (Baril and Dickey 2014; Bickerman 2018), where it is expected that mediators will become arbitrators or pass the case to arbitrators, thus ensuring a certainty of settlement, accepted in advance by the parties.

- *Number of actors:* Personal or collective (team, large group, country).

  Without claiming to be exhaustive, this section will review *who* may be involved in mediating, as well as *where* and *how* these mediators operate. Three main categories stand out: informal, ad hoc, and institutional mediators.

Informal Mediators

These mediators may not call themselves mediators, but do engage in mediation or an activity very close to it. They could be anyone who, in everyday life, helps parties to listen and understand each other and co-create a solution to which everyone agrees. Here is a glimpse of the variety of these informal mediators:

- *A student:* Between classmates.

- *A teacher:* Between students, colleagues, parents and teachers, teachers and students.

- *An office colleague, boss, union official, or staff representative:* Between people at work, with customers or suppliers.

- *An agent, broker, or representative:* Stepping in at a given moment as an objective facilitator, and not as a defender of a particular cause.

- *A solicitor:* Between the parties in conflict.

- *A local elected representative:* Between their constituents, between the latter and economic actors or the government.

- *A governor:* Between local and federal public authorities, or between two local authorities, or in their relations with economic actors.

- *A policeman or policewoman:* Between two conflicting spouses, between squatters and owners of the premises, between protesters from opposite sides (Cooper 2003).

- *A member of the military during a peacekeeping mission, or a humanitarian in crisis:* Between belligerents, between the latter and the civilian population.

This list highlights numerous roles, functions, and professions that involve informal moments of mediation. According to a strict definition of mediation, only people outside and independent of the parties are considered as mediators. But in reality, mediation is employed by a range of people (as above) and occupies a much larger role as a method to pacify relationships or solve a particular problem. Rather than being in a position of authority or adviser or negotiator in their own name with their own motivations, informal mediators do not intervene for their own interests or to favor one side over the other. However, there is always a slight risk of sliding into other forms of intervention, such as arbitration. This is why mediation, as elaborated in this book, calls for professionalism, principles, ethics – methods, even though it is sometimes legitimate and useful that everyone can, on occasion and without formality, serve as a mediator.

The concerned parties need to accept the mediator as such, as well as the mediator's approach to mediation. In informal mediation, most often, the mediator intervenes without formal acceptance for their role: mediation remains implicit, taking place even without the parties being aware of it. In cases where the process is more explicit, if an informal mediator presents themselves with a sincere desire to settle a problem which is not theirs and which has weighed on the parties for some time, and if the parties trust the mediator to understand both sides, the mediator will be welcomed and appreciated. Thus, if informal mediators have acquired the know-how, they can sincerely and efficiently leverage the potential of mediation. But it is not enough for mediators to show their good will: the parties need to also accept them, at least implicitly, in this role. Sometimes the parties may prefer to receive advice or obtain a decision ruled by an authority, or may not want anyone to interfere in a conflict that they prefer to settle themselves.

Let us now explore two major models of "formal" mediators, which are designated and considered as such by the parties involved.

Ad Hoc Mediators

On particular occasions, an external third party is responsible for helping the parties find a solution to the specific conflict between them.

Who will be in charge of the price of raw materials?

A long-term contract guarantees the prices at which a multinational company supplies certain raw materials to another company. The contract covers the quantities and prices – around one billion dollars over five years. The price of these raw materials soars on the markets, to exceed by more than 30% the price set in the original contract. The producing company requests that the selling price be reassessed accordingly. The buyer refuses, relying on the long-term commitment made in the initial contract: proposing an increase of only 4%. The disagreement lasts several months. On both sides, lawyers prepare for trials; everyone believes they can convince the judge. However, mediation is finally accepted. A few sessions, over a two-week period, lead to an intermediate price reassessment, the setting of minimum purchase quantities, and a revision clause for periodic price increases or decreases, depending on the market conditions. Mediation has allowed each company to continue their commercial relationship without market fluctuations becoming a burden.

It is better for the parties to spontaneously agree on the profile and name of a third party, but sometimes an external authority – the public administration, a judge, a common hierarchical superior – designates a mediator with the parties accepting, *nolens volens*, this choice. The main characteristic of ad hoc mediators is that they halt their operations at the end of their mission.

Mediators: Doomed to Disappear ... or to Serve as Scapegoats

Boutros Boutros-Ghali, then Secretary-General of the United Nations, commented on his experience as a mediator in international conflicts: *"If your mediation succeeds, you must disappear because the [conflicting]*

States will say that they have been able to solve their problems alone; and if your mediation fails, you must agree in advance to serve as a scapegoat. I am used to it. I have done this all my life ..." (Boutros-Ghali 1995).

There are many areas where ad hoc mediators intervene, on a private basis, on behalf of a principal or within the framework of mediation centers, from global issues to the most modest disputes (Bensimon and Lempereur 2007).

- *International relations:* During a political crisis or armed conflict, a special envoy is appointed by the United Nations, or a regional organization (African Union, Arab League, European Union) in order to promote reconciliation (Mitchell and Webb 1988; Faget 2010; Colson and Lempereur 2011).

- *Relations between companies:* Via independent and specialized mediators, or through corporate mediation centers (Salzer, Fefeu, and Saubesty 2013).

- *Industrial relations* and labor disputes, or interpersonal conflicts between fellow employees (Colson, Elgoibar, and Marchi 2015; Euwema 2019).

- *Between the police and the community:* In the United States, for example, a number of police departments have partnered with mediation organizations to offer this service and improve the relationship between law enforcement officers and the communities within which they live and work (Walker, Archbold, and Herbst 2002). Research also investigates the role of mediation in police work (Cooper 2003).

- *Between neighbors:* Small conflicts can be mediated thanks to local mediation associations and to strengthen local democracy (Faget 2010; Susskind and Lempereur 2017).

- *At school:* School mediators (adults or students trained for this purpose; Cardinet 1997).

- *Within the family:* Family mediators (Parkinson 2014).

These official, but ad hoc, mediators are generally experienced people, recognized for their wisdom or impartiality, or accepted as such and trained in mediation. They are sometimes retired professionals (Lempereur 1998b) or freelance consultants. Another approach is to involve several mediators – the co-mediation model – as illustrated in the following example.

A college of mediators in New Caledonia

By 1988, and for several years prior, the French overseas territory of New Caledonia had been shaken by a series of clashes between supporters and opponents of independence. On April 22, the crisis culminated in the hostage taking of 27 police officers (*gendarmes*), detained on the island of Ouvea by independence activists. On May 5, a special commando unit of the National Gendarmerie engaged in an assault, releasing the hostages, but at the cost of 21 casualties. New Caledonia was on the brink of civil war. Prime Minister Michel Rocard dispatched a team of mediators to the area, coordinated by Christian Blanc. This team was composed of different mediators with complementary profiles (legal, administrative, spiritual leaders). They engaged and listened carefully to representatives from the different ethnic groups of New Caledonia. They succeeded in bringing the parties together and convening a negotiation which successfully ended with the Matignon Agreement on 26 June 1988.

Whatever the outcome, these official yet ad hoc mediators halt their mission once the problem has been resolved, or the stalemate has been confirmed.

Institutional Mediators

Here, mediators are part of a mediation organization, which guarantees continuity. The mediators are formally employed by an organization (public body, company, etc.) and its external partners (consumer, user, customer, supplier, etc.) seeking to rectify a complaint that they find justified in law or in equity. In addition, large organizations have appointed mediators in charge of managing internal disputes among their stakeholders.

We owe the invention of institutional mediators to the Swedes, who created the *ombudsman* in 1809: a *man* in charge of a mission (*ombuds*), in this case the search for justice between the State and its citizens. A similar function has developed in neighboring Nordic countries, such as Finland in 1953, then in the United Kingdom and the United States in the 1960s. In 1973, France created the Mediator of the Republic to facilitate disputes between the government and its citizens. Many universities have created ombuds services.

Why appoint institutional mediators? The intention is to establish a human link between an individual and an organization, which at first glance looks like a bureaucratic machine. Even in organizations that strive to respect rights, an individual might feel lost or powerless, when faced with decisions that seem unfair or seem to impinge on their rights. In these cases, mediators can help to exercise, between a person and an organization, an *ex post* review of the quality of the decisions. Even if the organization appoints and remunerates the mediators, it needs to guarantee their independence of judgments and actions, for them to seek fair solutions between the organization and the applicant. In fact, taking into account the current craze for mediation, such services will only serve the long-term image of an organization, if they also benefit from real resources and skills (Lempereur 1998b). Many leaders of organizations sincerely appreciate that "their" institutional mediators exercise critical functions and contribute to conflict reduction and to stakeholders' improved satisfaction.

Whichever organization hosts them, institutional mediators generally employ a method characterized by the following:

- Written mediation, carried out on the basis of a complaint reported by one stakeholder (for example, the employee or the user on one side, the department concerned on the other).
- A compliance review of contractual rules or established law.
- A fairness test that mediators perform.

- An opinion of the mediator (or of the mediation commission), which makes suggestions that the parties remain free to follow or not. This advice sometimes paves the way for a new negotiation.

An additional advantage of institutional mediators lies in their ability to recommend, within their organization, the implementation of the solution advocated at the end of the mediation they just conducted. There is thus a coherence between the problem posed, the proposed solution, and the people or organizations involved in the implementation of this solution.

Institutional mediation also aims to propose generalizable solutions, fully integrating the possibility that they constitute precedents that can be referred to later. Because of their role, institutional mediators inevitably reveal patterns in the interpretation of, and solutions to, some recurrent conflicts; as a result, they create some predictability of outcome. In addition, they derive recommendations from their activity, which they communicate where appropriate within their organization, or even make public in annual reports. These recommendations often help to revamp organizational structures and procedures.

Finally, in general, it is the institutional mediator (and not the parties) who proposes solutions in the form of opinions or recommendations. Institutional mediators thus fit into the "mediator as adviser" model that we will develop next. As evidenced, this typology of mediators – informal, ad hoc, institutional – echoes a diversity of mediation practices.

A Variety of Mediations

The above categories illustrate a diversity of mediation *models* (Lempereur 1999a), with various *methods*, and translate into multiple *practices*.

Models, Methods, and Practices

What do we mean by these three expressions?

Models – By "models" we do not mean examples to follow, but rather broad types of mediation approaches, featuring the characteristics representative of most mediators (Lempereur, 1999a). We can distinguish, for example, *mediators as advisers* or *as facilitators.*

- *Mediators as advisers* try and find solutions for the parties. Such mediators, also called *evaluative,* provide, after listening to the parties, suggestions which they find relevant, balanced, and fair. Parties remain free to follow or not to follow this advice, to modify or adjust it.

- *Mediators as facilitators* help the parties find their own solutions. Such mediators, also called *facilitative* (Brown 2002), do not offer any solutions, but try to make solutions emerge from the dialogue between parties. They invite parties to explain their views and hopefully acknowledge each other. Like midwifes, they make them ready for, or facilitate, a joyful birth at the ripe time. They consider that parties always understand their problems better than a mediator so that they can deliver their own best possible solutions themselves.

- *At the crossroads of the two models* are the *evocative mediators,* who are *providers of ideas* – but not givers of lessons. Based on their own personal experience, mediators add to the ideas of the parties, if the parties did not get them by themselves. This is done not as "advice" but as a "gift of ideas," without prejudging whether the parties will perceive these solutions as suitable or not. In short, these mediators wonder aloud about the adequacy of this or that solution. Knowing that they are not a party to the conflict, they offer without advising, insisting, pressing, or pretending in any way to alone hold the keys to the just or fair solution.

Depending on whether they claim to be an *adviser* or a *facilitator,* mediators do not use the same resources. According to a classical typology (French and Raven 1959), mediators can leverage different power resources vis-à-vis the parties: they can demonstrate *expertise* that the parties trust; their status may grant them special *legitimacy;* the parties can *value their relationship* with them; they may have *crucial information* which they can make available to the parties; or they can *reward or exert pressure* on the parties.

Methods – Within these three overarching models, mediators make method choices. That is to say, they select reasoned approaches to achieve their goals. This is flexibility within the framework. There are many method choices, and we will come back to them. For example, is there, at the opening, an oral agreement or a written contract on the rules of the mediation process? Do we communicate in writing or orally, face to face, by videoconference or by phone? How is the time dedicated to analyzing the past allocated in relation to that spent exploring possible avenues for the future? Is the final agreement drawn up by the parties, their lawyers, or the mediators themselves under the supervision of the parties?

Practices – At a more detailed level, within the choices of methods, each mediator brings their own personal "way of proceeding." Mediation style may also vary in the same person, depending on the situations encountered. Mediation styles will crystallize in the details of the choice of words, the ways of welcoming, the handling of space and time, the questions asked, the use of silence, the transition from oral ideas to putting the solution in writing, and other various initiatives of mediators.

Some Variables

The extraordinary diversity of mediation practices is due in particular to the large number of possible choices regarding the methods. To illustrate this diversity, the following tables present the main variables, which offer endless combinations. As of now, some light will be shed on the key choices.

The question of the free acceptance of mediation – or, on the contrary, when it is imposed – deserves to be raised immediately (before being further examined in Chapter 4). What happens, depending on whether the parties hear a suggestion (*"How about going to mediation?"*) or receive an injunction (*"You must go first to mediation!"*)? In fact, when the judge says to the parties: *"I strongly suggest that you go to mediation,"* they are more or less forced to do so, even if the judge adds: *"Do you agree?"* In mediation sessions, we have frequently heard expressions such as *"we did not want to displease the judge."*

TABLE 1.1

Before the mediation takes place	
Named as such – The upcoming process is explicitly labeled: "a mediation."	*Not named as such* – We proceed the same way, but without specifically calling it "mediation."
With much prior information on mediation given to the parties – The parties have received more or less lengthy information on the principles, procedure, objectives, and rules of mediation.	*With little prior information on mediation given to the parties* – The parties engage in mediation with little or no information on how mediation works.
With formal acceptance of the mediation – The parties say "yes," orally or in writing, for the initiation of a mediation process, after a more or less lengthy reflection.	*With superficial acceptance of mediation, without any deep understanding of what mediation is* – The parties experiment with mediation, "to see," without prior in-depth reflection, or because the judge or another authority has invited them to do so.
With contractual or legal obligation – Due to the law or a mediation clause in a contract, the parties are required to attempt mediation before they engage in legal proceedings (depending on the country, such clauses may apply in bankruptcy, labor disputes, or divorces).	*With acceptance not linked to a contractual or legal clause requiring mediation* – Once a conflict has arisen, the parties decide by mutual agreement to engage in a mediation without having previously committed to it.

A hypothesis often put forward is that only mediation that is genuinely accepted at the outset leads to an agreement. However, the probability of an agreement is fairly close in both cases. If there is an obligation to mediate, whether the parties wish it or not, they need to at least try a mediation process. When a mediation is well conducted, the parties feel recognized, realize that there is a shared purpose to understand each other – and eventually reach an agreement, more often than expected.

TABLE 1.2

From whom? And with whom?	
Internally – Mediation concerns internal relations within a group (family) or an organization (company, public body).	*Externally* – Mediation concerns the external partners of a group or an organization: customers, suppliers, users.
With official institutional mediators, mediation bodies, or mediation centers.	*With informal mediators, or independent mediators on ad hoc missions.*
With a single mediator.	*With a team of mediators* (co-mediators).
In the presence of the parties – The parties involved are present in person.	*In the absence of the parties* – Only their representatives attend (lawyers, elected representatives, agents, etc.).
In the presence of all parties concerned.	*In the presence of only some of the parties concerned* – Only the main ones, as involving all of them would complicate the process.

When the parties are not there in person and are represented (by a friend, a spouse, a lawyer, etc.), it is necessary for mediators to find out, at the start of mediation, the representatives' decision-making power. They will thus know, when the discussion turns toward the search for solutions and then the approval stage, if the agreement will still have to receive external approval, or if an agreement can be reached here and now, with the agent being empowered to decide for the principal.

The presence, or absence, of many actors involved (multi-party mediation) poses particular difficulties:

Sometimes, the stakeholders are numerous

- *Divorce* – Father and mother ... but also children? Or a grandparent who could help with child custody?

- *Succession* – All heirs? The main ones? A distant cousin? The loyal housekeeper who receives a symbolic share?

- *A co-ownership* – All co-owners of the condominium? Only co-owners most concerned by the work proposed in the garden?

- *An infrastructure project* – The mayor, any neighbor, or some of their representatives? What about environmental groups and business owners? Do we need to bring a state official or representative? Maybe one from the construction company? (De Carlo and Lempereur 1998; De Carlo 2005; Matsuura and Schenk 2016)

- *A major policy change* – What if we need to redefine political districts, or a state or federal policy? (Lempereur 1998c)

Various criteria influence the choice of the number of people to solicit. The concern of facilitating the exchanges can favor, at least initially, a small number of actors. It is also important to involve the main protagonists likely to influence the decision. Conversely, in the spirit of inclusion, some mediators favor the idea that the participation of a maximum of actors, even "the least" important, will contribute to the legitimacy of the final result and, therefore, to its smooth implementation. Age, state of health, legal capacity, or availability are also criteria. In the most complex multi-party mediations, it is preferable to sequence meetings over time: the first meetings, conducted with the key players, will reveal who else needs to be involved to obtain their reaction – and possibly their agreement.

The question of the number of people around the table is all the more important as participants do not share the same information, or in the same way, if they are being observed by other parties (Colson 2004, 2007). During mediation, even if one of the parties wants to express themselves spontaneously, it is important to be as inclusive as possible – the other party or parties, their counsel, mediators themselves? Any presence is a filter to information sharing. Admittedly, the hypothesis is that mediators, by definition, are benevolent toward everyone, have little influence on what is said and what is not said. For example, fearing retribution, some parties may hold back on expressing themselves: *"What will my lawyer think? And the other lawyer, could she hold against me what I intend to say?"* As a result, mediators may turn to the "caucus method," which we will further discuss in the book: caucuses (probably stemming from an Algonquian word *caucauasu*; Online Etymology Dictionary 2020) are private meetings with a given party, to allow for a free flow of information.

If the temptation exists to restrict the circle of the parties present at mediation, it needs to avoid creating the opposite risk involved in the absence of certain parties, who could disavow an agreement obtained without them, and consequently hinder its implementation. Two types of absences should be noted:

- *The absence of decision-makers.* It is not surprising that they do not accept the agreement reached, without them, by the other parties. An agreement is only binding on those who build and then sign it. Hence the importance, at a given moment, of the presence of all the actors concerned.

Litigation between a real estate developer and a co-owner

The developer of a housing complex is in litigation with a new co-owner, about leakage from roof terraces. Responsibility could be attributed as much to the developer (waterproofing qualities of the products used) as to the co-owner, who may have damaged the terrace by installing a chimney, which was not originally planned. Never mind, the developer is covered by insurance: co-owner and developer agree on behalf of the insurer. However, if the latter is absent during the mediation and does not sign the agreement, its implementation is unlikely.

- *The absence of decision influencers.* Certain essential actors do not appear at first sight: without being directly involved, it is nevertheless they who, behind the scenes, are pulling the strings. Decision influencers are not always easy to detect, but when they have been uncovered, it is useful, with the agreement of the parties, to invite them to mediation.

TABLE 1.3

From whom? And with whom? (continued)	
In the presence of parties alone – Parties are not accompanied by anyone who could offer advice.	*In the presence of supporting parties –* Other people are present to provide informal (friend, family, ally) or formal (expert, lawyer) advice.

Child custody

When mediating a divorce, one of the spouses seems to agree with the other but opposes a solution that seems reasonable and corresponds to their interests. They repeatedly reject the agreement. They end up revealing that their opposition reflects the pressure they are under from their own parents. Rather than going around in circles, it is better to initiate an in-depth discussion with the grandparents – the hidden interlocutors – and identify their concerns. Their involvement will help to find an agreement that integrates, if possible, the needs of the children, the mother, the father, and the grandparents.

Lawyers' presence or absence deserves special attention, as opinions differ: "Lawyers are welcome all the time," or "at certain times during mediation," or "above all, no lawyers present during mediation!"

- Some mediators are convinced that only the parties should be present, because it is their own story: the challenge is to restore their power, without outside interference. The parties will always be able to consult their lawyers outside the sessions.

- For other mediators, when the parties have already taken on lawyers, it is useful for the latter to be present at the sessions, so that they too know and understand what is experienced and said in the relationship between their client and the other party. Indeed, often, lawyers do not have access to "the other party," but only to their own client or the other's lawyer. They are therefore far from knowing everything that takes place in this relationship. If they are present, they will better understand what comes out of the process and thus better advise their client.

Several means of communication are used in mediation, which contributes to the diversity of mediation practices. Let us recall the main ones.

- *Writing* – The vast majority of institutional mediators deal with written documents. Parties and mediators exchange letters and memos. Although registered mail with acknowledgment of receipt remains advisable to keep a record of documents exchanged, documents sent as e-mail attachments have increasingly become the norm. If, from beginning to end, exchanges of information go only through e-mails, this "cyber-mediation" might miss the root causes of the conflict and fail to analyze the behavior of each party, given the lack of direct interaction.

- *Telephone* – Of course, telephone calls can routinely help to rapidly clarify a given item. Sometimes, given the urgency, mediation can only be done by phone, the necessary documents or proposed agreements being sent by e-mails in parallel. For example, disputes over the purchase or sale of securities have to be settled quickly. In other disputes, it may happen that a phone call from a mediator is sufficient to help overcome the reluctance of a given party to join the mediation meeting.

Defective household appliance

Unhappy with a valuable appliance that the store refuses to repair, a customer turns to a mediator. A phone call from the mediator to the store manager was enough for the customer to be welcomed there the same day in order to find a solution, without the mediator needing to further intervene.

TABLE 1.4

What is the compensation framework?	
Self-funded – The parties assume the cost of mediation.	*Subsidized* – All or part of the cost of mediation is covered by the institution.
Paid – Mediators receive a fee for their services.	*Volunteer* – Mediators do not receive any monetary compensation.

With what means of communication, and what meeting formats?	
Written – By exchange of letters, in paper, or electronic format.	*Oral* – Face-to-face, by videoconference, or by telephone.
With individual meetings at the start – Mediators first receive each of the parties privately.	*With a joint meeting at the start* – Mediators first receive all the parties together.
Along the way, individual meetings alternate with joint meetings.	*Throughout the mediation, the same type of meeting continues* – either individual or joint.

- *Videoconference* – Enhanced systems of videoconferencing (Zoom or otherwise) have now bridged the gap between e-mail exchanges and face-to-face meetings. At the same time, parties and mediators can hear and watch each other, while also showing and even editing documents shared on the screen. This fairly new medium, which became "the new normal" in 2020 because of the COVID-19 confinement in many countries, has proved an effective way to save time and carbon emissions, as parties can meet while being in different parts of the country – or on different continents altogether.

- *Face-to-face meetings* – Nevertheless, this mediation mode remains the favored mode of interaction between parties and mediators, as they optimize the exchange of information and allow participants to grasp "the mood in the room" – the unsaid elements that help sense whether the mediation is heading in the right direction. These meetings take several forms between the beginning and the end – individual with each party, in sub-groups, bringing together all the parties – each with its advantages and disadvantages. These different types of meetings will be elaborated on in Chapter 5.

TABLE 1.5

What about the time factor?	
A unique encounter.	*Several successive meetings.*
Brevity of meeting – For example, 1.5 to 4 hours in criminal or family mediation.	*"Marathon" meeting* – Mediation proceeds continuously over a weekend, a few days, or even weeks. For example, a dispute between banks in different countries – brought to court for two years – was resolved within a week by intensive mediation.
Short in total – Mediation focuses on a meeting of a few hours.	*Long-lasting in total* – Mediation spans several days, even months or even years.

Where?	
In a "neutral" space – A place equidistant between the parties, the premises of a mediation center or a town hall.	*At the place of the dispute, or on the premises of one party with the agreement of the other* – For example, on the construction site where the damage occurred.

Agreement and post-mediation	
With suggestions for solutions from the parties.	*With suggestions for solutions from mediators.*
With a final written agreement – Written by the parties themselves, or their lawyers, or mediators, or a combination of the above. This written agreement can be approved by a court to ensure enforceability.	*With a final oral agreement.*
With the existence of a follow-up – Verification with mediators of the next steps of implementation and completion of the agreement.	*Without follow-up* – Follow-up is left to the parties themselves.

(continued)

TABLE 1.5

Agreement and post-mediation	
With post-mediation debrief – The mediation, once completed, is the subject of an analysis of practices, and of exchange between mediators.	*Without post-mediation debrief* – Without organized exchanges of reflection between peers on past mediations.

Of course, a given mediation can simultaneously combine a set of elements taken from both columns of the tables above. This diversity is further increased if we look at the variety of mediation sequences, an aspect covered in greater detail in Chapters 5 to 7. This sequence varies, depending on the number of parties, the habits and training of the mediators, the technical nature of the case, the refusal of one of the parties to physically meet the other, the tensions between the parties, etc. Finally, this variety also contributes to the irreducible diversity of personalities: no mediator is like another, depending on their training, their specialization in this or that sector, their past experiences, their personal qualities, openness and attentiveness, authority, or objectivity. Mediation is a deeply human process with many variations (Fiutak 2009).

Conclusion: An Overflow of Methods or a Lack Thereof?

Mediation illustrates the 2000 European Union motto: "United in Diversity" *(In Varietate Concordia)*. Behind a constant – the desire to contribute to the peaceful resolution of conflicts between parties, based on their acceptance of an approach characterized by its dynamism and plasticity – appears the variability of practices. However, this mediation effervescence should not obscure several risks.

The first risk is the trivialization of mediation, of its use in any situation, leading to some *mediation mania*. It is useful to identify precisely when and why to engage in a mediation process, or otherwise rely on other intervention mechanisms. This refers to the relevance of mediation, and its application criteria, which is treated in Chapter 2.

Aboard an airplane, a pointless mediation

The use of micro-mediation can reflect the growing difficulty of fellow human beings to communicate directly with each other in order to settle small disputes. On planes, when a passenger was annoyed by a neighbor (conventionally, the knee kick in the seat, or the backrest too tilted during a meal), the matter would be settled directly with the fellow traveler. Airline companies have noted the increasing propensity of passengers to ask for help from flight attendants, rather than attempt a direct resolution of their conflict by relying on the elementary rules of civil request by conversation.

A corollary to the previous one, *the second risk is the absence of methods:* whether they may be ignorant of the existence of methods, or, on the contrary, disturbed by the apparent relativism that draws from a diversity of possible methods, would-be mediators might rely on their own instincts only. This risk concerns each of us when we are called upon to take on the role of informal mediators. But the other models – institutional mediators and ad hoc mediators – are not immune to this pitfall either.

Moreover, *a third risk is unsuitable methods;* i.e. mediators apply patterns and reflexes inherited from their previous professional experience in other functions. This is the case, in particular, of the institutional and ad hoc mediators, who find themselves minutely supervised when planning the mediation but in the end are left fairly on their own during the actual mediation process.

Even mediation professionals may lack methods

- Criminal mediators, sometimes chosen from among former judges or police commissioners, might see mediation as a subset of a criminal lawsuit, without necessarily reaping all the potential of a more methodical approach including gaining a mutual understanding of the causes that led to a criminal offense.

- Some mediators, who are often efficient in the search for solutions, seem less focused on the reconciliation between people. In this case, it is a question of working, also, if necessary, on the relationship on top of the concrete problem at stake.

A mediation process entails its own methodological requirements. To ignore them, or to apply inadequate ones that are fundamentally foreign to it, is to risk the failure of mediation, or in any case to deprive oneself of assets in favor of the resolution of the conflict.

Hence this book: it is not about proposing *the* method – as if only one method exists – but rather about synthesizing *methods,* drawing from enough sources and tempered by enough experiences to be applied flexibly to most contexts. It is not a question here of limiting oneself to a single model, but of being inspired by several, to unfold an approach that allows each mediator to find their own ways of engaging in mediation. In doing so, we will try to bring as much to experienced mediators – who are sometimes so comfortable employing *a single method* that they end up ignoring others that may be useful – as to beginners – who venture in this delicate path with, depending on their personalities, either the misleading feeling of knowing it all or the paralyzing impression of not knowing anything.

To structure this method, mediators and parties in conflict can rely on what we call the Seven Pillars of Mediation, which we will develop in the following chapters.

The Seven Pillars of Mediation

1. *Solicit the Parties* permanently so that they take ownership of the resolution mechanism, by mobilizing active communication between them and seeking progressively some mutual recognition.

2. *Secure Principles*, that is to say the "rules of engagement," which will allow everyone to stay on course with problem-solving.

3. *Sequence Phases* in this process, with various stages, from the establishment of mediation to, if possible, an agreement.

4. *Seize the Problem,* and its various data, by an in-depth analysis of its dimensions.

5. *Seek Paths* to solutions, so that parties discover what might work for them.

6. *Surmount the Pitfalls* that arise and hinder a resolution throughout the process.

7. *Seal the Points of agreement (or disagreement),* with the aim of gradually bringing to light a peaceful and realistic solution, to be implemented by all parties.

CHAPTER 2
THE PERTINENCE
Weigh the Pros and Cons of Mediation *Before* Engaging in It

In what kinds of situations can one choose mediation as a way of resolving a conflict? What are its many advantages, but also its limitations? These are the fundamental questions that the parties in conflict as well as mediators may need to ask themselves. This chapter will help to determine the adequacy of mediation as a process of intervention. Indeed, third parties can act in various ways, so it is useful from the outset to offer an overview of the spectrum of intervention.

Mediation Among Other Types of Third-Party Interventions

When one or both parties conclude that it is no longer possible to engage in direct negotiation, a third party's intervention can become necessary. A wide diversity of types of third-party intervention coexist; eight of them will be introduced here (see Figure 2.1).

Eight Approaches of Third-Party Interventions

These intervention methods are arranged on a continuum from more autonomy for the parties toward more control by the third party.

1. *Ally* – It is wise, when a party lacks self-confidence and recognizes the need for support, to ask a third party to sit next to the party or attend

FIGURE 2.1 The 8 A's: Mediation within the spectrum of third-party approaches.

the meeting as part of the audience. Though this individual – or a supporting group – is not a substantive expert, and remains silent, their presence offers comfort.

2. *Attorney* – When a situation involves a legal dimension, it is wise to have input from someone who understands the law – its technical and relevant language and its challenges – and who can represent the involved party. The latter, of course, is free to adopt or reject the attorney's contribution.

3. *Ambassador* – In some situations, it is wise to resort to a third party who will be a representative, either because they are well versed in a particular area (for example, a regional subject matter expert) or because they know either one or both of the parties.

General Staff of the National Burundian Defence Forces (Wolpe et al. 2004; Colson and Lempereur 2011; Lempereur 2021)

At the start of the 2000s, in the aftermath of a civil war having claimed the lives of 1 out of 20 Burundians, the delicate national reconciliation implied, in particular, the integration of the defense and security forces. For months, the representatives of the regular army and the armed movements remained stuck on many questions, such as rank harmonization and position allocation. During a series of formative retreats gathering the head members of all the former belligerents, third parties (including two of the co-authors) were involved. They acted in a diplomatic fashion, using methods of conflict resolution, as ambassadors do. They also brought military experts, who played the role of *advisory* aides. Subsequently, the parties succeeded in unfreezing the situation and in settling all the details by themselves, without third-party support. During this period, the third parties remained available as *attendants* in the background to offer all the help that the parties would have judged useful; they were ready to intervene "if necessary," but the parties did not need them. Their simple availability proved sufficient.

4. ***Auxiliary or facilitator*** – When direct negotiations are deadlocked, parties might need a third-party facilitator who will act as an intermediary. By asking questions and sequencing the steps of problem-solving, this type of third party paves the way to breaking the existing logjam, thus enabling parties to conceive and produce their own solutions.

5. ***Adviser*** – Faced with the same difficulties of relationship deterioration and deadlock, parties may need to resort to a person who, in addition to providing methods and process tips, will offer their evaluation, i.e. substantive guidance on questions at stake. Because of the Adviser's expertise and experience, the parties will seriously consider their recommendations, which again they are free to adopt or refuse.

6. ***Arbitrator*** – When the parties have not been able to come up with a binding solution – despite the involvement of one of the preceding outsiders – and there is an urgency, weariness, and/or desire for a decision – it may be necessary to designate a third party in whom the parties place their confidence, and whose decision they agree *a priori* to accept. This form of "private justice" exists in sports as in many civil disputes.

7. ***Adjudicator*** – If a "private third party" cannot decide their case, parties can turn to a "public institution" that wields a conclusive function, such as the judiciary for legal disputes. This adjudicator – typically, a judge – will have to conduct due process, and therefore keep the parties involved to a certain extent before deciding, and for this reason differs from the last type of third-party intervention: Authority.

8. *Authority* – As a solution to the conflict, parties (either or both) may decide to ask an authority figure to make the decision. By doing so, however, the parties usually completely lose control over decision-making. The authority's solution can become necessary in an urgent situation that requires a quick decision with or without consultation.

Conflicting medical diagnoses

In a hospital, sometimes doctors make different diagnoses. They cannot negotiate indefinitely, because the patient's health would suffer. They therefore agree to rely on the head of the department, whose special expertise is *authoritative*. The hierarchical authority is asked for a decision on how to move forward with the patient's medical treatment.

Complementary Approaches to Wisdom

Mediation involves a third-party intervention between the facilitative and the evaluative modes. It can be hybrid and borrow from the other modes, especially up the ladder toward more autonomy, as the above-mentioned Burundian example showed. In other cases, mediation, when it fails, may open the way toward more authoritative modes of intervention. Mediation and these eight approaches (8 A's) are complementary forms of wisdom, and depending on conflicts and contexts, each can prove pertinent in order to manage disagreements and reach a decision.

Facing Borderline Pathological Cases

Pathologies of conflict exist. Certain groups or people only exist in systematic opposition to another group or person, affirming their identity in confrontation. The conflict becomes their reason to live. As René Girard describes (1972, 1982), in certain contexts, the identification of a scapegoat prevails, with a permanent denunciation and a destructive, adversarial logic. Often, other psychological pathologies – schizophrenia, deep depression, dementia, etc. – prevent people from coping.

Mediation implies a minimum amount of possible dialogue and comprehension, creating a threshold past which mediation becomes impossible. Here, the authority's solution – a judge, a doctor, or a psychiatrist – might be necessary.

The Desire to Impose, Avenge, or Punish

Often, when suffering has been extreme in a conflict, the victim *wants* to make a case, to impose a sanction, to avenge, or to punish. Research has shown that in these situations, though mediation may not have been initially wished for by the parties, after having gone through it, the mediation process was actually able to satisfy them beyond what they envisioned.

Impose – When one party considers themselves to be right, they may want to get a sanction imposed, without paying attention to the desires and justifications of the other party. As mediation necessitates a minimum amount of listening and comprehension, it does not respond well to a pure demand of imposition. However, experience underscores that parties in this state of mind, when they are involved in mediation (for example, at a judge's request or in application of a contractual clause of compulsory mediation), can evolve if they find in the other party a recognition of the legitimacy of their claim for compensation.

Avenge – The culture of "an eye for an eye, a tooth for a tooth" refers to a logic of retaliation, which mediation stays away from. However, seeking vengeance implicitly expresses a demand for justice that mediation can help to recognize and reformulate. Mediation can be appropriate as a place where a lucid diagnostic of a situation emerges, including the suffering inflicted and felt, and consequently where the terms of a proportionate and legitimate compensation for the damage committed are discussed.

Punish – This demand differs from the logic of retaliation, as it does not aim to make the other suffer what we suffered, but to sanction through legal proceedings. This punishment is deemed to compensate for the misdeed – retributive justice – and to prevent its future recurrence – deterrence justice.

It requires the intervention of an authority – hierarchical, judicial – whose role is to deliver a penalty – judicial sentence. Even when a willingness to punish exists, criminal mediation is used, notably for minor offenses (Lempereur 1999c). It provides an avenue of action for cases that would be otherwise dismissed. For example, it increases the chances that the "small" delinquents will understand their impact on the victims and acknowledge their wrongdoing through an apology. It also empowers the complainant, who can shape the compensatory measures.

When Timing Counts

Speed is a primary criterion in some types of decision-making, in everything from the most mundane situations – settling a disagreement between teams at a sporting event – to the most serious – assigning responsibilities in the management of an industrial accident, or in hostage situations. Faced with a problematic situation where time is of the essence, and as mediation is not the fastest approach, it is often not the most pertinent.

Is a player offside?

In a soccer match, could the two teams discuss, negotiate, or mediate for hours to arrive at a shared decision on whether or not a player is offside? Night would fall on the field without the match continuing. With the support today of video replay, accepting the referee's decision is preferable to guarantee speedy decisions and to resume the match, even if it does not satisfy a particular player or team and feeds the newspaper columns the next day.

Thus, each time the situation demands a form of swiftness in decision-making – to avoid prolonged blockage, deterioration, even a human disaster – intervention by an authority proves itself essential. This aspect is reinforced in a situation where the decision also involves precise technical, scientific, or legal issues: turning with confidence to a subject matter expert allows everyone to save time.

The fact remains that this preference for speed is carried out to the detriment of other criteria, including the *quality* of a decision – notably its perceived legitimacy by the involved parties. A prompt decision, without taking time to exchange, inhibits a deep reciprocal understanding, leaves the underlying causes of the conflict intact, does not guarantee that the most appropriate decision will be made, and nor does it prevent the recurrence of conflict. There is, in defense of mediation, a tension between the speed and sustainability of the decision, between immediacy and legitimacy. Mediation, because of its slow and more careful decision-making style, favors comprehensive conflict resolution. In this spirit, an authority, like a judge, can order an "urgent" mediation, which will make it possible – by immediately taking the useful time of reciprocal explanation – to unfreeze a situation. As long as it is conducted "within a specific timeframe," this mediation can not only be urgent, but quickly finished, successfully or not. For example, before deciding if the occupation of a factory is legal or not, a judge may order a swift mediation between the parties before making a decision.

What is at play deep down concerning whether or not to resort to mediation is the organization of exchanges. Mediation complements other approaches of conflict intervention by providing an original division of labor. On one side, decision-making stays with the parties. On the other side, mediators are in charge of the process and the organization of exchanges, allowing parties to concentrate on the problems, without being concerned about "Who is going to talk after whom?" and "Have I been listened to and understood well?" Mediators become like translators from English to English and from feeling to feeling, helping the parties to listen and understand each other, even when there is no particular decision to make. While the mediator focuses on the process, the parties are able to concentrate on their relationship and the problem at hand. The mediator ensures that the process is appropriate to increase the chance of resolution at every moment.

Faced with multiple approaches to third-party interventions, why choose mediation? The following paragraphs will explore a series of justifications which complement more intuitive criteria, linked to our culture and personal values. Research and experience distinguish between two types of justifications favoring the use of mediation: the first is linked to the past to overcome; the second focuses on a future to (re)construct. Let us examine both.

A Past to Overcome: Seven Justifications in Favor of Mediation

This first series of justifications focuses on barriers from the past that prevent progress in the present. What typical blockages can a mediation surmount?

Communication and Relationship Breakdown

A parent has not seen their child for 10 years. An owner does not respond to an urgent request from a tenant. A business does not deliver an order despite multiple messages. In every case, one party avoids contact for multiple possible reasons: the fear of blame, aggression, or shaming by the other party; the desire to no longer suffer from (physical or verbal) abuse; the difficulty of fulfilling a contract; the other's rejection; or even a position of strength resulting in denying any demand.

Accepting the presence of a neutral person between oneself and the other constitutes a first step in renewing the dialogue. Sometimes, simply learning that "the other" proposes mediation is perceived as a sign of opening and suffices to relaunch direct negotiations resulting in a solution, without the need for external mediators.

In cases of a complete relationship breakdown, it proves useful to involve a third party, who plays the role of a messenger between the parties. There are two possibilities:

- *The parties agree to meet one another:* The mediator reunites them in joint meetings, except if the choice is made to hold private meetings.

- *The parties refuse to meet one another but agree to communicate through the mediator:* The mediator meets them in turn and engages in "shuttle diplomacy." By carrying the messages between the parties and giving their own perceptions or suggestions on the evolution of the relationship, the mediator plays the role of a mutual spokesperson. As a result, either the parties change their perceptions of "the other," and agree to meet, or the process proceeds without any physical meeting.

In the latter case, mediation does not serve to renew the relationship between the parties, but to establish enough contact for the resolution of the problem: the parties do not wish to meet each other; they simply want to resolve the problem. In fact, experience shows that there are four different scenarios, in terms of focus and results, defining a *Mediation Matrix* (see Table 2.1) that reflects the Responsible Negotiation matrix (Lempereur 2018).

1. *Mediation with no progress on the relationship or the solution.* In this case, the intervention by an outside authority, like an arbitrator or adjudicator, becomes likely. However, sometimes the conflict has ripened, and even after the mediation ends, parties might resume direct negotiations.
2. *Mediation with a solution, but without a relationship.* "Problem-centered mediation" is transactional, i.e. only concerned with the substance of a conflict, but not with the quality of relationships among the parties in dispute. Without building a relationship, however, there is a risk that the solution will be short-lived.

TABLE 2.1 The Mediation Matrix

		(3) Relationship-centered mediation	(4) Full potential mediation
Focus on **relationship**	**Yes**		
	No	(1) Unsuccessful mediation	(2) Problem-centered mediation
		No	**Yes**
		Focus on problem-solving	

3. *Mediation with a renewed relationship, but without a solution.* Some mediations only aim at restoring relationships between parties, without trying to achieve a resolution of the substantive issues at hand. A "relationship-centered mediation" is seen as a process of transition so that a direct relationship can resume between parties. This renewed relationship allows the parties to find a solution on their own. A metaphor that could be helpful to clarify this situation is a "jump-start" cable that a fellow driver uses to help start a stalled car. The person offering the cable is not physically pushing the stalled car, but they are serving as a catalyst that enables you to continue on your own.

Corporate relationship and sensitive confidentiality

Two companies in a sensitive technology sector were ready to engage in long and costly litigation proceedings, with an unpredictable outcome. Mediators were able to restart communication between them. As soon as their leaders had renewed the thread of their former relationship, they asked mediators to withdraw in order to broach highly confidential questions. In the absence of mediators, the parties drafted a final contract that contained some clauses known only to them.

4. *Mediation with a relationship and a solution.* This is mediation that delivers its full potential in terms of relationship building and problem-solving; it yields both relational and transactional results. Though it may look like an ideal to achieve, parties may wish to renounce it when there is already a solution to the problem *or* a resumption of relationship. So much the better if mediation succeeds in these two spheres of action; but both the parties and the mediator will remember that sometimes there can be a solution without relationship; and the converse. A renewed relationship is like the cherry on top, but the second scenario, whatever discomfort it brings, can emerge, even if the hope was to purge the past and to reconstruct a common future together. Maybe the only future that comes out of mediation is the one, limited but important, that stems from the implementation of a workable solution to a particular problem.

Negative Emotions and the Risk of Escalation

Pretending to ignore negative emotions is to risk an impasse or an explosion later on (Lempereur 2003b, 2014a). Therefore, sharing them can serve a constructive purpose in conflict resolution, especially when a good faith effort is made to express them with, and not against, the other. There is an emotional release that, once performed and received by the other (who shows empathy, if not sympathy), prepares to come to terms with rational arguments. The venting person can then turn to rational problem-solving as the next step.

Yet, these toxic emotions – fear, sadness, anger, shame, etc. – when unmanaged, often damage relationships. Emotions can overwhelm not only those who experience them, but also those who are exposed to them: "You are not going to complain again …," "Calm down!" In these examples, the listener reacts to emotions by refusing to acknowledge them, which can significantly exacerbate the expressed feelings. Or, the interlocutor can mirror these emotions (one's tears generate the other's tears) or transform them (one's fear provokes the other's anger). If the emotional spiral deepens, the parties can no longer focus effectively on the issues.

In particular, negative emotions nurture excessive aggression, whether they are unilateral or, most often, reciprocal. Aggression is communicated in writing (sending a certified mail to neighbors, former spouse, or associates; threatening e-mail to multiple addressees) or orally (tone of voice, screaming) and is accentuated by word choice (irony, accusation, shaming, threat, insult), as well as body language and demeanor. The protagonists thus find themselves in an escalation that they no longer understand or fully control.

To stop this cycle, each party requires the first step from "the other." They can all wait a long time like stone statues. In this blocked context, mediation is appropriate because an external third party, whom everyone agrees to meet, builds a bridge of "ceasefire" across the gap of negative emotions. This image of mediators with the white flag or blue helmets applies as much to wars between countries as to conflicts between groups and individuals.

Mediators, ready to understand everyone, screen aggression; they *translate* the messages – transmitting the content without an aggressive tone – that thus become audible and acceptable to the other.

In these cases, mediators themselves need to know how to recognize, accept, and welcome emotions, consider them, name them, and channel them without rejecting them (Chapter 8). They witness the drama of both the emitted emotion and perceived emotion, as well as their intermingling (Lempereur and Colson 2004, chapter 6). They bring each of the parties to the mutual awareness of *"How have our emotions overwhelmed our relationship?"* We have often seen, in criminal mediation, for example, how a few hours of discussion can lead each person to recognize sincerely: *"We both got angry ..."* After this de-dramatization, the mediator can focus on the "relationship-centered mediation." Once the link is re-established, the mediator withdraws and leaves the parties to deal with the problem between themselves, if possible. Or, in the framework of a "problem-centered mediation," they continue to help the parties formulate the needs underpinning their emotions and look for solutions together.

The Imbroglio of Accumulated Problems

In most cases, the parties do not have *one* problem to deal with, but *many*. Additionally, they may have different problems in mind, each of which is valued more or less according to their own priorities. If they cannot manage to sort out this imbroglio by themselves, mediation can be useful.

The supplier, their client, and the implementation of a contract

In this conflict, Client A considers the rule of law to be the uppermost consideration; on the other hand, their Supplier B emphasizes the lack of information, non-compliant work techniques, and personal attacks. In the dialogue, each person repeats the important points for themselves, while carefully avoiding addressing those of the other.

PERSON A: Article 42 of that regulation provides, in case of transportation, that the manufacturer is liable.

PERSON B: But you did not give us any information about the quality of …

A: Anyway, six years ago, you gave us a hard time about … We did not come to terms with it.

B: What are you talking about? Are you the one complaining? Did you see how you received our representatives? You called them every name under the sun!

A: At our company, we favor directness. When we have something to say, we are frank about it.

B: But the delivered products were rigorously compliant with the contract.

A: I have already told you that Article 42 … provides that the manufacturer is liable.

A and B end up repeating themselves, and the dialogue goes around in circles (also see Chapter 6).

Anyone can observe these parallel "monologues" in conflict situations, both in negotiations and in court proceedings. It aims only to present to the other side the arguments that affect us, without responding to those put forward by the other side. It is a stubborn repetition of the same words, without going into detail or explaining each of the points that are important to the other. This "non-dialogue" evokes a reciprocal avoidance that fails to deal with the problems of the other party. On the other hand, thanks to mediation, dialogue orchestrated by a third party – the "*trilogue*" or "trialogue" – brings the problems perceived by one and by the other into the exchange. In mediation, increasing importance is given to recognition of the essential role of the mediator as the organizer of the meetings (Lempereur 2015c), orchestrating a sequence where a typical agenda includes both parties' priorities. During this process, the mediator enforces the agenda and helps to clarify different points and how they are connected, so that each party successively goes after important points for oneself *and* for the other.

In the previous example, mediators devoted a time slot for speaking when the parties could successively explain themselves on the following:

For A:

- The application of Article 42

- Traces of old disputes (*"Six years ago …"*)

For B:

- The reality of the lack of information

- The greetings of representatives perceived as insulting

- The compliance verification of the delivered products

From there, and subject to good faith in the statement of concerns by each person, the mediator invites each party to integrate what poses a problem for the other. This reciprocal recognition, by accepting possible disagreements on the interpretation of the facts, contributes to the emergence of potential solutions to the problems invoked by each party.

In addition to this juxtaposition of priorities, another source of complexity is that mediation succeeds in managing the existence of *many intertwined, independent, but linked conflicts.* What appeared to be *one* conflict, is, in reality, *many underlying* conflicts. In court, where a conflict hides other ones, judges find themselves quickly annoyed: solicited for a particular dispute, they cannot rule on another one, even if it is linked to the first one. Mediators, on the other hand, embrace the complexity of the diverse elements of the conflict.

On a farm: One thing leading to another

A court commissions a mediator to help find an agreement between a farm in financial difficulty and its creditors. Throughout the course of a session, the mediator realizes, while listening to the farmer, that the latter is confronted by two other conflicts: with his wife in the settling of a divorce, and with his brothers for the succession of their parents' farm. The mediator, feeling that the conflicts are related and knowing that resolving one may help to unfreeze the other, takes on work with the farmer and his wife on the one hand and with the farmer and his brothers on the other hand. They thus arrive at two distinct agreements, one on the divorce and one on the succession. These two conflicts settled, the financial capacities of the farmer improve: an agreement occurs with the creditors to keep up the establishment and restructure the repayment of debts. The resolution of the financial conflict with the creditors results from the prior resolution of the two other disputes.

If there had not been mediation, each conflict would have been managed in an isolated manner: the conflicts regarding divorce and succession would have persisted as much in negotiation as in court. As often happens in cases of bankruptcy, the farm would have been liquidated at a low price, and the creditors would have ultimately been repaid less than what they received in the long-term agreement allowing for the continuation of agricultural activity.

Mutual Misunderstanding

The parties involved in a conflict often do not understand one another: they live their past as a coherent whole, and the other, whether it is a person, a department within an organization, an ethnic group, or a nation, is placed on the "negative" side. The other is of bad faith and is the representative of the "axis of evil." French philosopher Jean-Paul Sartre (1944) summarized it: "*Hell is the others.*" How did we arrive at this Manichean Yalta between the other and me?

As Chapter 6 will elaborate, the mediator helps to uncover it, as much for themselves as for each of the parties, by verifying through their questions if each party listened to and understood the other. The goal here is that a step-by-step, mutual comprehension of what has been perceived differently in the disagreement should come to light. The mediator will explain an essential distinction between *understanding* and *agreeing*: one party can understand how the other functioned – recognizing how the other feels – *and* still not agree with them. A party who understands can, at the same time, continue to express a different narrative of reality, of the distribution of responsibilities, and of the consequences to draw from it in order to find an acceptable solution to the conflict.

The reciprocal ignorance and incomprehension increase when individuals, groups, or organizations in conflict belong to radically different cultures: national cultures, but also professional cultures – such as an engineer in conflict with a legal expert. An extra factor favoring mediation requires the availability of a "multicultural" person, knowing the different, present "worlds" well, who is likely to play the role of cultural interpreter so that each party better understands the other. This essential role of cultural intermediation, for example, is taken on by criminal mediation associations in Paris.

Interpreting the culture of the Other, my fellow human being

- At the Paris-based Mediation Training Center (CMFM), an effort is made to assign at least one mediator (if there is a co-mediation) of the same cultural origin as the party in conflict.

- In the framework of the Association of Criminal Aid (AAPE), a mediation case involved a French mother and an Algerian father. The mother had no contact with her children – who were living in Algeria – for more than a year. The association took care to integrate a mediator of Algerian origin in the mediation team. During the entire mediation, the Algerian party looked only at the Algerian mediator and addressed only him. At the end of the meeting, a first agreement was made, and the French mother was immediately able to talk to her children by phone, before meeting them later.

- At the juvenile courts in Paris and Nanterre, African students residing in France, with members of Étienne Leroy's Cultural Anthropology Laboratory of University Paris I, endorse the role of cultural intermediation between the judge and children of African origin.

The Absence of Precise Rules or Established Laws

All situations where a simple, clear, and unanimously accepted rule is lacking are a potential breeding ground for conflicts. Each party invokes "their" rule, or "the right" interpretation of the obscure rule.

Adolescence: Who decides?

Concerning teenagers, no absolute rule exists concerning the hours of going out and returning home, the possibilities of long trips alone or in a group, or whom they choose as friends. Often, parents, assuming their parental responsibility, establish rules that are contested by their teenage children. The latter, already feeling like adults, affirm their new identity by confronting their parents. Each side, feeling legitimate, camps on their reciprocal positions.

When direct exchanges become difficult and include a constant interrupting of one another, the need is felt to organize the exchanges and establish new rules of the game: it is a call for mediation.

This call also concerns areas where the rapid advancement of technology does not allow people to always take their time to respond judiciously; the same applies to copyright in the dissemination of works on the Internet. To a greater extent, the settling of conflicts resulting from Internet transactions creates a need for mediation by the Forum of Internet Rights to organize online or face-to-face mediation between Internet users and Web service providers. The mediator, who helps in the interpretation and legitimacy of an implicit or explicit rule, assists the parties to agree upon the rules they all find acceptable.

Absence of a Suitable Space

Individuals like groups or organizations in conflict find themselves separated by the front lines. A *no-man's-land* comes between territories that became impenetrable, each person being banned from a stay in the other's space. For example, two departments in a quarrel within the same company are situated at two different sites; no one goes to the offices of the other "camp" anymore. A few meters suffice to raise a wall of separation. Colleagues in conflict, although separated by only one floor, may lack a neutral space to speak with one another safely.

In all these cases, faced with protagonists refusing "to go" to the space of the other party, the mediator offers a suitable neutral space for the meeting. This place materializes if the parties accept to physically meet: the mediator suggests an office, a cafeteria, a table surrounded by comfortable chairs, a discreet hotel in a neighboring nation, Geneva, etc. or any other favorable location (*cf.*, on this logistic aspect, Chapter 4 on mediation preparation). Mediation often assumes the careful choice and preparation of a meeting space that parties lack.

In some cases, this suitable space may be symbolic. The parties refuse to meet or are not financially able to do it; in this case, the mediator acts as the shuttle between them, carrying messages from one side to the other so that the exchange continues.

Adam Curle in Biafra: A mediator-shuttle

Mediator, indispensable author, and first tenured chair of *Peace Studies* at the University of Bradford, Adam Curle (1916–2006) was the shuttle throughout the war of Biafra (1967–1970) between Biafrans and the Nigerian government to prepare solutions to end the crisis.

Distrust of the Other and Confidence in the Third Party

In a situation of conflict, past experience leads a person or a group to be suspicious of the other. Based on a negative experience, one fears the worst:

- *With the same interlocutor:* A party was "fooled" once, and no longer wants to take a chance. Once bitten, twice shy.

- *Or with other interlocutors in a similar situation:* A party suffered from harmful events elsewhere and does not wish to risk a recurrence.

Past painful experiences drive caution and reluctance, which manifest themselves even when the causes have vanished. With attentive and benevolent ears, the mediator probes and explores what has happened, uncovering the sources of distrust in order to move forward. This suspicion may appear during joint or private meetings. An understanding of real or perceived risks helps to elaborate guarantees or other acts likely to restore confidence.

Distrust of the other pushes someone toward a third party, who might not be discarded the same way. When the mediation idea emerges in a suspicious party's mind, another question is quickly raised: who would be this neutral person who inspires enough confidence to overcome such ingrained suspicion? Often, the confidence in a potential third party precedes the very idea of mediation. As one first thinks of someone trustworthy, the idea of mediation comes later.

The American hostage crisis in Iran

In the aftermath of the 1979 Islamic revolution in Iran, with the arrival of Khomeini in power, a grave diplomatic crisis was precipitated when US citizens were held as hostages at the US embassy in Tehran in 1980–1981. There was no confidence between the two countries. On both sides, an outrageous rhetoric obstructed all contact. Algeria, on the other hand, enjoyed the confidence of both sides. Algerian diplomacy opened channels of communication between the two camps, working toward the resolution of the crisis.

These seven justifications above underline how mediation helps to *go beyond an* unsatisfying *past,* bereft of communication and trust, dominated by an escalation of negative emotions, the imbroglio of problems and reciprocal misunderstanding, marked by the absence of shared rules and a meeting space. Mediation happens at a particular juncture in order to understand the past and try to move toward a promising future.

A Future to Reconstruct: Seven Justifications in Favor of Mediation

Facing conflict, the finality of mediation for parties is less about agreeing on the past than about helping them build a future suitable for each of them. What is at stake is the durability of the agreement, which mediation takes into account by responding to seven new justifications, this time to move forward.

Preserving Relationships

One needs to "separate the people from the problem" (Fisher, Ury, and Patton 1991) in a conflict. Even if some conflicts concern mostly the resolution of a problem, nevertheless the human, or intersubjective, component reveals itself as decisive in finding a way out of the problem.

In other cases, the damaged relationship is more important than the problem itself, which is only a symptom. Thus, addressing it constitutes a principal objective of mediation. It is not conceived as a moral question, but as a contextual necessity. Reality puts people or groups in contact, brought to stand alongside one another and to interact not only because they want to, but because they cannot do otherwise, at least in the near future. Here are many examples.

- *Ex-spouses* – Two hypotheses can be distinguished. The first one requires a more sustainable relationship.

Divorce with children

Parents need to maintain relations, even minimal, to better assume their respective role as parents. Children will be grateful that their mother and father know how to talk to one another and continue to exchange views, without tearing each other apart. All this is in the interest of the children.

Divorce without children

The ex-spouses wish to conserve a cordial or at least efficient relationship. Even if they do not see each other again, it is in their interest to maintain a relationship in the strict framework of the divorce procedure, which they hope will be the least painful possible.

- *Neighbors* – Unless you move to isolated regions, you will inevitably rub shoulders with neighbors, with whom it is preferable to maintain cordial relations so as not to make daily life difficult for yourself.

Neighbor on the same floor

Despite the racket from their party until five in the morning and the damage they caused to the walls of the corridor two days earlier, my neighbor and I have an interest in speaking civilly to one another in the future in order to manage co-ownership issues.

- *Students, teachers, parents* – Our children spend much time at school. It is also the workplace of teachers. From elementary school, to middle and high school, students, teachers, and parents are linked for years. Preserving the quality of these relationships is fundamental for all (Cardinet 1997).

Insults at school

Student of this professor or professor of this student, I think about tomorrow. I still recall this moment of tension where we lacked respect and nearly got physical. I have a hard time speaking to the other. But, tomorrow, we will meet again in class and it will be unpleasant. I would prefer to not go there, or to call in sick. But seeing one another again is inevitable: still six months before the end of the year. Ah, if only there were mediators! Could they help us?

- *Employers and employees* – By definition, a corporation supposes continuity; beyond conflicts, everyone needs to work together.

Work methods in a company

Employee of my boss, or boss of my employee, I no longer tolerate this lack of respect for the work methods I propose. They do not understand anything no matter how hard I try to explain it. As for firing or resigning, I do not even consider it. But tomorrow, the atmosphere will remain horrible. Ah, if mediators were able to make them understand the advantages of these new work methods!

- *Between organizations* – Businesses, governments, and associations maintain ongoing working relationships (clients, users, suppliers, partners, associates) which are not in their interest to cut off.

A company and its supplier

A company notes the increase in late deliveries, errors related to orders, and changes in taxes without previous information from its main supplier. Things become so bad that the company is nearly thinking of changing suppliers. Terminating relations: why not? But what will be the cost associated with a new supplier? Facilitating an exchange of explanations between the two companies, mediators help to shed light on the temporary difficulties of the supplier – the unexpected departure of the director of production. The supplier agrees to the preferential conditions of its client regarding *future* deliveries, once the director of production is replaced.

- *Between countries* – It is advantageous for neighboring states to maintain good relations. If tensions appear, it is in the interest of the international community to mitigate them through mediation efforts.

A border dispute

A border dispute has poisoned relations between two countries for years. But is it only a border problem? What about these ancient historical tensions that have not been dealt with? Is it not time to evoke endured and inflicted sufferings in order to work toward a reconciliation? From the viewpoint of neighborly relations, beyond fixing the borders once and for all, what about reflecting on exchanges across these borders: developing trade between the two economies, student exchanges, learning both languages, creating sister cities, etc.? A third party can help to support confidence building at least until direct negotiations can take place.

The concern to maintain or rebuild an acceptable – and ideally, satisfying – relationship is at the core of many mediations. Its success is measured by the results of the restored relationship, to the extent that parties themselves judge relevant.

The Need for a Process of Problem-Solving

Sometimes, negotiators, charged with resolving a conflict, skip steps to announce "their" solutions without having set up an extensive inventory of problems and needs of "the other." The result is suboptimal if compared to the solution that negotiators could obtain if they had followed a methodical process of problem-solving:

- Description of facts, while comparing the versions of each party

- Understanding the motivations, needs, interests, and constraints of each party

- Invention of all possible solutions in response to the needs of one another

- Considering the involved parties and contexts

- Finally selecting a balanced solution among all possible options, which is justified and takes everyone's needs into account as much as possible

It remains difficult for negotiators to split themselves in two: to know how to negotiate the resolution of a problem on one's behalf and, at the same time, to structure the exchanges in anticipation of such a resolution. Thus, an additional justification favors mediation: it stems from an already evoked "division of labor." On the one hand, negotiators are in charge of the substance, and on the other hand, mediators are in charge of the process and its successive phases (see Chapters 5 to 7).

The Need for Confidentiality

Whether talks take place in the family, the neighborhood, the district, at school, or at the workplace, safe free speech needs to be protected. Parties are often concerned about maintaining discretion around a conflict and its resolution, fearing for their public image or their personal reputation. Confidentiality proves to be an important criterion of choice. In contrast with other modes of conflict resolution, mediation prioritizes confidentiality, as it is essential to confidence and trust.

Petty crimes: I will repair the damages. To protect my honor, please do not talk about it!

There are 30,000 cases of criminal mediation in France every year. Petty crimes include slander, assault, and shoplifting. If they become public, the offenders risk ruining, for life, their reputation. Within mediation, confidentiality allows parties to say difficult things about oneself or the other, to react to one another, without the information being used against anyone. Mediation can thus result in apologies, followed by mutual recognition, as well as reparations for the reprehensible act. However, confidentiality does not cover infringements of public order. Here is why mediators temper the principle of confidentiality, as Chapter 3 indicates, with the principle of respect for the law. For example: *"I commit to confidentiality and invite you to do so. But if there was a violation of public order, I would be obliged to disclose it to the prosecutor."* Each person knows the limits of confidentiality guaranteed by mediation because they have been clearly spelled out by the mediator.

To protect oneself from the risks of leaks in the media, the advantage of confidentiality in mediation is valued in the political field, as in economic matters, between companies.

Good Time Management

All of the above underlines how long it takes to overcome, peacefully, a conflictual situation, because a multiplicity of factors need to be taken into account: (re)establishing the relationship, receiving and considering emotions, describing contents, dealing with needs, imagining appropriate solutions, and obtaining commitment. From this point of view, the comparison between mediation and negotiation reminds us of the fable *The Tortoise and the Hare* by La Fontaine: the hare-negotiator tries to rush the exchange, to finish it quickly, but without ripeness. The tortoise-mediator, on the contrary, meticulously progresses, step by step, grasping the deep sense of words pronounced by each person … and guess who crosses the finish line first?

But the image of the tortoise has its limits. Indeed, mediation is not slow: it is much faster than a court ruling, as it presents several advantages. First, long periods of time elapse before a judge addresses a case, except for emergency interim proceedings. Second, once the decision has been made in the first resort, appeal remains possible, again postponing a decision to a potentially distant horizon. From start to finish, it is not rare for a court ruling to require several years. Mediation can be started in a short time, and take from just a few days to a few months in the most complex cases. Therefore, if it succeeds, it saves years to the benefit of all parties.

Besides, if it takes some time for a case to be litigated, the time dedicated by the judge to review it is short, really too short: the parties have the feeling that "their" case is expedited in minutes, stuck between dozens of others. In front of a civil judge, the parties' arguments are so brief that deep explanations are impossible. It is true that mediation will take more time: first to understand (one another), then to listen to one another until a solution is reached. In brief, in litigation, the frustration of the waiting time for a decision adds to that of a shortened hearing. By contrast, mediation intervenes more quickly, and then, as Talleyrand says, knows how "to take one's time."

Other forms of external decisions (the vote, a hierarchical decision, etc.) are settled quickly – limited time for a debate before a vote or for an explanation to a hierarchical authority. But again, parties often feel they lack the time to explain themselves, as in court. The way mediators manage information exchanges will thus be perceived as a loss or gain of time, depending on the length of time it takes to renew the relationship, to dig into a problem deeply, and to brainstorm solutions.

Thus, mediation manages time well. It consumes a little but utilizes it well.

Cost Control

On average, the predictable cost of mediation remains significantly less than that of a legal procedure. It is a frequently cited justification in favor of mediation. Litigating a case, especially if it involves an appeal, requires legal specialists, like bailiffs and lawyers, whose services prove expensive. Naturally, if mediation is engaged in parallel with a trial, the costs of one add to the costs of the other, especially if mediation does not result in an agreement; but if it succeeds, the trial is ended, sparing a much greater financial cost for the parties. In mediation, lawyers act as advisers and often charge more reasonable fees, because the time they save allows them to engage in other activities (Lempereur and Scodellaro 2003).

What about the mediator's compensation? In general, *informal* mediators are not paid. Institutional mediators are paid by their organization and not by the parties. What about ad hoc mediators? Many practices exist, responding to different contexts. Certain associations give unpaid services to their members, like the French Mediators' and Arbitrators' Association (AMAPA), which settles conflicts between audiovisual professionals. In this case, mediators voluntarily give their time. If not, as for all services, private advisory firms or liberal professions charge a flat fee, hourly fees, or an amount that depends on the total amount that is contested in the mediation. Certain complex affairs require a lot of time, not only for preparation but also in sessions; they require experienced and specialized mediators, whose services are valuable, and therefore expensive for parties. Even in this hypothesis, if two parties agree on the name of *one* mediator, rather than each one appointing a lawyer – thus *two* professionals – the incurred fees remain lower and are split between them.

It is up to each person to appreciate the value of the service rendered by paid or unpaid mediators (see Chapter 4). It would be dogmatic to consider that a mediation solution should necessarily be free. The more individuals, companies, and organizations are accustomed to work with lawyers whom they pay well and from whom they demand a lot, the higher-quality services they will expect from mediators. Inevitably, a mediation market is put in place, and the law of supply and demand will apply. Reputable and experienced mediators will naturally be more costly. It is important to follow the evolution of the mediation costs, because the risk is that mediation will be viewed as an expensive process, like arbitration. Free mediations will persist in ad hoc mediation under the form of *pro bono* action and will continue to prevail in informal and institutional mediations.

Search for a Well-Accepted, and Thus More Sustainable, Solution

The scenario is frequent in negotiation: two parties sign a direct, rapid agreement between them, but it is revoked a little later by one of them or not executed at all. Why has an agreed-upon commitment not seen the light of day? Have the parties truly explained themselves in depth? Have the identified solutions put an end to the problem? Have the parties really claimed ownership of the agreement? All these questions shine light on a powerful criterion in favor of mediation: a solution will be all the better accepted if none of the parties feel it is imposed on them.

In conflictual situations, emotions and tension between parties enable an entrenched position to emerge: mine. Here, only "my" solution can be the right one. The conflict, where one digs in one's heels, is also a way of preserving one-sided self-esteem: "*I am a good person. The one who is at fault is the other.*" On the other hand, if mediation works, the parties find sufficient time to explain their perspective to the other and to really understand one another. The self-esteem of both parties is preserved and reinforced. Each person is considered, and more easily recognizes some legitimacy in the other's words and actions. The mediation process helps the parties to formulate acceptable solutions that were not imaginable at the beginning, but that emerge when one better understands the deep motivations of each party.

A divorce – "$2,000 of alimony, too much!"

In a divorce, the husband refuses to grant a $2,000 monthly payment of alimony to his ex-wife. She demands this sum, producing a budget of her monthly needs and those of their children. In mediation, the husband reveals that he understands the necessity of this sum, but his new partner considers that it would be offering an undeserved luxury to his ex-spouse. He needs the solution to be understood by, and acceptable to, his new partner. It is thus not as much the financial aspect that annoys him, contrary to how it appeared at the start. Once these respective needs are clarified, the parties come to imagine appropriate responses to it.

During the mediation, an acceptable solution for the parties (but also for the new partner in the background) emerges. First, the ex-husband transfers a $1,000 alimony to his former spouse, who will manage this sum for herself and both children. Second, he will grant up to $1,000 to cover a part of the rent, which he will transfer directly to the real estate agent. This final clause ensures that the money is not used for another purpose. The agreement is thus durable, responding to the needs of both parties.

This example underlines that beyond negotiators – the ex-spouses – *quasi-negotiators*, however absent from exchanges, exercise an important influence on the choices of official negotiators (Colson 2007). A party's refusal in mediation is sometimes rooted in the fact that another stakeholder, absent but *decisive,* is not taken into account in the solution. That is why the mediator's approach claims to be as inclusive as possible. To assure a durable agreement, it is important to map out all the relevant protagonists who might be impacted by the consequences of the agreement, block it, or, on the contrary, encourage it.

The following example illustrates the advantage of mediation in finding solutions that integrate the needs of all parties and in organizing the agreement's sustainability by anticipating changes in circumstances and their potential consequences for the initial agreement.

Inheritance: To sell or not sell the house?

A sister wants to keep the family home of five rooms where she was living with her parents, now deceased. Her brother wants to sell the house to collect half the purchase price that he inherits. Mediation reveals the following:

- For the sister, the emotional need to conserve the family home and the practical need to find accommodation

- For the brother, the need to finance the acquisition of a small apartment in the same town to house his two kids, who are attending university

From there, the mediator brings the parties to imagine solutions not formerly envisioned. The property will not be divided. The sister will let her nephews, the students, occupy half of the house. She will keep the family home, while her brother will not incur any expenditure to house his kids in town. At the end of the children's studies, the sister will pay a rent to her brother or progressively buy his part of the house.

Because the solutions are elaborated by the parties themselves and respond better to their multiple needs, as well as those of others, they are not only well accepted but also more easily implemented. Naturally, for solutions to be acceptable they also need to appear equitable – fair – to both parties in the unique context of each situation. This important principle of fairness is analyzed in Chapter 3.

Control of the Parties Over the Final Decision

If one chooses an external decision system – arbitration, ruling, or vote – uncertainty increases as our control over the final decision diminishes. Choosing to rely on a third party is accepting in advance that their decision can disappoint us, not conforming itself to our expectations, hurting us, and even frustrating everyone.

On the other hand, the advantage of mediation – as in negotiation – is to leave the power of the decision to the parties themselves, evidently consistent with public order. In this sense, mediation prolongs the negotiated space where the parties retain their autonomy and engage one another freely. It is only as a last resort, mediation failing, that the final outcome requires an external decision-making body imposing itself from this point forward. In that respect, mediation makes parties aware of their responsibilities and decision-making capabilities. They control *their* decision. Certainly, they can refuse, if necessary, an agreement that they would consider unsatisfying; but the flip side to this freedom is that they can otherwise accept it and agree to implement an agreement that is suitable to them.

Nevertheless, it happens that a party, facing mediation, feels a form of disempowerment. Two principal causes explain how mediation can by perceived as interference. One is the tactlessness of mediators, who fail to act like facilitators when necessary and rather overplay the role of advisers, to the extent of appearing as moralizers and know-it-alls. The other reason concerns the inadequate choices of mediators. In Africa, for example, mediations proposed by a former colonial power will in general be badly received by the representatives of an independent state, quick to interpret them as a neocolonial maneuver.

Avoiding this parties' feeling of disempowerment is an ongoing concern for the mediator. Thus, it is up to them to walk the talk and constantly prove by their behaviors and moves that they do the utmost to help the parties to find their own solutions and, in the final analysis, to recall that the ultimate decision belongs to them, and not to the mediator.

*

Committed to overcoming a painful past and building an acceptable future, mediation will be pertinent each time that the relevant conflict will bring together some of the 14 justifications presented in this chapter. There is no need for all criteria to be verified; but the more there are, the more relevant mediation will prove. Needless to say, the fact remains that at the onset of mediation the parties may express fears and doubts. Are mediators neutral? Are they independent enough of all the interested parties? Do they not risk showing themselves more sensitive to the point of view of the other than to mine? Are they competent? Will they keep what I tell them confidential? Are they going to impose their own visions of things on us? Hence the importance, for the mediator, as for the parties, to keep in mind some key principles regarding structuring the functioning of mediation. This is the goal of the following chapter.

CHAPTER 3
THE PRINCIPLES
Set Up Operating Principles
Before Acting

A responsible mediation method is essentially structured by principles (Lempereur 2015a, 2016b). Each of them contributes to the intrinsic value of mediation, to its proper operation as well as to the trust that the parties – and, more broadly, the general public – accord to this mode of conflict management. The parties, as well as the mediator, owe one another the greatest clarity on the principles that guide their respective exchanges and relations. As a result, everyone achieves a better understanding of their respective roles.

Before describing these principles, let us emphasize how much simply *knowing* them in theory proves insufficient. First, it is important to explain them and get buy-in from the parties before the mediation takes place: everyone explicitly needs to agree on the operating principles and be willing to put them into practice. These principles are worth keeping in mind both in the pre-mediation phase, before the parties meet with the mediator, and in the mediator's opening statement in the presence of the parties. Depending on the context, the mediator will adapt their statement of principles – to render it either succinct or detailed – which in itself is a form of *agreement to mediate* and corresponds to a reciprocal commitment to the "rules of the game" that will govern subsequent exchanges (Lempereur 2003d).

Second, these principles need to be practiced throughout the mediation by both the mediator and the parties. The principles are the backbone of the dialogue among all the protagonists. This chapter thus calls for a double responsibility, on the part of both the mediator(s) and the parties.

Our mediation experience, assisted by research insights, brings to light seven leading principles. Such principles do not define mediation in absolute terms to maintain a degree of adaptability in implementation, but each one anchors *a strong preference*. However, in some contexts, each principle may be in tension with a complementary, if not opposite, tenet.

The Principle of Independence
Versus the Reality of Situations

Strictly speaking, the mediator's *independence* requires they do not depend on any party in any way: emotionally, financially, hierarchically, politically, etc. This principle is crucial so that the mediator does not feel obliged to favor this or that party, because their own situation *would depend* on it. It aims at avoiding the risks of a conflict of interest, and also of roles.

However, this principle has exceptions, in particular, concerning informal mediations. As we discussed in the first chapter, many of us are brought in our daily lives to intervene like informal mediators with family, within a company, or any other organization, where multiple links of deference, even dependence, exist. The application of this principle therefore demands a fine understanding of concrete situations: everyone needs to be conscious of their existing relations with others and to step back, so that the mediation outcome stems from the parties. On the contrary, a risk appears if my possible dependence as a mediator on one of the parties calls into question my ability to be an "independent" mediator in the mind of the other.

Mastery of the "in between"

I work in the textile sector; Janet is my boss, and I supervise the work of Leo, an employee in the clothing workshop. I can become a mediator between Janet and Leo in a dispute only if I assume, temporarily, my independence, and if the parties perceive me as capable of doing so. This in-between ability is not inconceivable, but still needs to be verified because there is a risk, in the course of the same conversation, of "changing hats" and slipping from the role of a mediator to the role of a subordinate (submitting and acting to make my boss prevail) or of authority (emphasizing my authority as Leo's supervisor).

To avoid any confusion, it is useful to indicate explicitly that we change "hats" by qualifying these roles and by indicating where we are speaking from. For example, by stating: *"I would like to leave my role as a mediator for a moment to talk to you as an adviser/expert/member of the union."* Then: *"I now come back to my mediator's role."* The involved parties can thus better understand "where" the third party is coming from and thus situate themselves accordingly. The informal mediator needs to be conscious of their multiple roles and the possibility of sliding from one role to another.

The principle of independence is all the more important as it meets – and in part conditions – the principle of neutrality.

The Principle of Neutrality
Versus the Resort to Fairness

A mediator's neutrality speaks to an absence of preference, as much vis-à-vis the parties as vis-à-vis any solution to the problem. But can one ever be totally "neutral"?

Proximity or repulsion

Throughout the course of a mediation, I feel irresistibly closer to the party seated to my right: this handsome man or this beautiful woman. On the other hand, on my left, I feel antipathy, even hostility, toward this narrow-minded person, whose face reminds me of a former boss. Antipathies and sympathies haunt everyone's lives, including the mediator's, who struggles to maintain equidistance.

In absolute terms, neutrality would assume the mediator's *indifference* when it comes to the parties, the conflict, its resolution or not, and to the choice of the terms and conditions of a possible solution. It is important to recognize that an idea of the mediator's absolute neutrality produces a myth, as research demonstrates (Mitchell and Webb 1988; Bercovitch and Rubin 1992): the mediator is less neutral than their pure intentions which lead them to mediate. Mediators have an interest, for example, that mediation takes place – because they are paid to facilitate it, or because they will be able to refer to this experience later as part of their accomplishments, or because they will draw useful data for their research if they are professors, or still because their participation serves a spiritual mission if they are clergy, or their self-esteem, etc. If a mediator desires that the mediation succeeds, it is also because this success speaks to their facilitation skills and their credibility in the field, or because the resolution of the conflict stops the indirect negative effects from which they suffer – as in the case of a nation that facilitates the settlement of a crisis between two neighboring states in order to stop the flood of refugees into their own country. Finally, mediators themselves often draw concrete benefits from the agreement, especially if the parties entrust them with the mission of surveying the implementation of the agreement, or because the agreement is favorable to them, as in the following example.

Between neighbors, an interested mediator

A co-owner seeking a quiet living space finds themselves disturbed by the noisy disputes of their two neighbors, who argue about storing objects in the basement. Relying on their good relations with both parties, they serve as an informal mediator. However, most likely, they have an interest in the case: either to keep the peace, or maybe to keep the basement empty or, further, perhaps they wish to store objects there. In all cases, the situation contradicts the principle of neutrality, but this does not prevent them from playing a positive mediation role.

Challenged by some for its idealism, and endorsed by others for the sake of objectivity, the neutrality principle is important because it stresses that mediators, despite their own feelings, values, and the interest that they may have in settling a dispute, *need to stay neutral in regard to the conflict*. Even if mediators have personal impressions, they keep these inside them, without revealing them. Whatever their inner state, mediators act in an irreproachable fashion during the process and exhibit *impartiality*, a principle that we will explore next.

The neutrality principle collides with another, the *fairness principle*, or the conception of what is just or not, beyond even the letter of the law. "*What is, thus, above justice? – Equity,*" averred Victor Hugo. If a mediator claims to be neutral, can they let the parties reach a solution that seems inequitable, either for one of the parties, or for a stakeholder not present at the mediation? Or can they venture to express their sense of fairness? The moment they raise the fairness principle, they move away from the principle of absolute neutrality.

In observing the practices of different types of mediators, depending on the case, mediators act by favoring either the principle of neutrality or that of fairness. Either a mediator conceives their role in compliance with the principle of neutrality, in which case the substance of mediation is uniquely the parties' realm, or they perceive themselves as the guarantors of fairness and, if a solution emerges that appears unreasonable, they will propose a time of reflection, suggest consulting advisers before committing, betray their viewpoint through their probing, and even leave the mediation to let the parties negotiate between themselves an agreement which the mediator finds inequitable. Between these two extremes and to allow the parties to reflect on these questions without taking part themselves, a mediator manages many resources – notably the art of questioning, which is broached in Chapter 6.

In order to surmount the dilemma created by the tension between these two poles – neutrality and fairness – mediators need to sequence their actions: first, by establishing neutrality so as not to be influenced by either perspectives of the parties; next, by calling for fairness, or searching for the most just solution possible. The initial neutrality is *sine qua non* for the later expression of fairness. In summary: *neutrality comes first*.

Neutrality is so much a matter of perceptions that a psychological perspective helps this discussion. Those who question the idea of a mediator's pure and unwavering neutrality are supported by recent discoveries in psychology. It might be easier to detect emotional lies – when one mimics sympathy despite real antipathy – than informational lies – when one distorts facts. If mediators lie about their inner state, for example if they "externally" parade their neutrality, while deep down disapproving of one of the parties, their real feelings might betray them. The idea that mediators can hide their deep sentiments is thus more of an ideal than a reality.

Suppose someone in conflict is hypersensitive and is thus inclined to develop feelings of paranoia and persecution. Despite all the efforts that are being made, they will scrutinize the mediator's neutrality. Mediators may in fact be neutral but may not be perceived as such.

For all these reasons, whether mediators demonstrate their own feelings and values or keep them locked inside, it seems reasonable to hypothesize that they will not be able to part with them and will thus never be neutral in a strict sense. The principle of neutrality is certainly meaningful but has its limits. Hence, practitioners often prefer to invoke another principle: impartiality.

The Principle of Impartiality
Versus the Need for Proximity

Deep down, the only way to operationalize neutrality – that is, to effectuate the positive effects despite the mediator's preferences – is by the impartiality of the process. Impartial mediators are those who, whatever their intimate opinion on the issues, *strictly maintain the equilibrium of the process*. Here, it is important to distinguish *neutrality* (*lived by mediators*, notably in their relation to the content of the mediation) from *impartiality* (*perceived by the parties*, notably in relation to the management of the process). Defined thus, neutrality and impartiality hinge on one another to characterize four typical configurations (see Table 3.1).

TABLE 3.1   The Matrix of Neutrality and Impartiality

Solution to the Problem:	Neutral	3	1
situation lived by mediators	Not neutral	4	2
		Partial	Impartial
		Process: the mediator's attitude as perceived by the parties	

- *Situation 1* forms the most desirable case: Mediators are totally neutral and indifferent in terms of solutions; they also maintain an impartial process. For the reasons that have just been explored, this configuration often remains theoretical: it is the model of the *ideal mediator*.

- *Situation 2* corresponds to *realistic mediators*: Even if they have preferences concerning the solution, or regarding one of the parties, or on the type of agreement to favor, the mediator ensures that they remain unbiased in the management of the process, which is balanced and beyond reproach from the viewpoint of the parties.

- *Situation 3* allows us to really explore the difference between neutrality and impartiality: Even though they have no substantively affirmed preference, the mediator fails – by lack of methods or experience, or by one of the parties' influence on them – to organize and maintain an impartial process. Their efforts notwithstanding, these *clumsy mediators* get carried away and are poorly regarded by the parties for their unbalanced process.

- Finally, *Situation 4* corresponds to *biased mediators*: Driven by their personal preference, the mediator manipulates the process in order to lead to one type of agreement rather than another. If the mediator takes the side of one of the parties, and favors them through the process, they lose the trust of the other.

The mediator's impartiality is put to the test by the different forms of identification or proximity that make them feel closer to one party or another. Here are some examples.

Identification with a social role – Because of their own life experiences, the mediator feels closer to the student or the teacher, the employee or the employer, the seller or the buyer, etc. Putting aside their own experience, the mediator needs to be careful to treat all parties with equal care and consideration. If necessary, they should organize a co-mediation by enlisting a mediator who has a different and complementary profile.

Co-mediation in the audiovisual profession

AMAPA (Mediators' and Arbitrators' Association for Audiovisual Professionals) favors co-mediation, which consists of putting a producer and a screenwriter as co-mediators in a case between two protagonists – a producer and a screenwriter. The risk of not doing this would be that one sole mediator, identifying in advance with the viewpoint expressed by the "colleague" party, rejects the other based on the fact that this is *"behavior typical of screenwriters or producers."* The risk that mediation is biased by a professional prejudice is minimized by having two complementary co-mediators.

Identification with the situation of a victim – When the past or present action of one of the parties regarding the other is viewed by the mediator as an expression of domination exercised by the strongest against the weakest, the mediator may feel the temptation of rebalancing in favor of the latter, in order to avoid giving the impression of supporting an injustice. This risk of partiality is important in criminal mediation. Between the author of a crime and its victim (harassed, threatened, extorted, robbed, injured, etc.), mediators feel closer to the victim in general: they are quick to support them, and to take a side against the offender, for the sake of teaching a lesson. Sometimes there is no crime, but an unbalanced relationship of power. Inversely, a mediator may identify in advance with the stronger party, when the latter derives their domination from law or a social norm.

I identify with the weak or the strong

- *I feel close to the weakest*: how can I feel impartial in this family disagreement, where a father, in order to punish his 11-year-old daughter who got bad grades, left her in the yard for the entire night?

- *I feel close to the strongest*: how can I feel impartial in this dispute where the supermarket director wants to sanction two members of the personnel who, of their own initiative, took toys off the shelf to offer them to children whom they found nice? ("If one gives merchandise in this way, without even referring them to the manager of the store, soon there will be nothing left, but to close the shop!") Yet, if as a child I suffered from a lack of toys, I can identify with the generosity of the staff.

Identification with one's physique, age, sex, race, ethnic origin, religion, clothing choices, etc. – We are not always aware of the biases or prejudices that shape and cloud our judgment. Mediators, as people, are no exceptions. They need to engage in continual self-reflection to pinpoint their prejudices, and exercise exceptional self-discipline to prevent conscious and unconscious biases from impacting their professional efficacy. Do they not identify with the husband rather than the wife – or inversely – with the young rather than the elderly, with the white rather than the black, with the elegant rather than the disheveled, etc.?

Identification with the cooperative, kind, welcoming – As much as there may be prejudices in relation to people, there may also be judgments concerning situations. Even as one reduces the harmful action of prejudices, many judgments may remain. As any person, mediators are subjected to commonplaces *(topoi)*, in the sense of Aristotle: they prefer the cooperative individual to the aggressive, the nice to the nasty, the accommodating to the quibbler. Mediators need to be aware of the temptation to prefer the party who, through all their gestures, mirrors and comforts them in their own approach, including searching for integrative solutions, making concessions, etc.

Faced with these forms of identification and similarity, there are three ways of conceiving impartiality that reflect three different mediator behaviors:

- *"I am neither for one nor for the other"* – Taken literally, this approach leads to unemotional mediators, avoiding any sign – mimics, gestures, words of comprehension, etc. – that can be interpreted as an agreement. They behave at a distance: neither with one, nor with the other.

They even become *distant*, which can be counterproductive. Pushed to the extreme, the principle of impartiality results in a dehumanized version of mediation.

- *"I am not more for one than the other"* – Here, the mediator is more involved, expresses signs of comprehension, and enters into the world of each party while consistently monitoring their actions and words to ensure equidistance: not showing themselves closer to one than to the other.

- *"I am for one and for the other"* – In contrast to keeping one's distance, this principle, which we call *multi-partiality*, consists of moving closer to one *and* the other, inspiring trust in one *and* the other through a balanced proximity. Traveling from one party to the other, the mediator claims to be *with one and with the other*, alternately showing empathy for the viewpoint of each person, to genuinely understand their needs and contradictions. This *multi-partiality* brings the parties to look at the mediator from another perspective. Instead of being felt as exterior, distant, even disinvested, the mediator is perceived as close, available, willing to take each one's place and being able to step into their shoes.

In this last approach, the mediator's empathy is permitted because it is aimed successively at one and the other party, and each of the parties knows it. Even better: the mediator's empathy vis-à-vis the two parties inspires empathy between them. And that is where the symbolic benefit of mediation resides. Before the mediation, party X may not have tolerated party Y. X has now discovered a mediator who understands X *and* Y. If both X and Y, who have differing perceptions, are understood by the same person who is using a multi-partial listening mode, they will begin to question the positions creating the divide. That is, if the mediator is able to understand me, but also "the other," the latter cannot be completely wrong. The mediator's actions make X pause and reconsider whether X is 100% correct. Maybe Y has their reasons; therefore, why not reflect and at least recognize them. Then, possibly, reconsider the positions from the start?

This multi-partiality nevertheless requires caution. The empathy expressed by the mediator toward each party need not be perceived by either as a surreptitious sign of preference for the other. This search for proximity and "non-indifference" needs to take place in a balanced manner among the involved parties.

The robbery of a purse

In criminal mediation, empathy is theoretically possible for the perpetrator of a crime – for example, recognizing the need for money, their family history, their willingness to impress their friends, etc. The risk is to upset the victim, who will ask themselves if this (supposedly multi-partial) empathy does not in fact negate their status as a victim and lessen the responsibility borne by the perpetrator of the reprehensible act.

Indeed, the underlying conditions that constitute the core of the mediation process, including recognizing the identities of each party, alternating active listening – moves which will be explored in the chapters to come – help mediators to avoid these traps.

The Principle of Confidentiality
Versus Potential Exceptions

The principle of confidentiality designates the secret binding the holder of the information and prevents them from transmitting it to outsiders. We will first highlight what makes this principle so strong – notably in contrast with public hearings in court – and then analyze certain circumstances where the exception to the principle becomes legitimate.

The Strength of Confidentiality

In mediation, there are *two forms of confidentiality*:

- *In the strict sense*, the principle of confidentiality applies *between the mediator and each of the parties, consulted jointly or privately*. What one party reveals to the mediator is not to be disclosed to the other party. As a trustee of the protagonist, the mediator is the sole guardian of the secrets confided to them. Thus, confidential information circulates only from party X to the mediator, and only from party Y to the mediator. Confidence and trust go hand in hand in mediation.

- *In the broad sense,* the principle of confidentiality extends to all the protagonists of mediation – that is to say, *the parties and the mediator* – vis-à-vis everyone else outside. Little by little, as trust grows, the parties manage to exchange more information between themselves, thanks to the mediator. However, no matter how much information circulates among the parties who participate in a mediation, this information is protected from the curiosity of outsiders by the seal of confidentiality. This principle extends to everything that is said during the process. It then commits both the mediator and the parties to keep the content of the exchanges for themselves, thus avoiding the risk of misinterpretation, transformation, or modification by others. This principle encourages sincere interactions, as the examples, below, illustrate. However, some exceptions, presented afterward, create a tension between this principle and the necessity or objective of transparency.

The major interest of confidentiality in mediation is to overcome an inherent contradiction in court proceedings: justice needs to be public – except in exceptional cases of closed hearings – but the risk of a biased audience can impede an exchange of information, which is indispensable to an objective understanding of a dispute, the identification of possible contributions, a shared solution, the mutual recognition of parties, and therefore the fundamental resolution of the disagreement. In front of a court, where "all you say can be used against you," one refrains from saying too much. Besides, it is tempting to charge the other and exonerate oneself from any wrongdoing, and even to disguise all or a part of reality. The legal sanction in sight also leads to an amplification of resentment, and a polarization of intentions. At each instant in judicial proceedings, the protagonists calculate the risk that the information that they possess, if they divulge it, turns against them, feeds rumors, or gives leverage or sanction to outsiders.

Because it is confidential, mediation avoids these pitfalls. In order to help identify a zone of possible agreements, mediation increases the flow of information between the parties themselves, and between the mediator and the parties, by limiting the risk of possible diffusion of confidential information outside this restricted circle. Mediators play an important role in this regard, as the following example illustrates.

A case of potential harassment

An employee complains about the fact that her boss overworks her with mind-numbing tasks, mocks her efforts, and frequently threatens to fire her. Because a legal approach naturally implies a limited scope of facts, evidence, and applicable rules, it focuses the magnifying glass on a minimal part of the reality: the alleged harassment. This limited scope is amplified while the rest is ignored. This *focalization-deformation* emphasizes the perceived reality of each party, while the objective and shared reality may be something else altogether.

- The perceived reality of one party includes various motivations: the need for recognition of one's work, wish for promotion, respect for personal life, serenity, etc. From this standpoint, harassment becomes intolerable and the focus of the problem.

- For the other party, their perceived reality includes another series of motivations: the efficient management of one's team, the necessity of performance, recognition and promotion, etc. This party also understands an intolerable reality: the accusation of harassment.

Because it is confidential, mediation, where anything may be broached, offers parties the possibility of speaking freely in order to perceive this shared reality and to focus on the disagreement without losing sight of the context. The action is placed in perspective. Thus, mediation respects the complex identities of people; it reveals them, because people open themselves to it more easily. Confidentiality, the keeping for oneself, is paradoxically what allows talking about everything, including the most intimate topics.

This case illustrates how legal action creates the risk of only unveiling a part of the reality, and even of obscuring it to strategic ends. It encourages bad faith and the fear of consequences if one proceeds in good faith. Instead of resolving the problem, it can sharpen it. It often rewards lies, omissions, and pressures. Although it aims to settle social issues and to end problems, it instead enables them to bounce back – if only in the minds of those who suffer from the feeling of injustice, because they know deep down what really happened. *"Tell the truth, the whole truth, nothing but the truth"* is one of the most beautiful fictions invented by the law. Lawyers know it. Since the sophistry of Greeks, plausibility has more success in the courtroom than the truth. "Perception is reality."

Mediation thus provides a venue for contextualizing the narrow truth that – in the heat of the moment – we believe is the only view of the situation. In this venue, one's speaking can encourage the other's speaking: confidence for confidence. Because one of the two feels safe enough to make the first move, dialogue begins. This is how the principle of confidentiality works in practice.

This principle justifies itself in the interest of not only private people, but also of organizations (Colson 2004, 2007). Companies wish to protect their reputation, as much as individuals. Through the judicial system, they would fight and spend considerable sums to protect their reputation by denying facts, however obvious they may be. In the confidential framework of mediation, knowing that their reputation would be safe, they may be ready to admit error and generously compensate the contractual failures that are theirs. Mediation favors sharing without fear of sanction. It thus allows the reparation of damages caused, in contrast to a legal proceeding, where through a lack of evidence or a brilliant plea, the truth can be distorted, and any damages consequently denied.

Conflict between two large companies

A large contract of a popular company on Wall Street resulted in the delivery of material containing serious defects. A lawsuit, public by definition, would have had devastating effects on the reputation of this supplier, without even taking into consideration the uncontrollable rumors that it would generate. The company preferred to enter into mediation because of the confidentiality it entails. At the end of the process, the company allocated considerable sums in damages, all the while repairing the defects caused as quickly as possible, but it was able to avoid exposing itself to the spotlight of the media and the markets. It took necessary measures to prevent the failure from recurring. The confidentiality of the mediation allowed the supplier to keep the trust of its current and future clients.

Hence, mediation commits parties to a discrete process of information exchange, in view of a confidential agreement recognizing and compensating for what is necessary but sparing the relations of the involved parties and their external image. As a result, an agreement is more sustainable for all concerned. In the case of failure, other paths toward solutions, including litigation, remain available.

Potential Exceptions to the Principle of Confidentiality

It remains nevertheless true that there are exceptions to the rule of confidentiality. Sometimes, the parties themselves do not want to keep everything confidential. Thus, it is important to give the parties a choice concerning the degree of confidentiality. At the beginning of a process, the mediator and parties need to agree on the rules concerning information exchange. Three types of arrangements are possible:

- *Agreement on non-confidentiality* – When the mediator and the parties are acting as representatives of organizations, it is often necessary for each party to share information within their organization.

Two rival factions

In one of the poorest African states, the mediator – a special representative of the Secretary-General of the UN – managed peace talks between the representatives of two armed political movements. Both parties and the mediator accepted in advance that the talks would be public and their content would be communicated to all the represented groups and organizations.

- *Confidentiality for the mediator and freedom of speech for the parties* – The mediator commits to keep all information shared during the mediation confidential. Then, they invite the parties to maintain the same level of confidentiality, but sometimes the parties wish to keep others in the loop: for example, a husband with his family or his children in particular; an emissary with her government; a business representative with management, or a union representative with union members, etc. Here, it is about discussing and arriving at a common agreement on the application of the rule. The principle of confidentiality is present at the start, but open to adjustments as long as all the parties agree.

- *Agreement on common information to be provided externally* – From the onset of the mediation, all parties accept confidentiality with the provision that an agreed-upon text or a list of information concerning the proceedings and contents of the mediation will be shared with external parties (for example, with the media, work colleagues, family, a lawyer, the judge) at the end of each mediation session. This more nuanced approach, which we recommend, avoids rumors and an escalation of the conflict by distorting "noises." It prevents the mediation exchanges and sensitive information from being divulged. Actors outside the mediation, who are able to better understand the complexity of the disagreements and the progress made, can thus contribute to the search for solutions for everyone involved.

One spokesperson for all the parties

A factor of success for many international mediations consists of appointing a sole spokesperson, common to all parties present at the table. During the Camp David Accords of 1978 that restored peace between Egypt and Israel, US President Jimmy Carter proposed to President Anwar al-Sadat and to Prime Minister Menachem Begin, who agreed, that outside communication be conducted only via the Presidential Press Secretary, Jody Powell.

In 1995, on the invitation of US President Bill Clinton, Presidents Alija Izetbegović (Bosnia), Slobodan Milošević (Serbia), and Franjo Tudjman (Croatia) met in Dayton (Ohio) to negotiate a peace accord for the former Yugoslavia. The State Department Spokesperson, Nicholas Burns, oversaw all outside communication.

The application of the principle of confidentiality has a limit: *the exception of public order*. Let us be clear on the perimeters of this exception.

- *On past events constituting a violation of public order* – Sometimes in mediation, parties divulge information that testifies to a past violation of criminal law, by one or both of the parties. In this case, mediators are held to confidentiality, as long as the facts do not contribute to a continuing offense. The mediator hears the parties under the seal of confidentiality; in this respect, professional secrecy applies here. If they are lawyers, this principle is even stricter. A mediator will not be able to disclose in court what has been revealed to them in confidence in mediation, even if they receive proof that could turn the case. Under that condition, mediation encourages parties to express themselves to the greatest extent possible.

- *On the current commission of a violation of public order* – Confidentiality does not apply as soon as it involves the continuation or commission of a crime. Mediation cannot serve as a façade for actions that violate the law. The mediator would be liable if they covered up reprehensible acts, even if the parties agree among themselves. The mediator needs to always do everything to prevent parties from using mediation and confidentiality as instruments of illegality. Here, not only are mediators not bound to confidentiality, but they are bound to disclosure. For example, if a mediator knows that the parties reached an agreement that violates the rules of public order regarding environmental obligations, not only do they have to prevent such an agreement, but if this agreement concludes without them and they know about such a clause, they have no choice but to denounce it to the ad hoc authority, even if this question remains controversial.

This legal exception to the principle of confidentiality maintains the trust in mediation in general and in mediators in particular. If trust demands mediators' confidentiality, it also demands that they respect the norms of public order. If mediators started serving illegal interests by using confidentiality as an excuse, public trust in mediation would be affected.

The Principle of Respect for the Law
Versus Spaces of Creativity

Mediation has always taken place *"in the shadow of the law"* (Mnookin and Kornhauser 1979). Mediators intervene in a normative landscape: that of national or international law. *Law is like Janus: it has two faces, one that is amicable and one that is coercive* (Lempereur 2012b). Mediation situates itself within the law on the amicable side. Mediators, without being auxiliaries of justice, contribute to *alternative dispute resolution* (ADR), as they carry on a form of legal "private justice" (Goldberg et al. 2020). As long as mediation works in a conflict, it reflects the law in its voluntary form within a system of problem prevention and resolution; but if mediation fails, the law, in its coercive form, will take over. Sometimes strictly calling for this coercive form of legal intervention is inevitable, and a broad knowledge of the law (as expressed by courts) will help the parties and mediators to find an appropriate solution (Lempereur 1990, 1995). But because conflict consists of other dimensions, explored in detail in Chapter 6, this principle of respect for the law is exercised in tension with the necessity of thinking beyond usual, legal frameworks; to fill in the gaps, to resolve legal contradictions, and to surpass divergent interpretations. It is here that the indispensable space for creativity exists, shaping the flexibility and adaptability of mediation.

Comprehension of the rule of law, including case law, appears necessary in the sound exercise of mediation, in particular for the legal aspect of the problems that illuminate parties' rights in a conflict. Two complementary principles emerge:

- Within the law, *there are norms of public order* (for example, protecting public health, the environment, banning child labor, commission of misdemeanors or criminal acts) that must be respected by mediators, as by every citizen. This corpus requires the increased prudence on the part of the mediator, who cannot become an accomplice to ignoring or circumventing the law. As indicated *supra* regarding exceptions to the principle of confidentiality, vigilance is required to prevent the violation of this first category of norms.

- The law also consists of *numerous negotiable norms* that do not concern public order. These dispositions exist in contract law to fill the gaps in case the parties did not address them explicitly, but they can be waived if parties wish to. Because these dispositions are negotiable, the parties have the right to opt out of them by a mutual agreement, or they can use them as a source of inspiration. For example, in some legal systems, payment for a commercial service must be done "within 60 days"; and it will be if the parties mention nothing about it in their contract, but they can also agree to a payment "within 30 or 120 days," or "upon signature of the contract" or "upon delivery." The rights that are at stake here are open to negotiations.

The law therefore is both a source of constraints (obligations of public order) and a motivation for parties' creativity (permissibility of negotiable laws).

Some conflicts, concerning relational or cultural aspects or a new domain for which the legislator has not yet developed any regulations, may lack any legal norms or may have norms of various degrees, from negotiable, up to becoming crucial to prevent the parties from acting in violation of public order. Thus, mediators need, at the very least, *a sensitivity to the potential legal dimensions of conflict* to orient them according to the two following categories.

Disagreements with a Direct Link to the Law, to Rights, and Duties

Two examples of legal links

- Plagiarism of intellectual works, counterfeiting, unfair competition, or use without authorization of a patent are banned and sanctioned.

- A father wants to cut two of his three children out of his will, but according to French law, he is prohibited from depriving some of his descendants of a minimum share of the estate.

Through the intervention of mediators, (who are not necessarily lawyers) or of a legal expert (the lawyer of each party), it is essential for the parties to know their rights and duties. Two scenarios appear.

- First, *the parties, informed of their rights, can choose to not apply* them if they are not of public order. These accommodations are produced in mediation, when a solution appears more satisfying to a beneficiary than that which would result in the strict application of the law by a court ruling. One is situated here in the domain of freedom of contracts and transaction, where one party, with knowledge of the cause, renounces the exercise of their rights by concessions judged desirable in a given context.

Three examples of agreements with the renouncement of rights

- A spouse knows that she would be able to obtain $1,000 alimony, but she agrees to $800, which is sufficient, and keeps her in a more relaxed relationship with her ex-spouse.

- An employee can expect a court to make a ruling on a severance pay of $40,000, according to legal precedents; but rather than find herself unemployed, she prefers an arrangement with her employer to immediately change jobs, reducing her work schedule, and preserving her rights to retirement.

- A real estate developer, whose construction work caused nuisances in the neighborhood, chooses to immediately fix the damages, rather than resorting – though this is his right – to his insurance, the premium of which would be strongly re-evaluated following this declaration.

- On the other hand, *the parties,* in mutual agreement*, can ask a judge for approval* of their agreement and to give it *legal enforceability.* Ordinarily, the judge's role is thus limited to confirming the legality of the agreement. However, a judge remains free to give their opinion, and to modify the agreement if the latter contradicts dispositions of public order.

Disagreements Without a Direct Link to the Law

In many situations, the principle of respect for the law – even if it applies – fades in front of non-legal dimensions of the dispute that encourage greater creativity.

Spaces for the imagination

- Three departments of a tech company – marketing, production, and finance – have been in conflict with one another for months. Some, taking the market into account, find the launch of an ultra-perfected new cell phone the best approach. Others, taking into account the cost of investment and the current unreliability of the system, are opposed to it. This conflict has strategic, technical, economic, and commercial dimensions (each choice being associated with its own legal consequences, which remain secondary).

- Within a political party, several factions collide in terms of agenda priorities for the next parliamentary session.

- Four brothers and sisters wear themselves out dividing the possessions that their parents left them. Doesn't each child have the best motives? For example, one of the sons explains that his mother said to him that this particular object – in the family for three generations – was especially destined for him. Another recalls that she cared alone for the parents during the final years, while the other brothers and sisters lived elsewhere. Sometimes, going to court on such issues will lead to a cold, narrow, and random application of the law, and will not allow any understanding of the underlying issues.

Therefore, mediation does not limit itself to the legal appearance of conflict (the visible part of the iceberg) but reveals its deep roots, its profound reality (the unseen, submerged part of social interactions). The ability of the parties to imagine solutions that respond to this submerged part is crucial. The mediator thus need not lock themselves into a restrictive legal interpretation of the conflict. What is "right" beyond the "rights" may also be delicate, as the following principle demonstrates.

The Principle of Fairness
Versus the Parties' Self-Determination

Sometimes, the agreement is established on legal aspects; rights are respected, but the result may be less than equitable. Integrating this principle in mediation requires a high vision of justice. In each particular instance, it is about producing a result that embodies what is equitable; hence the need for the mediator to consider, in light of their personal convictions, whether an agreement reached also embodies fairness. But how to proceed when fairness as perceived by parties differs from that perceived by the mediator? When invoking the principle of neutrality, this question is particularly pertinent when the parties themselves agree with one another – according to the principle of self-determination – but when their provisions go against the mediator's sense of equity.

Equit(y)-ies

The following real-life examples highlight the contrast between what seems equitable to some and what is not necessarily perceived as such by others.

Agreements in mediation – acceptable or not?

- *Case 1* – Two spouses, during the course of a divorce, reach an agreement according to the terms of which the father, who lives 900 miles away, no longer sees his three-year-old son and in exchange receives all property assets.

- *Case 2* – One morning, a delivery driver brings a medical certificate to work, exempting her from driving due to sickness. But her boss orders an urgent delivery; the driver accepts and causes an accident. Although not responsible – because of the hierarchical coercion – the employee feels guilty about the extent of the damage, estimated at $40,000, and out of shame, she agrees to resign.

- *Case 3* – Mrs. K., whom her husband beats every day, accepts the rule he proposes, according to which he will no longer beat her, except if he considers it necessary "given the circumstances."

- *Case 4* – To satisfy the workload of a start-up, the CEO agrees to work in the office from 7 am to 11 pm, including weekends if necessary. If not, she will have to resign.

- *Case 5* – A copyright conflict pits a producer and a scriptwriter against each other. The financial damage suffered by the scriptwriter is estimated at $2,000 by the two parties, but the scriptwriter consents to a $1 symbolic compensation.

Clearly, conceptions of fairness clash with one another, and the parties' choices result in solutions that many would judge inequitable. The parties' "agreement" obviously betrays power dynamics where the stronger party seems to impose their will. As much as the law helps in bringing back fairness in an agreement, by application of rules of public order, the values or feelings of the parties can help to include it as well.

In *Case 1*, a father cannot part with the right to see his child for life; this right is not negotiable, that is to say alienable, buyable, or saleable. Even if this father were ready to apply such an agreement, he has the right to rescind it later on. *Case 3* illustrates a same legal limitation: the prohibition of violence against people makes the potential agreement violate the law and public order. Every deal to the contrary is unenforceable; even if an agreement intervened, it would have no legal value. In these two cases, beyond the rule of fairness, mediators find a better ally in the respect for the law and the rules of public order to prevent such agreements. Mediators would be legally responsible if they endorsed them, not because they are unjust (which they are), but because they are illegal. *Case 4* seems to reveal rules of public order, but legal regulations on the limitation of work hours for employees may not apply to a CEO. The principle of fairness thus takes over: mediators need to decide if they want to engage the parties in evaluating the equity of such an agreement. *Case 2* properly reveals fairness: nothing can prevent anyone from resigning from a position. If no pressure is exercised on the driver to push her to resign, and if she is fully aware that nothing obliges her to do it, she does not have any less right to leave the company at her own discretion. Still, mediators find themselves faced with a dilemma that we will explore *infra*: should the delivery driver be considered the ultimate judge of fairness for what concerns her, or should the mediators bring their own conception of a just solution? The same principles apply to *Case 5*: if, from a legal point of view, the scriptwriter has the right to financial compensation, he also has the right to decide to abandon it. This approach seems shocking, but it might be justified by other motivations: getting a symbolic recognition, keeping a good relationship with the producer, not preventing future collaborations, etc.

These examples above highlight how much the mediator needs to measure whether they are operating under the premise of fairness only, or in accordance with the subdued fairness under the law and public order. Another orienting principle is that of "coexistence," or "living together": mediation, deep down, needs to allow parties to continue to coexist on a voluntary basis. Recognizing this principle will sometimes bring solutions in contradiction with the perception of fairness of one party or the mediator. But an agreement can sometimes embody the principle of coexistence, while not that of fairness. If no imperative disposition of positive law applies, it is up to each person to mobilize their personal sense of what is just. It will thus be necessary to examine who is asking for fairness.

Whose Fairness?

The use of the word – "fairness" – seems to suggest that only one type of fairness exists. Actually, perceptions of what it means vary significantly.

They fluctuate from culture to culture, from one time in history to another, from person to person, and, of course, according to the circumstances of each case. The definition of equity differs according to mediators, parties A, B, or C, philosopher Y, or judge X. A mediation outcome can be built on many approaches, and feelings that stem from the parties, and from the mediator. Let us explore multiple hypotheses.

- *Fairness is left for the parties to define* – Certain mediators deem it essential that the parties maintain their freedom to choose throughout the mediation, no matter what the balance of power is between them. This self-determined agreement takes priority over the mediator's perception of fairness, as long as public order is preserved. The mediator considers the parties to be adults and does not wish to project on them their values or their own feeling about what is just or unjust. It is a *liberal vision* of fairness, making parties responsible for their choices, at the risk of producing results perceptible as unjust, even if approved.

- *Fairness is evaluated by the mediator* – In this interventionist conception, the mediator openly expresses their opinion when they consider the decision approved by one (or both) parties as inequitable. They act like benevolent parents, or even like judges. For example, the Mediator of the French Republic and institutional mediators have, by law, the personal responsibility to give an opinion on the fairness of a solution. They are obliged to seek and verify the existence of fairness in the agreement: "*Given the set of elements brought, it would seem equitable to …*"; "*We verified the different elements of the elaborate agreement by and between the parties, and this agreement seems equitable to us …*" If this agreement does not seem equitable to the mediators, they inform the parties, and can even choose to withdraw from the mediation. It is a *social vision* of mediation, attached to promoting fairness in compliance with either what the society feels concerned about – in the case of institutional mediators – or with one's personal conception – in other cases. But such a vision poorly suits sophisticated parties, who can feel patronized by mediators.

- *Fairness is established by the parties and the mediator* – Far from the clear-cut previous models, in practice, the principle of fairness often manifests itself through a dialectic of exchanges between the parties and the mediator. Throughout the mediation, the mediator questions the parties regarding the motivations that ground their expectations. These questions bear witness to the mediator's inquiries into fairness as perceived by the parties. In this *pragmatic vision*, the principle of fairness is *co-constructed* in an agreement through shared work.

○ **Fairness in an Amicable Divorce Procedure**

"Mr. So-And-So, how does the alimony that you claim fit with the income of Mrs. So-And-So?"

"Mr. So-And-So, by asking for the sole custody of the children and by wanting to limit the mother's visitation rights to only two days per month, how does it allow her to play her role as parent and to express her love for them?"

• *Fairness is shaped by the parties, with the mediator* – Between the liberal vision and the pragmatic vision, the mediator might call for *an integrative vision*. This aims for the elaboration of a decision immediately satisfying the parties – in the liberal sense of their individual needs – *and* also more in the long term, preserving their relations with one another – in the sense of a durable social equilibrium. The mediator, through questioning, urges the parties to construct a decision together in order to attain a fair balance as much as possible. Without uttering the word "fairness," they urge the parties to decide on its existence, to search for an agreement that respects it. The mediator, by their questioning, invites the parties to a collective search, rather than by asserting a version of fairness that overlooks the wishes of the parties. This type of mediator is comparable to an architect who questions their clients on their needs and submits successive plans testing the waters and assuring, at the end of the process, that the definitive home plans suit everyone, all the while guaranteeing the solidity of foundations and walls. Such a mediator plays an active role, and by their Socratic method alone allows the parties to discover an adequate application of what is equitable in their given case. This approach requires great skills on the part of mediators to preserve the creative tension between the search for fairness and the support to the parties' self-determination.

o *What justification criteria would you like to apply to assure a balance of benefits between what each of you will receive and give as a parent to your children after the divorce?*

How will you write the agreement in such a way that it is equitable in the eyes of each of you two?

Now that the agreement has taken shape and its writing is completed, what is your degree of satisfaction with its legitimacy? Do you want to reflect on it, and give your response after some reflection time?

Without making a decision in the heat of the moment, I suggest each of you take some time (hours, days, or weeks) to make sure it is a good agreement for you.

Would you wish to contact your lawyer, your children, your respective relatives, so that they provide you with their advice and guarantee you the feasibility of the clauses, implementation, etc.?

This final approach, integrating the necessity of respecting parties' self-determination, as well as the social function of mediation as an instrument of social justice to avoid abuses of power to the detriment of one of the parties, pushes the mediator to make the parties reflect upfront about their agreement and about its *quality*, giving them time to consult before making a definitive decision.

Certain mediation analysts fear, however, that such an approach might threaten the potential of finding an agreement: by wanting a perfect agreement, there is a risk of not finding one at all. If the parties do not take advantage of promising opportunities when an immediate agreement seems likely, the door may be opened for a perpetual reassessment and procrastination, which could prevent any agreement from ever emerging.

Fairness in conflict is not simply founded on what is just, but also on what is finished.

Taking into consideration these risks of postponement, we advise to resort to a "*draft agreement*" that contains elements to which parties are ready to give their consent. If the fairness of an agreement seems contestable, it is useful to leave a *small time for reflection*. Inviting parties to verify the balance and fairness of the agreement increases the chances that it is respected and subsequently implemented.

The Principle of Self-Determination *Versus* the Mediator's Push

Mediation is, above all, the business of the parties; it is a *negotiation* by other moves, facilitated by a third party. Mediators help parties to come to the table, to better communicate together and to search for mutually satisfying solutions. From beginning to end – before, during, and after – mediation is characterized by its voluntariness. It is enough that one of the parties does not play the game, or wants to leave it, for mediation to stop. In sum, *ownership* is key, and mediators work at every moment so that parties remain in charge, so that they understand that the mediator does not make mediation work for them, but that they make it work.

Does this mean that the mediator remains passive? Of course not! But sometimes the mediator needs to step back and resist the temptation of pushing the parties in a specific direction or to an agreement. The more the parties understand that the mediation is voluntary and that every solution needs to be agreed upon, the more the mediator's efforts – at all stages – will be effective in enabling the parties to understand that for their own interests, they hold the key to mediation and its success.

Before mediation starts – When a party is willing to try mediation, sometimes the other may not see its usefulness, either because they think the dispute can be resolved by simply prolonging the negotiation, or because they have decided to bring the case to court. In this delicate phase where one party drags their feet, nothing can force them to a mediation. The mediator's role is to demonstrate the advantages of mediation but also its limits (Chapter 2), all the while noting that each party remains free to refuse mediation and that, even if they engage in it, they will always be able to put an end to it, for example, at any time, in favor of litigation. The reminder of the voluntary character of engaging a mediation imposes itself on the mediator from the get-go to gently bring reluctant parties to accept mediation.

At the beginning of the mediation – Let us concede that both parties are ready to try mediation: the mediator still needs to clarify the mediation framework. The mediation principles – independence, neutrality, impartiality, confidentiality, respect of the law, and fairness – are some guarantees that facilitate a voluntary involvement of parties throughout the process. It thus falls as much upon the parties as upon the mediator to continuously mobilize these principles and to ensure they are respected. In this spirit, it is convenient to explicitly reaffirm these principles before the mediation starts (Chapter 4), or at the very least at the start of the first mediation (Chapter 5), in order to obtain the agreement of the parties on them before initiating the in-depth discussions. However, these principles cannot be imposed as such on the parties: it is important for the mediator to not simply present them to the parties, but to elicit their voluntary adherence to their application, through an *agreement to mediate*.

During the mediation – Listening techniques that a mediator uses during the exchanges encourage parties to express themselves and highlight the central place of their opinions throughout the entire mediation (Mnookin and Lempereur 2014). The mediator is the expert of the Socratic method, but steps aside to let the parties take the floor, and only comes back in the game in order to ensure that nobody is forced, nor prevented from speaking, and that each one's will is respected. The mediator ensures a balance in the dialogue, avoids untimely interruptions and the abuse of harmful influences, because these forms of constraint may disempower one or both of the parties, giving them the impression of having lost their freedom of choice. The evidence of the voluntary character of mediation is that it happens that one of the parties wants to leave the mediation table. Sometimes, for good reasons, the mediator exercises delicate pressure on this protagonist to return.

This approach requires exquisite nuance. On the one hand, the mediator avoids giving up on the process, as soon as a party signals even the mildest of dissatisfaction. On the other hand, the mediator cannot become coercive, pressuring either party to remain at the mediation table. Ideally, parties only return to the mediation table because they recognize it is in their interest to do so. The ensuing process is equally voluntary, malleable in accordance with the wishes of the parties, in contrast to a judicial process that authorizes neither improvisation nor modifications at the convenience of "litigants." Likewise, the search for solutions is incumbent upon the parties: whether or not they share information; whether or not they block one another through positional bargaining or choose to concede what is secondary to save the essential; whether or not they devote themselves to brainstorming in order to overcome initial barriers; and whether they propose justification criteria to decide in legitimate ways as opposed to the use of power.

When the ultimate decision materializes – The most formal mark of the voluntary character of mediation is that ultimately, the parties are free to accept the solution that is in sight – or not. Either party can refuse to adhere to it. If the final decision were imposed by the other party or by the mediator, then there would be no self-determination. Even if the mediator, facing a deadlock, is sometimes tempted to let go of their role of process facilitator in order to venture in the domain of substance by proposing one or many solutions, they know that their solutions are only some among many possible others and that the only ones that count are those on which both parties agree. Whether the mediator proposes solutions or not, whether they intervene on fairness or not, whether they are powerful or not, the principle remains that each party possesses the ultimate power regarding the final decision.

It is precisely mediation's voluntary character, from beginning to end, that offers the best guarantee of voluntary implementation of the agreement. There is no need to coerce implementation where agreement is willingly given. The parties do not commit carelessly to a solution, because once they say yes, they are held to it. The willingness to adhere to a transaction embodies the legally binding willingness to implement it. Once the adherence is conferred by the two parties' mutual yes (*mutuus consensus),* both parties can only agree to undo it upon by a mutual no (*mutuus dissensus).*

It needs to be thus clear to the parties, from the start of mediation, that they are not obliged to reach an agreement, or to give their agreement, but if they do it, they will have no choice but to execute it. This is the magic of a freedom that constrains itself, because it was freely given.

This voluntary character that spans all mediation from its inception to its conclusion, in its success as in its failure, demonstrates its place in *the negotiation space*, where the power to decide is incumbent upon the parties and nobody else. Mediation is the ultimate attempt to reach a negotiated decision, to avoid resort to a decision-making third party, to a private authority (the arbitrator), or public authority (the judge) who will substitute their decision for the parties. The failure to reach a mediated solution is always a sign that the parties are finding it difficult to identify, by their own examination and through self-determination, a possible solution to the problem that they face. This failure to find a solution is as much the responsibility of parties as that of the mediator, because mediation itself emanates from their double responsibility.

*

The seven principles presented in this chapter form the backbone of the mediation methods. The mediator needs to share them with the parties to make them theirs, and above all to combine them so that each supports the other at the right time. It is this combination that produces the infinite mediation styles situated on a continuum formed by the following models:

- *Either a mediator focuses less on content*, favoring neutrality and impartiality, refusing to intervene other than on the process, thus ensuring the parties' self-determination, ownership, their creativity in coming up with solutions that work within the law;

- *or a mediator focuses more on content*, favoring active multi-partiality, engaging with the facts and problems; suggesting solutions, checking their conformity to the law and even to fairness, and does not hesitate to gently push the parties in one direction.

Mediation theories reflect a spectrum of interventions that look contradictory at first sight, claiming both neutrality and intervention in fairness.

Rather, it denotes a complementarity, a creative tension between principles, even a management of two terms of polarity over time. It confers upon the mediator a freedom and responsibility for their ethical choices that adapts interventions to the circumstances. Still, the mediator needs to learn how to make their personal ethics explicit to the parties, because this information is likely to influence the process. In fact, it is highly desirable that the parties be made aware in advance – and choose themselves if applicable – if the mediator will intervene by favoring absolute neutrality, or establishing fairness, or ensuring coexistence to help the parties reconstruct a common future.

CHAPTER 4
THE PREPARATION
Structure Pre-Mediation
Before Starting a Session

Once mediation is considered, it is important to move from theory to practice. Preparation will usefully precede action. Experience underscores the importance of this pre-mediation stage, which greatly determines the success of the mediation to come. Solid foundations are necessary for a well-constructed building. On the one hand, it is about preparing for the mediation itself and, in particular, identifying a mediator. Who feels responsible for this preparation? It may be one of the parties, all of the parties, a judge, or an external stakeholder, such as a family member. And how is a suitable mediator to be selected? According to what criteria? A mediator (or the organization they belong to) may volunteer. However, the choice of the mediator needs to be accepted by the parties, which constitutes a key concern of the pre-mediation stage that this chapter will explore. On the other hand, each one of the protagonists needs to prepare for what is important to them: both the parties and their eventual counsel, as well as the mediator(s). How to get ready? This chapter will provide you with operational answers.

An Itinerary for the Pre-Mediation Phase

The idea of mediation needs acceptance by all the involved parties. Likewise, the choice of a mediator requires agreement. The mediator will also prepare, if necessary, an agreement to mediate.

Birth of an Idea: A Bet

All mediators acknowledge that there is a game of *"who is going to start?"* Who will escape the vicious cycle where each party waits for the other to initiate mediation? *"That the other party takes the first step"* is sometimes posed as a prerequisite, perceived as an indispensable sign of respect. But it is also less of a risk: it is more comfortable to refuse an offer than, if one initiates the first move, to endure the affront of refusal. These feelings, conscious or unconscious, make this initiative delicate – sometimes to the point of preventing mediation altogether.

Proposing, Accepting, Refusing Mediation

Prejudices are often projected on the very offer of mediation and its acceptance. Suggesting – or not – and accepting – or not – become a power issue, a struggle of egos. The *"who proposes to whom?"* conveys ambivalent perceptions of strength or weakness. Indeed, a mediation offer from party A to party B is perceived as

- a strength by some: *"Party A feels sure of itself since it fears neither mediation by a third party nor confrontation with party B"*;

- a weakness by others: *"Party A feels hesitant because they prefer the support of a mediator to engaging in direct negotiation, or to starting litigation."*

Monsignor Gaillot: I am ready if the Pope ...

Due to his activist and media-friendly stances in favor of marginalized people, French Bishop Gaillot was sanctioned by the Catholic Church and lost the Diocese of Évreux in 1995. In the conflict that pitted him against the hierarchy, Monsignor Gaillot declared that he would accept mediation if the supreme authority of the Church – then Pope John Paul II – made the first move.

Likewise, the acceptance of mediation may be perceived as

- a strength by some: *"Party B feels confident. They are not scared of confrontation and the upcoming exchanges"*;

- a weakness by others: *"Party B recognizes the precariousness of their position by agreeing to resort to a third party"*; *"They fear that the case will end up in court."*

What is the point of experiencing mediation as a setback, a negotiation failure, or the weakest strategy? Rather, you can experience it through two positive lenses:

- *Wisdom:* Every human being, with their dignity, their values, and their history, can legitimately – because they are "human" – not arrive at an agreement, either in their own name, or as a representative of a group (sometimes of millions of other human beings). This is why systems of hierarchical or legal decision-making exist. But before resorting to the authorities, would it not be wise to take a chance on a benevolent, neutral specialist in human exchanges, who can tackle difficult and painful situations? This third party, instead of deciding on your behalf, employs useful methods so that each party retains their dignity in being able to decide for themselves.

- *A breath of fresh air:* Rather than locking oneself into a prolonged painful present, isn't it interesting to think of a mediator as an impartial catalyst of innovative logic, a new alchemist of relations and unexpected solutions?

Who Proposes Mediation First?

There are three possible scenarios, none of which are fully satisfying:

1. *One of the parties proposes mediation* – Spontaneously, one side invites the other to engage in the mediation process: *"We have had trouble coping,*

let us organize a meeting where each one of us will voice our concerns; a facilitator will help us achieve a mutual understanding." The risk, in this case, is that the origin of the idea – one of the parties in conflict – will cast a shadow on the very suggestion of mediation. The suspicion that characterizes a conflict situation makes one party suspect a trap in everything proposed by the other party. This cognitive bias, called reactive devaluation (Ross 1995), is likely, especially if the other party is unfamiliar with the mediation idea. Hence, in order to reassure the parties, before the mediation starts, the mediator needs to give enough explanation about the sincerity and objectivity of their mission, which serves all parties.

2. *Solicited by one of the parties, the mediator suggests mediation to the other party* – To avoid the pitfall of the previous case, or because any contact is impossible, or still because the party in question feels incapable of explaining the mediation approach correctly, they ask the mediator to contact the other party and get their agreement to begin the mediation process. But, in this second case, the reactive devaluation can tarnish the mediator themselves, who may be accused of partiality because they were contacted and identified by "the other" party. If the mediator is not careful, they may end up reinforcing this suspicion from the moment they make contact with the other party, on the phone, for example: *"I was contacted by Mr. X, from Company H, who has a problem with you, concerning, etc."* The other party may fear an antagonistic alliance between the mediator and the other party: *"The mediator will without a doubt defend the other against me, since they are calling me, on behalf of the other!"* To avoid this risk, when the mediator contacts party B after having been solicited by party A, they can do the following:

- *Introduce themselves* immediately (and, if necessary, the mediation organization to which they belong), *before* making a reference to party A.

- *Mention* – if necessary, as a hypothesis – *the problem at stake*, by highlighting a lack of information and the need to listen to B right away to know what it is about. It is indeed risky to take the first version of the problem literally. Demonstrating this concern to B will help B to understand that the mediator is keeping a fair distance from A and does not identify with either of the parties.

- *Ask questions* regarding what B thinks, as a way to directly respond to the reluctance or questions that may come up. By recognizing the equivalent validity of the version presented by B and by raising the eventual misunderstandings on the mission proposed to both parties, already at this stage it is necessary to appear as a model of listening and understanding, a preview of the manner in which the person would be welcomed in session.

- *Give the first elements of information on a potential mediation process and on the mediator's role.* In particular, the mediator invites B, like A, to explain themselves completely, and assures that each party, even in disagreement, will be listened to. The mediator will then seek, with both parties, solutions that respond to their needs and work with both of them.

- *Describe the advantages of mediation,* without actually hiding its limits (Chapter 2). It is useful, in particular, to remind a potentially reluctant party of the success rate of mediation (two cases out of three) and to underscore that public authorities, like judges, recognize the usefulness of this approach. But B could ask, *"How can I be sure that an eventual agreement will be respected?"* In reply, the mediator will then mention that a mediated settlement can be approved by a judge, which makes it enforceable, without the need for a trial.

3. *The mediator is proposed to the parties by an external actor* – In this final configuration, mediation is proposed by an outside authority – a common friend, social worker, judge, commission of conflicts within a sport federation or a political party, the European Union, the United Nations Secretary-General, etc. This approach avoids both preceding pitfalls: the perception that the mediation hides questionable intentions. On the one hand, parties who are prisoners of knots that they can no longer untie can view mediation with relief. On the other hand, it also provokes, for certain parties, the impression that one "forces their hand." The recommendations in the preceding hypotheses thus equally apply: the prescriber or the mediator mentions them with each of the concerned parties.

It therefore falls upon each party to determine for themselves, with a full awareness of both the degree of urgency and the ripeness of the conflict, whether or not to proceed with mediation.

How to Approach a Party's Resistance or Refusal?

The causes of resistance and refusal of mediation (as analyzed in Chapter 2) are diverse. Let us briefly recall them: parties suffer a feeling of failure or powerlessness; they fear revealing details of the conflict to an outsider ("to air dirty laundry in public"); they fear being robbed of their free will, of having to accept a solution imposed by an external authority; etc. To give mediation a chance, it is important that the mediator listens to these fears and responds to them with finesse. The refusal of all mediation draws on three big categories of causes, which call for different strategies:

1. *Legitimate reasons to prefer another system of conflict resolution* – A party can prefer the pursuit of direct negotiation, the decision of a hierarchical supervisor, the arbitration or judgment via the rule of law despite the risks, even the end of all action due to weariness or hope that time will do its work. "There is no problem that an absence of solution cannot resolve," maintained French politician Henri Queuille (1884–1970). Once a party has evaluated the advantages and limitations of the conflict resolution mode that they contemplate, their decision demands respect.

African tradition of palaver

A French CEO, a former commercial judge, gives an example of his experience as a supervisor of a public works construction site in Africa. One day, two African workers find themselves in conflict about how to store material. A third party listens to the version of each person, reflects, then rules in favor of one. But the same worker who received the favorable decision scowls and expresses their dissatisfaction. The boss of the construction site is surprised by it: "Oh come on, don't you understand that I ruled in favor of you?" The worker responded: "Yes, but … we did not discuss!" This reaction makes the French CEO reflect: what is the satisfaction of winning the case worth for B, if A did not understand the reasons? What is the decision worth if it is not preceded by a human exchange that sheds light on it? The CEO kept this episode in mind during the rest of his career in France.

2. *Causes tied to a lack of understanding of mediation* – The reasons why mediation is being proposed need to be clearly explained and understood. If one party resists the use of mediation, is it clear to them that their concerns would be addressed in the process? That mediation respects the parties' freedom of choice and leaves the final decision to them? As already outlined, it is important to keep in mind that "the other party," who has been invited to the mediation, may be suspicious about the intentions of the party asking for it, as well as the mediator's themselves. Therefore, being clear about the role of the mediator is equally important.

3. *Causes tied to skepticism concerning the mediator's ability or independence* – The idea of mediation is perceived positively; but the choice of mediator is questioned. *"Who will know how to understand me?"* This brings us to the following question: *"Whom to choose as a mediator?"* A mediator's professionalism and sense of responsibility may push them to suggest to the parties to turn toward another mediation center, or toward colleagues whose personality, experience, or culture will fit the situation better. The issue remains to identify the right person with whom the parties will work in trust.

Sometimes, this trust in a potential mediator precedes the idea of mediation. Because the parties know Mrs. X or a certain mediation organization that they trust, they overcome their preconceived notions and pre-mediation gets off to a good start. The choice of mediator is crucial for mediation to be accepted, and the mediator is the principal catalyst of this acceptance: *"The first thing to do when I see the parties for the first time is to establish my legitimacy."* The parties need to feel that the mediator is up to the task.

Choosing the Mediator

When mediation is suggested, irrespective of whoever initiated it – friend, lawyer, member of the family, one of the parties – and the idea of mediation is accepted, the question quickly emerges: who?

From the Idealized Mediator to the Best Possible Mediator: Question of Trust

"Deep down, the mediator needs to have so many qualities, it is like looking for a five-legged sheep!" a speaker once declared during an academic mediation symposium.

Parties in conflict often search for the *"ideal"* mediator – knowing, of course, that who is ideal varies from one party to the other! – as well as an *idealized* one, in the same way someone might seek the perfect spouse. Thus, the conflict is transferred to the choice and even the personality of the mediator. The choice of a mediator constitutes a first symbolic agreement between the parties. Conversely, the failure to agree on a mediator marks the perpetuation of conflict.

A social conflict in audiovisual media

During a prolonged strike, the parties spoke to each other about mediation and looked for a mediator, a person who would understand them and, at the same time, someone who was an expert in their domain. The unions and management examined a series of names and did not reach an agreement on any of them. The mediation never took place.

At a given moment, finding the best possible solution among people we know or people recommended to us becomes the priority, knowing that a mediator is a human being, fallible like every human. The fact remains that a minimum of trust is necessary. This trust draws on a diversity of factors: age, profession, gender, race, technical specialty, their geographic or cultural proximity, the first contact, and the recommendation by another person or an authority worthy of trust. Other criteria may also include the mediator's reputation or recognized moral authority.

Trust in the person

- The Bishop of San Cristobal is proposed as a mediator between the Mexican government and Zapatista groups.

- The government proposed to the Truck Drivers Unions and to the Federation of Freight Road Transporters Mr. X, inspector for the Transportation Commission, as a mediator in a collective conflict.

- The treasurer of Association Y proposed a founder, Mr. H, as a mediator in the conflict in which the chairman of the board opposed the CEO.

- Two leaders of multinational companies settled their disagreement with the support of an informal mediator, another well-known leader, of a different economic sector.

Trust in an organization often confers trust in a mediator who is affiliated with it. If the mediation moves forward, when a mediation association or center is contacted for the choice of mediator, it is because of their general reputation. The parties may put forward wishes to engage a particular mediator but for the most part rely on the mediation association or center to choose for them.

Trust in the organization

- The community of Sant'Egidio, a Catholic organization based in Rome and at the origin of many successful mediations, proposed certain members as mediators between different Algerian political parties, between belligerents in Burundi, etc.

- In France, in each territorial department, the delegate of the Mediator of the Republic benefits from the legitimacy of this independent administrative authority.

Beyond the central question of trust, other criteria matter: the mediator's training, their technical skills, expertise in a domain, knowledge of the context, of the cultures, etc. The diversity of these criteria prevents the proposition of a general rule of choice. Similarly, how does one rigorously estimate the experience of a mediator? Their legitimacy? Their ability to respond to the parties' expectations? In the end, there comes a moment when the parties retain a mediator who is available and who best suits them.

What Are the Reasons for the Mediator to Accept or Refuse Mediation?

The question of choosing a mediator leads to another question: According to what criteria may a solicited mediator accept or refuse such an assignment? Contrary to an institutional mediator, whose status, in general, prevents them from refusing mediation, the informal or ad hoc mediator enjoys this freedom of choice. The mediator is selected according to their skills, field of expertise, network, reputation, ethics – even their self-esteem. If the proposed mission puts the mediator in a difficult position on one of these points, it is their duty to either refuse it or signal what seems delicate, so that the parties are informed of it and can decide with full knowledge of the issue.

Proximity of the Mediator to a Party

Solicited by two companies, a mediator informs them that two decades earlier, they worked for one of the companies for three years. If, after having learned this information, the two parties nevertheless accept them, they will not blame them later, and the mediator will feel at ease for having mentioned it. In such a case, one of the representatives of the company might say: "Well, do you truly think you can be impartial?" The mediator confirmed their impartiality and conducted the mediation until the parties reached a solution.

Here are some examples of when a mediator would not take a case:

- The mediator feels too close to one of the parties, and for personal reasons, it would be difficult to deal properly with the other party.

- During pre-mediation, the mediator notices that one of the parties, in bad faith, accepts mediation only to gain time but does not intend to advance the negotiations.

- Still before the mediation, a party indicates in good faith that they want a court decision: in fact, the party believed that mediation constituted an obligatory step before returning to litigation.

- The mediator realizes that the conflict contains an essential technical dimension (for example, computer failures in relation to a defective material) that is more relevant than the human relationship; judging themselves too far removed from the domain or technically incompetent, they prefer to refer them to another mediator who possesses the required knowledge.

- The mediator has a particular personal interest that puts their independence at risk (for example, the mediator happens to be an architect, and could be brought one day to work for one of the parties).

- Quite simply the mediator, already occupied by some ongoing mediations, fears not being available enough for the parties in the mediation process.

What Should the Compensation Be?

Reaching an agreement on the mediator's possible compensation is also part of pre-mediation. Practices are diverse, to which Chapter 2 alluded. To summarize:

- *Voluntary work* – As for all activities where "goodwill" makes sense, mediation attracts "men and women of goodwill," desiring to make themselves useful. This includes any available person, having a life experience – notably at the dawn of retirement – and/or from a particular domain within which conflicts generate a need for mediation. Voluntary work is often seen in criminal mediation and for district, neighborhood, or school mediation.

- *A free public service* – Institutional mediators are paid by the central administration, local governments, or big institutions – or businesses – and propose their services free of charge.

- *Diverse forms of payment* – The fact remains that mediation is work – in the noble sense of the term – difficult and demanding work requiring concentration, competence, and commitment. Leading a conflict resolution process requires significant self-sacrifice and humility on the part of the mediator, who has to temporarily renounce their own logic, beliefs, etc. in order to empathize with each party. At the same time, payment for these services needs to take the financial capacity of the parties into account. This group of factors produces an extreme diversity of systems, from a flat rate to hourly pay, sometimes with scales varying according to revenue or the importance of the matter.

If the parties reach an agreement on the choice of mediator and if the mediator accepts the mission, another essential step in pre-mediation consists of structuring the agreement to mediate.

Preparing the Agreement to Mediate

The agreement to mediate is an agreement – oral and written – according to which the parties and the mediator (or the organization to which the mediator belongs) settle on the general configuration of the mediation to come: the place; the time that will be devoted to it (the estimated duration of work sessions, the date of completion); and, finally, the mediator's fees, if applicable. In informal mediations (Chapter 1), in general, there is no explicit agreement to mediate. Sometimes, a simple letter of invitation addressed to the parties suffices, but even here formulation is important.

Letter inviting parties to mediation – testimony of a mediator

"Usually, I write a single letter to all the parties so that they see I am writing the same thing to all of them. In this letter, I note the agreement of the parties to try to settle their conflict amicably, through mediation. I high-light their willingness, if I perceived it throughout the first contacts by telephone, to really be involved in the search for a negotiated solution. If not, I insist on the necessity of such an involvement in order to reach a mutually satisfactory agreement. At last, I indicate to the parties my com-mitments toward them: impartiality, listening, availability. The objective of this letter is to prepare the parties for the spirit of mediation." *Martine Balayn, a mediator in Var, France.*

For one thing, the agreement to mediate stipulates the rules governing the process that the mediator will recall in the presence of the parties when the mediation begins (Chapter 5). Here is an example stating the mechanisms and risks in conflict and the subsequent need to respect some communica-tion rules.

A mediation contract proposed by a freelance mediator

"When we are in a conflict, negative feelings (anger, urge for vengeance, 'to make them pay,' to win by making them lose, etc.) can dominate our communication with the other party whom we designate as responsible for our misfortunes.

Frequently, facing a conflict, we construct walls – to protect us – between the other party and ourselves. The weapons we use to defend ourselves or to fight (accusations, intentions ascribed to the other party, threats – veiled or not, irrevocable judgments, critiques, insults, slander, sarcasm, etc.) provoke the shutting-down attitude of the other side, caus-ing them to refuse to listen, to understand, and *a fortiori* to be nice to us.

This negative communication mode

1. favors violence (attacks and counterattacks);
2. drives conflict or maintains it, provoking an escalation of the tensions;

3. can poison our life by making us lose time, money, energy, and relationships.

Other ways of resolving conflicts and expressing oneself exist [...]."

The following examples illustrate the reciprocal commitments that structure mediation:

"I commit, throughout the mediation ...

1. to approach mediation with an open mind;
2. to express in the first person, 'I', my vision of the problem, my point of view, my needs, my expectations, in good faith and without violence in regard to others;
3. to avoid all hurtful behaviors or words and accept that each one of us can talk about all subjects if we wish, as long as each side is respected;
4. to listen attentively to the vision of the problem, the point of view, the needs and the expectations of the other party, until the end, without interrupting them, and to seek to understand, before, if it is possible, responding;
5. to welcome what is said knowing that 'understanding does not mean agreeing';
6. to proceed with the willingness of everyone, and efficiently cooperate with the other party to attempt to resolve, with them, our conflict in a peaceful manner."

"Co-mediators commit

1. to be impartial;
2. to respect the confidentiality of what is said during the meetings;

3. to do their best to evaluate the relevance of mediation and to verify the agreement of the parties;

4. to evaluate the mediation process in order to pursue, suspend, or interrupt mediation;

5. to respect the mediation framework and especially to make the parties respect the rules of communication where each one speaks in their own name and listens to the other until the end."

"We acknowledge having been informed of the objectives and conditions of mediation

We are informed of the fact that we – each of us – have the right to put an end to the mediation at any moment after having met with the mediator(s). We commit ourselves to the search for satisfying agreements for each of us, and we agree

1. to respect the terms of this pact;

2. to respect the confidentiality of discussions and exchanges, confidentiality that will only be communicated outside the mediation following a common agreement, and in particular, that the information shared upon common agreement will not be able to be used in court;

3. to not introduce contentious procedures during mediation except for procedural acts aiming to protect oneself from limitation periods;

4. if necessary, to ask our lawyers to call upon the court for the suspension of legal proceedings already engaged at the time of mediation, that will not exceed a three-month period, renewable once [...]."

Chapter 5 will explore more rules and principles that are useful to present to parties when a mediation session opens, in order to establish a fruitful process. Now that the parties have agreed to mediation, each one must prepare for it.

A Preparation Itinerary for the Parties' Mediation

Which parties, first of all? Which allies, advisers, or lawyers can be associated with the process? These points need clarification before making recommendations for efficient preparation by the parties.

What Is the Scope of the Concerned Parties?

Pre-mediation includes reflection on the "seating arrangements": what is the perimeter of the concerned parties? Who needs to sit apart and why, and who needs to be involved in the mediation process and to what extent? Let us shed light, using three examples, on the importance of the distinction between having protagonists at and away from the mediation table.

Stakeholders Attending or Not – Example of Children

In a pending divorce, the spouses are the sole decision-makers. But how to consider the children in the process, who are equally affected by the outcome? In Germany, for example, it is common to invite the children to ask them their opinion. In France, in general, underage children remain absent from mediation. This choice in no way prevents certain mediators from hearing the children, with the agreement of the parents and depending on their age.

Empty chairs

Even if they are not present at the mediation table, children are a critically important topic in the discussions, so that sometimes the mediator will symbolize their presence by one or several empty chairs. The mediator thus invites the divorcing couple to consider that James, seven years old, could be seated on the chair to the left, and on the one to the right would be Sonia, his sister – three years his senior. The mediator asks the parents to discuss what they imagine their children would say in response to selected questions. This staging better integrates the children – although they are physically absent – in future decisions for which they may need to be consulted at some point.

However, it is important to consider a possible conflict of loyalty. If the children are absent, it is to protect them from being torn between their two parents and from hearing things that may cause them pain. Of course, in general, children would like to be as close to one parent as to the other and to remain loyal to both. That is why mediators, rather than having the children participate early in the conversation, prefer to organize a meeting at the end of the process, so that the parents can explain their common decision.

The problem intensifies in stepfamilies. In addition to the parents who are divorcing, should the new partner(s) who shares their life with the children also be invited? Their presence is only allowed if the parties agree.

This complex situation is similar to that in a company where interested members (i.e. members of a team or department) may be absent from the mediation table. Whatever the domain, it is important to determine in the pre-mediation stage if there are protagonists, either part of the problem or part of the solution, who may need to be invited to the process, even if for only part of a session. This way, the mediation will not only gain time, but also effectiveness.

Absent but Informed Stakeholders

Harassment complaint within a company

Sometimes, when colleagues have difficulty working with one another, the conflict results in harassment or discrimination complaints. Management may wish the concerned parties to settle the problem themselves, via an external mediator. However, perhaps the conflict has vitiated the atmosphere in the department in question. So, even if the content of the exchanges remains confidential in mediation, it is useful and "liberating" for the rest of the team members to know that the colleagues in conflict have started a dialogue to attempt to resolve the problem. Likewise, it is important from the onset of the pre-mediation stage that other members of the department are kept in the loop by the parties in regard to the result of their mediation – just like the children of the divorcing couple in the previous example. These stakeholders, absent but informed, are invited to support and consolidate the agreement on a daily basis.

Representatives with a Limited Mandate

In mediation, one or many parties may send authorized representatives. During pre-mediation, or at the latest when the mediation gets started, it is necessary for the mediator to verify that all representatives really have the authority to sign an agreement; if not, it is necessary to clarify who the decision-makers are within the concerned organization.

Mediation between corporations

The authorized representatives present during the mediation had not been able to reach an agreement, because each party had reached the red lines that were set in their respective mandates. The mediation was then paused, and each party reported back to their company leadership. The two CEOs of the companies, absent from mediation but kept informed of the proceedings, met with one another as a last resort. The dialogue created during the mediation contributed to a better understanding of the situation from both viewpoints and reduced the gap between the CEOs, thus making an agreement through direct negotiation between them possible.

Solicitation of Influential Stakeholders

During the pre-mediation stage, it is important to identify and analyze all the potential stakeholders who would be likely to influence – in a positive or negative manner – the mediation process. Possible protagonists include the following: an expert in the given domain, an insurance company representative, a specialized lawyer, a former director, a founder, a union leader respected by all, or a family member. Their reflections and recommendations might prove as useful to the parties as to the mediator, who will consider, if appropriate, calling on these protagonists to intervene.

The Parties' Individual Preparation

Faced with the issue of personal preparation, a choice exists – that we respect – between pure spontaneity (*"We'll see what issues come up, when they come up …"*), which has its value, and, on the other hand, prior preparation. From experience, we recommend that parties prepare themselves before attending a mediation session. We propose three increasingly intensive formats of preparation. Each person chooses the format that seems the best adapted to their case, notably in relation to the importance of the stakes.

Preparing Interactions

This is the minimum degree of preparation – focused nevertheless on an essential component of mediation. Mediation is first a dialogue, even a trialogue if we include the mediator. That is why the quality of information exchange is key, as well as preparation for it. Each party benefits from planning, in advance, what they wish to say and how they wish to express it, as much as to the mediator as to the other party. In addition, the order in which issues are discussed also matters.

I prepare my communication:

I prepare a list detailing

1. what I would definitely like to say;
2. what I could also say;
3. what I prefer not to say, or then only to the mediator during a private meeting;
4. the questions to ask the mediator;
5. the questions to ask the other party.

As important as it is, only preparing the communication does not always suffice. Here, a second format of preparation can be helpful to parties.

Analyzing a Difficult Situation

Preparation helps parties to step back from the whirlwind of their conflict and clarify what is really important to them and what they wish for the future. It is important to retrace the chronological order of the conflict, including what caused it and the reasons why it escalated. If each party takes some time for this reflection, everyone will better understand the origin of the problem, which will ensure a better organization of exchanges and a smoother progress toward a possible solution.

This preparation format, which is more detailed than the previous one, has the major advantage of forcing each party to contemplate, in advance, two points of view: their own and that of the other side. This double perspective allows equal room for shedding light on our story and for better understanding the other party's story. In fact, what counts in general, from the onset of a conflict, is not as much the *intentions* behind certain words or actions as the *impact* they have on the other. This preparation for difficult conversation consists of reviewing eight questions (inspired by Stone, Patton, and Heen 1999).

I analyze a difficult situation

1. What is the *impact of the other* on me? (My work colleague did not respect me, she insulted me in public, she damaged my professional reputation, etc.)

2. What were *my own intentions*? (I wanted her to focus on product defects, to underscore the risks the business took, etc.)

3. What could have been *the other's underlying intentions*? (Maybe my colleague was so anxious about the success of the project that she unleashed her own stress on me, or did she simply want to defend her work, her efforts, etc.?)

---

4. What was *my impact* on the other? (I may have been insensitive in the choice of the time to speak or in what I said, to the extent that the colleague believed I was accusing her of being responsible for the product defects, etc.)

5. In summary, what is, from my point of view, *the contribution of the other* to the current problem?

6. And what is, in my view, *my own contribution* to the current problem?

7. In order to overcome the problem, which *solutions could the other* agree to in order to fix the problems? (What reparation for the past, what commitment for the future, etc.?)

8. And what could be *my possible solutions* for a better future? (What reparation for the past, what commitment for the future, etc.)

This preparation connects facts, but also feelings, impressions, and challenged values. The distinction between the perceived impact (in general negative) and the initial intention (maybe there was no willingness to harm) is essential to overcome our reflex reaction to accuse the other and to excuse ourselves. As the reality is often less binary, it is incumbent on each party to reflect – in light of their ethical choices – and recognize their potential contribution to the chain of events.

Methodical Preparation

With mediation defined as negotiation facilitated by a mediator, an even more complete format of preparation (Lempereur and Colson, edited by Pekar 2010) distinguishes three essential dimensions:

1. *Who?* The *people* dimension. The relationships and emotions between protagonists.

2. *What?* The *problem* dimension. The object of the dispute, its stakes, and content.

3. *How?* The *process* dimension. The practical organization of the meeting, in particular, information exchange.

These three dimensions reveal 10 assets for preparation that we invite the parties to analyze before the mediation.

I get prepared: The 10-assets preparation method

On the people dimension:

1. *Interpersonal relations:* I identify and collect information on everyone who will be present at the mediation table; I establish a diagnostic of my relationship with the other side; if necessary, I see how I can improve this relationship so that it allows us to work together toward a solution; does the other come accompanied? If yes, who would accompany me since I would not want to be alone?

2. *Vertical relation, or mandate:* If I represent an organization during mediation, I discuss the constraints of the mandate that I received from my principal or my organization; I analyze if other parties present at the table are equally authorized representatives and will have to, like me, report the results of the mediation.

3. *Stakeholders map:* I notice if other protagonists, although absent from the mediation, have some stakes in the outcome. What relationships do they maintain between them and with the parties? Some of these absent stakeholders may be able to bring us some resources for a common solution: how to solicit them? Others may spoil the implementation of our agreement if they perceive it as unfavorable for themselves. How to predict this difficulty by integrating them into the solution?

On the problem dimension:

4. *Motivations:* What are my underlying needs, or interests? My priority objectives? What do I try to satisfy in this mediation? And the other party – from their side, what are their needs, interests, and crucial objectives? I try – for me as much as for the other party – to move beyond superficial positions, public declarations, or rumors.

5. *Solutions at the table (SAT):* What elements of the solution can I contribute? And the other party? And the other identified stakeholders?

And the mediator, if they agree to contribute? I reflect on my order of preference between many possible solutions concerning what I would like to obtain and, also, what I would like to offer. I try to be creative.

6. *Justifications:* What objective criteria can I invoke to anchor my request, or refusal, to the other party? It can be a law, contract, precedent, technical demonstration, expert opinion, bailiff report, tradition, market value, etc.

7. *Solutions away from the table (SAFT):* What happens if the mediation fails? What can I do away from the mediation table? And the other party – from their side, what can they do? (We can go to court, or let the conflict simmer, or I can take unilateral measures, or the other can, etc.)

On the process dimension:

8. *Organization:* How much time do we have? Are there particular deadlines (from their side, from mine, fixed by an external party, etc.)? How are we going to structure this time? Given the topics to negotiate, what would a smart agenda look like? In terms of the work methods, is it better to settle issues step by step, or to look for an overall deal? Would I ask to see the mediator individually, or only with the other party? The mediator will have their ideas on these points, but it is important that I also reflect on them.

9. *Communication:* How to manage the information exchange? (cf. see above, "I prepare my communication").

10. *Logistics:* What material conditions are useful together to facilitate mediation? Where do we meet one another? In what room? Around what type of table? Will we be able to leave the room or have something to eat and drink if necessary? Will the privacy or security be sufficient? Do I really have all the documents and objects that I need with me? And so on.

This preparation plan is equally helpful for the mediator, who can explore the point of view of each of the parties around the table.

Whatever the preparation format, this preliminary reflection is not necessarily shared in session, neither entirely, nor immediately. It represents a roadmap that a party uses to move forward.

Lawyers and Advisers of the Parties

Parties may be accompanied by various allies or advisers, a technician in the case of a defective machine, an expert in the concerned domain, a union delegate, a family member, etc. It is important to inform the other party and the mediator of their presence in order not to create an unexpected situation of imbalance. The number and type of advisers attending the session sometimes necessitate a "negotiation" in advance. Each one of these advisers, according to their specialty, might find some inspiration in the preparation methods described in the previous section. Precisely because they are specialists of a domain, these advisers will try their best to ensure the fairness of the diagnostic and of the solutions, if necessary initiating a head-to-head with the party they accompany to show the limits of this or that reasoning. Among these advisers, the most frequently used, lawyers, merit particular attention.

Lawyer at the Service of Clients: Negotiator Before Litigator

With their client, the lawyer combines two complementary roles: negotiator of a transaction and litigator in front of the court. But before being a "lawyer" (advocate) of a client, they are counsel (adviser). Reducing them to the sole role of defense lawyer and seeing them a priori as such is misleading. In contrast to the risks of a trial, the search for a negotiated solution allows, in general, for faster closure at a lower cost, which better serves the interests of the client. Negotiation is also in the interest of the lawyer: faster and more satisfied, their clients will recommend them to others and hire them again in the future, if necessary.

To carry out this transaction, the parties' lawyers will negotiate together. But sometimes, each one "defending" their client, they will not find common ground. They might fear that if they invite their respective clients to more concessions, the party would retort: "Are you *my* lawyer, or that of the opposing party?" The client will imagine a coalition of lawyers against them, both motivated by a financial interest to engage in a long and costly process. Parties may even be tempted to change lawyers. This sequence underscores the interest, for the lawyers themselves, to resort to a mediator, who will lead the work of questioning in order to clarify the legal dimensions as much as the other technical, cultural, and human aspects, etc. of the conflict. A mediator will make the parties aware of their legal risks, the strengths and weaknesses of their views, and their share of responsibility. If the client follows the recommendation of their lawyer to engage in mediation, the question is then posed about the role of the lawyer in the process.

The Presence of Lawyers in Mediation: Three Typical Configurations

Let us distinguish three configurations in pre-mediation:

1. *Parties come without lawyers:* The question thus does not seem raised. But the mediator may note that the development of the case raises crucial legal questions, for example, regarding donation, inheritance, prenuptial, or co-ownership rules. If this is the case, the mediator will invite parties to contact a specialized lawyer.

2. *One of the parties disposes of a lawyer but the other party does not:* This hypothesis raises a series of issues that can be tackled as follows: simply raise the difficulties that this asymmetry entails; solicit the party without a lawyer and ask them if they agree to the other party being accompanied by a lawyer; or invite the party without a lawyer to recruit one in order to restore the balance; ask the party with a lawyer if they would agree to not come accompanied, in order to restore the balance; finally, invite both parties to discuss among themselves and come to an agreement on the presence or not of lawyer(s) in their mediation.

3. *In the final configuration, each party has a lawyer:* Many practices are observed, without determining if one is more pertinent than another. They are as follows:

   • Consult all lawyers – in general separately – before the start of the mediation to listen to their legal analysis.

- Propose to the lawyers that they agree with the parties on their presence or absence.

- Solicit lawyers in anticipation of their presence in mediation, taking into account their usefulness as a receiver of all information that will be communicated and as a source of opinions (support, moderator, defender, solution creator, etc.).

- Convince lawyers to be absent from mediation, so that the exchanges are not tainted by, or restricted to, a legal perspective, and bring each party to directly interact with one another without their words being conditioned by the presence of their lawyer or the lawyer of the "opposing" party.

- Finally, solicit lawyers to guarantee their presence only at certain key moments, for example, at the start, at the end, or during critical turning points.

For the lawyer, the choice of attending a mediation or not is a difficult one. If they are present, they risk obstructing a direct discussion between the parties, or even interfering in the process, complicating the work of the mediator. If one lawyer is there, the other lawyer might also need to be present for reasons of equity, and the risk increases that the mediation session will be transformed into a "pre-trial." If the lawyer is not there, their client may feel weakened, and the lawyer may feel ignored, even useless; the mediator needs to ensure that their absence is not interpreted as a denial of their usefulness. If they are absent, their role is not any less valuable: during the preparation of their client for mediation, along the way, and at each time that the client wishes. Then, at the end of the process when a solution is drawn up, their talents in giving advice and contract writing are fundamental. In family matters (with high emotional stakes) and in small litigations with minimum financial stakes (neighborhood, consumer, community administration, etc.), lawyers in general are absent. However, lawyers are often present in other types of cases.

The Evolution of the Lawyer's Role as a Mediation Adviser

By participating in the mediation, the lawyer increases the difficulty of their task as an adviser, since upon meeting the other party, they often discover a reality different from the image that had been described up until the present: the viewpoint and "truths" of the other party become obvious. Up until meeting the other party, the lawyer only knew their own client's version of the conflict. The lawyer remains, of course, their client's adviser, but from now on manages many more elements that emerged during mediation, including many that go beyond purely legal ones – because the conflict lies elsewhere, beyond the legal realm, in a history, in a human interaction. Thus, the aspects – economic (a debt to settle), technical (a delivery of a defective machine), psychological (a promise that was not kept), linguistic (ambiguities of the terms of the contract or oral exchange) – appear for which each party shares some responsibility. The solutions, therefore, will no longer be only legal: they will be sought from the lens of these different dimensions. Thus, the lawyer moves from the role of legal counsel to a larger and more gratifying role, adding to the legal aspects the range of other aspects that make up the conflict and with respect to which a fair balance will be sought. Thus, the lawyer receives "a new mission that is to their credit, similar to that of a judge: being, with the other party or the other lawyer(s), creator of what is just," according to the beautiful expression of a French magistrate.[1]

Whether a lawyer is present or not, the lawyer's role is fundamental as a legal expert on the content of the agreement that materializes. The lawyer helps their client to avoid an unbalanced agreement that would amount to less than what a court decision would grant. However, the lawyer also keeps their client in check from the dangers of overconfidence, because sometimes the latter may think, wrongly, that a judge would be more favorable to them than what emerges from the mediation process. The lawyer, as a continual adviser, helps the party evaluate the risks and opportunities of a refusal or acceptation of a potential agreement. They analyze the concrete results of

---

[1] Alain Damecourt, Meeting of attorneys at the Center of Mediation in Val-de-Marne Bar, 1998.

mediation sessions and the validity of the transaction, including its quality and balance. As Chapter 2 underscored, the parties themselves remain the decision-makers in mediation: it is up to their respective lawyers to shed light on this choice with constancy and comprehension.

The Compensation of the Lawyer-Adviser in Mediation

The conflicts of economic interests between lawyers and their clients are frequent (Lempereur and Scodellaro 2003). In mediation, a renewed approach to the question of lawyers' fees is needed. The absence of a clear pay scale for a negotiated or mediated approach could encourage lawyers to orient any case toward litigation. In fact, some lawyers fear that the mediation development replaces court procedures and leads to loss of their livelihood. It might explain their reluctance to turn toward mediation approaches, to the detriment of their clients but also to themselves. Other lawyers, on the contrary, now develop a mediation activity at a higher hourly wage and inform their clients of the relevance of mediation, underscoring the savings they will gain, when compared to the costs, length, and unpredictability of a trial. We have received the testimony of many lawyers who have brought many clients to mediation and who benefit from an increasing clientele supporting their reputation and skills in the amicable management of disputes.

The Lawyer Prepares

The lawyer's preparation can use one the formats proposed earlier. This preparation will help them regarding the following aspects of their mission:

- Advising their client on whether to accept mediation or not: The lawyer sheds light on the comparative merits of mediation and the legal procedure.

- Recommending options to their client that seem adequate, concerning the lawyer's presence or not during the mediation sessions; what is expected of them; their role and the rules concerning their interventions.

- Preparing the necessary legal elements and relevant documents which will be useful during the mediation sessions.

- Informing their client of what, in the rule of law and justice, constitutes their advantage and what, on the contrary, favors the other party. In mediation, lawyers have a strong responsibility to be as equitable as possible.

- Whether the lawyer is present or not, sharing their opinion with their client, as well as with the mediator, during the entire mediation process.

Preparing for the Mediator–Lawyer Relationship

This aspect also deserves to be examined in pre-mediation. Over the past 20 years, this relationship has evolved significantly. Originally, mediators, fearing that lawyers would try to control the mediation process as if in a courtroom, tended to exclude them, particularly in family mediation. Lawyers, having a biased, hazy image of mediation, kept themselves out of the process, leaving the parties to manage on their own. This rift has progressively left room for a consensus in progress: the mediator contacts lawyers before mediation and negotiates their role with them. Whether the lawyer attends the mediation sessions or not, the mediator and lawyer develop a mutual consideration and work together in the interest of the parties. To crystallize the place and role of lawyers in mediation, we propose the following seven approaches.

The place and role of lawyers:

Seven approaches observed in mediation*

1. *Expression of the legal point of view from the start* – Lawyers explain the law first, then let the parties explain themselves. Either lawyers remain present or are kept in the loop during the mediation process.

2. *Silent presence* – Lawyers are present in the room but remain silent. There can, however, be individual meetings (in the absence of the other party, for consultation) at the request of the lawyer, their client, or the mediator.

---

*This summary is based on the observation of best practices with the collaboration of Sylvie Adijies, lawyer and mediator at the Paris Mediation and Arbitration Center (CMAP).

3. *Permanent free speech* – Present as the parties, lawyers intervene when they want, without, however, "pleading" their case. They are careful to not take over the substance from the parties.

4. *On the basis of request only* – Lawyers express themselves only at the request of the mediator or parties. If they wish to intervene, they need to ask to speak.

5. *Silent presence first, then intervention* – Lawyers remain silent during the first phases when there is an analysis of the causes of the conflict and the needs of the parties during a slow progression that goes from the past to the present (Chapter 6). They actively participate in the following phases concerning the search for solutions, which begins in the present and moves toward an acceptable future (Chapter 7).

6. *Mixed models* – Inspired by the above, these models are a combination of moments of silent listening and interventions at the request of the parties, the mediator, or the lawyers themselves.

7. *Absent but informed lawyer* – Although absent from the mediation process, lawyers remain available by telephone or e-mail; they are kept informed of what happens during mediation.

By reaching an agreement in the pre-mediation stage with the mediator on one or more of the scenarios above, the lawyer-adviser knows which of these roles they will play, even if it means adapting it between the beginning and end of the mediation.

A Preparation Itinerary for the Mediator

The parties and their advisers are prepared. The mediator certainly does not want to be out of step and needs to reflect on the following elements: the principles and rules to be followed during the mediation, the in-depth stakes of the case, and the method and the organization of the mediation process – see Chapter 5. On the one hand, having a clear idea about what principles to invoke helps to prepare the content and make good choices regarding process, and vice versa: analyzing the stakes in depth allows one to discern what principles will be particularly useful, and what process will be the best adapted. Although these dimensions are presented here in different sections for clarity, of course, they remain linked.

Being Clear on Questions of Principle

Although the situation differs depending on whether the mediator is the informal, ad hoc, or institutional type (Chapter 1), the mediator's preparation will benefit from reviewing the following seven questions of principle.

As a mediator, am I sure that ...

1. I will know how to show the parties, who may still be unsure about the usefulness of mediation, its advantages as well as its limits?

2. I will know how to present myself and share my personal approach – that of a facilitator or adviser, for example – with the parties?

3. I will know how to integrate the structuring principles of mediation? Presented in Chapter 3, these principles guide the strategic choices of the mediator. For example, the principle of neutrality *versus* the call for fairness, or the principle of confidentiality *versus* the potential exceptions.

4. I am ready to lead mediation alone? Maybe I need to appoint a co-mediator, or consult or invite an expert to the table who will help me sort out technical aspects of the case?

5. After focusing on the seating arrangement, who, beyond the parties directly concerned, need to be there? Do they need to be present during the entire mediation or at least at some key moments? In particular, I contacted the parties' lawyers (if there are any), and we reached an agreement on their role.

6. I have prepared, if necessary, an agreement to mediate to give to the parties? (The examples presented in the first section of this chapter may be used.)

7. The conditions of my salary – where necessary – are clearly defined?

Preparing for the Problem Dimension

Mediators have important choices to make concerning the analysis of the problem itself, its context, and its protagonists.

- *Collecting a maximum amount of information before meeting the parties* – Some mediators favor this approach because it allows for a more precise and greater understanding of the problem before meeting and listening to the parties. In particular, this quest for information includes cross-checking many sources and verifying the reliability of collected elements.

- *Keeping information to a minimum before meeting the parties* – Other mediators prefer to present themselves as "free from all external influences" in mediation: they want to directly discover the case, first-hand from the parties either by meeting the parties or in writing. They then express their concern about objectivity, their willingness to not be oriented toward a diagnostic biased by given – or filtered – information according to a certain point of view. To verify the reliability of version A, they will listen to B, and vice versa. If necessary, only after having heard the parties, the mediator may consult other stakeholders: family members, specialists, other concerned people, etc.

- *Or adopting the third type of approach* – The ideal, if one is capable of it, is to combine the advantages of the two previous approaches and thereby avoid their disadvantages. It is about collecting the maximum amount of information before the mediation to be able to explore all hypotheses and at the same time being capable of coming to the mediation table with a clean slate, fully ready to listen to the parties and discover a new story.

Once the mediator makes the choice about how to proceed, they can use one of the three formats of preparation presented in the preceding section, adapting it, of course, to their role. If necessary, the mediator fully prepares for the mediation by using the 10 preparation assets, which will give them a comprehensive picture of the situation.

To accelerate and sometimes perfect their preparation, the mediator may want to ask each party to send a short text (prior to the first mediation session) describing, from their point of view, the problem's facts, their wishes, or any other key question that seems important to them.

Proposing such a document serves a double purpose. *Primo*, the parties do not always spontaneously prepare "their" mediation: this small questionnaire invites them to do so. *Secondo*, it presents the mediator with a surplus of information that will be useful in the mediation process.

Possible questionnaire sent in advance by the mediator to the parties

Confidential

1. Describe to me, from your point of view, the situation with the other party and your wishes.
2. Describe to me, from your point of view, what you think that the other party would say about the same situation, and what their wishes might be.
3. Are there questions that come up? Which ones?
4. Are there questions that you would like to ask the other party? Which ones?
5. Are there questions you would like to ask me on mediation itself? Which ones?
6. From your side, what would you be ready to do or say in order to strike an acceptable balance?
7. Likewise, from your point of view, what could the other do or say?
8. What other elements would you wish to share with me before the mediation begins?

Of course, knowing this information does not prevent the mediator, at the start of the meeting, from asking each party to share their perspective with the other party (since up until now, all this information was confidential and only for the mediator).

Reflecting on Good Styles of Intervention

Chapter 1 called attention to the diversity of intervention styles. Each mediation situation may necessitate one style rather than another, and this is why it is important that the mediator reflects on these choices during the preparation phase.

Three Levels of Intervention:
People, Problems, and Process

The three dimensions discussed earlier structure all conflicts. The mediator needs to reflect upon which of the following justify more emphasis than others, according to the particular case and the different moments of the mediation process.

- *The people* – Beyond the problems to resolve, any conflict concerns people, their relationships with one another or outsiders, their emotions or sufferings, lack of communication, individual or social identities in play, lack of recognition of these identities, etc. All these elements often count for more than the problems themselves. According to the situation, and with the hopes of resolving the problem, the mediator might widen the perimeter of mediation to focus on the people and work on their mutual recognition and create a relationship imbued with a sufficient degree of trust. The potential of mediation largely resides in its capacity to address well the essential human dimension.

- *The problems* – This is about the objects of conflict: the fundamental issues, facts, perceptions of reality, subjects that pose a problem, and solutions to implement. It is obvious that parties solicit the help of a mediator to deal with this second dimension: what solution to apply to the precise problems they are facing (an unpaid bill, night-time disturbance, etc.). The mediator will, of course, address the problems but knows that their role needs to integrate the other two dimensions.

- *The process* – How to proceed? Any mediator, even an amateur, quickly recognizes the importance of negotiating people and problems. The more seasoned they are, the more they recognize the essential dimension of the process: how to organize the meeting and the exchanges? How to manage this painstaking labor originating from a painful past to try to construct a better future? The mediator ponders the methods, the most suitable models for success, the steps to follow, the principles to respect, and the obstacles to surmount. These essential aspects will be described in more detail in Chapter 5 and in the following chapters.

With regard to process, a choice needs to be made and communicated to parties during the preparation phase, so that no one is surprised. Another question needs to be asked here: Does the mediator intend to proceed with joint sessions only or will they hold private meetings (caucus)?

Three Models of Mediation Sessions: Private, Joint, or Mixed Meetings

During the preparation phase, it is important that the mediator decides how to structure the sessions – either a joint or private meeting – during the first encounter and then for the rest of the mediation.

1. *Only private meetings* – Most of us have heard of "shuttle diplomacy," which consists of an emissary going to a capital and talking to a belligerent party, then taking a plane to another capital to meet another party, and then taking several round-trips between the one and the other, in the hope of getting an agreement. Henry Kissinger famously used this approach, which requires enormous efforts to persuade each party in private, in order to get an agreement by discovering a possible zone of agreement between parties without the parties ever meeting. Sometimes the parties do not even have diplomatic relations; or these relations are so strained that a joint meeting, with its risks of emotional outbursts, would add to the problem rather than resolve it. In this model, the mediator proceeds by alternating successive, private meetings.

   In fact, sometimes the pre-mediation stage starts with private meetings. Mediation continues until an agreement is reached, or not, without joint meetings ever taking place. This first approach is useful when parties are geographically distant and incapable of traveling, when they refuse to meet one another even if they desire to settle the problem, when they fear each other, when the conflict is purely material and they are not looking to renew a relationship (a guarantee to reimburse, a car accident to resolve with an insurance company), etc. When the relationship between parties is either non-existent or unimportant, this method makes sense. However, it quickly shows its limits in the long term between neighbors, colleagues, business partners, etc.

2. *Only joint sessions* – When it is important for parties to restore the relationship, even in a small way, it is difficult to communicate only through an intermediary. It is crucial for the parties to relearn how to talk and listen to each other, to rebuild coexistence. The earlier this happens, the better. Proceeding via a joint session from a common introduction is already a way of getting the parties together. Mediators may use informal settings, like a lunch or dinner. Certain mediators go as far as to refuse individual sessions, finding that the risk of damage to the relationship outweighs the advantages. If the obvious advantage of private sessions is being able to confide information or potential solutions in the mediator through the "secret of confession," the disadvantage lies in increasing the distrust of the absent party toward either the mediator or the other party. Absence fuels the imagination, and when there is conflict, this can be risky. To avoid these risks, certain mediators do not meet any of the parties in private from the beginning until the end of mediation. What one party hears from the mediator, the other party hears as well; transparency is total. This second approach, advocated and practiced, for example, by Robert Mnookin of Harvard Law School, demands experience and skills: the mediator needs to know how to manage the most difficult moments in a session, including those with intense emotions. However many mediators want to be able to interrupt a joint session and allow for the possibility of the parties to benefit from the advantages of private meetings; they might favor the hybrid approach below.

3. *Alternating joint meetings and private meetings* – The interest in keeping the parties together, as much as possible, is obvious. Our advice is to favor the use of the joint session. However, there are circumstances when private meetings are justified. Here are six of them:
   1. *At the very beginning*, if one of the parties considers mediation, while the other has not thought about it yet.

2. *In the pre-mediation phase,* to convince a party to accept mediation.

3. *During the process of mediation,* to give a party the opportunity to share confidential information with the mediator.

4. *In an emotional situation,* to avoid escalation between the parties and give each side the opportunity to catch its breath and get things off its chest, to allow the mediator to talk to one party without having them lose face in front of the other.

5. *In a situation of undeniable asymmetry,* in which one party is prevented from expressing themselves, to assure a space for both parties and avoid predatory attitudes, which are reproducing the same dynamics that fueled the conflict in the first place.

6. *In a situation of intractable disagreement,* to examine if there is a zone of possible agreement and to remind the parties – in a more direct manner – the concrete consequences of failure.

Thus, there are plenty of occasions when interrupting a joint session in favor of private meetings is justified. Notably, this approach was advocated by the late Frank Sander of Harvard's Program on Negotiation. Without wanting to strongly invite mediators to adopt one approach rather than another, let us recall the risk of private meetings to distill or harden distrust, and to deprive the parties of a common meeting space. Not to have joint sessions is, in some way, to lessen mediation's value and impact.

The choice of joint or private meetings is not without consequence for a final aspect of the mediator's preparation: where the mediation will take place.

Setting Up a Mediation Space

When convening a meeting, logistics are important. In fact, any sign of proximity between the mediator and one of the parties could be interpreted as a sign of preference, thus diminishing the trust of the other parties not only in the mediator and but also in the mediation process itself. Consequently, it is useful for the mediator to arrive before the parties, to make sure that the meeting space is conducive to fruitful exchanges. By arriving earlier, the mediator gives themselves time to modify the arrangement of the room, if it is not suitable.

Seating arrangements will respect the following basic principles, echoing the very spirit of mediation:

1. *Equal access of the parties to the mediator* – This principle is materialized by an equidistance between the mediator and each of the parties. Mediators avoid sitting closer to one party than to another, as this greater proximity could create a suspicion of connection or partiality toward the party in question.

2. *The mediator is there to help, not to reign over the parties* – Many mediators sit behind their own desk, with both parties sitting in front. This setting creates a power imbalance in favor of the mediator, who is physically positioned as a source of authority.

3. *Mediation is not simply about striking a deal, it is about mutual recognition and, if possible, resuming relationships* – Parties need to sit in a way that allows for eye contact and direct communication. Nevertheless, mediators need a space arrangement such as they can engage directly with the parties, and be able to control the flow of the exchanges, especially in cases of acute antagonism.

It follows then that the good, old *Round Table of King Arthur and his Knights* has many advantages. Thanks to the openness of the space, the mediator can more easily connect with both parties, and the parties with one another. The mediator can intervene if necessary. A flip chart behind the mediator may prove useful, not for marking details of facts, but for noting down problems and issues to be discussed in order to understand one another and, then later, to note down some of the solutions clearly in black and white.

Depending on the objectives of the meeting, we could set up the space without a table as well: three people can meet one another in a "salon" configuration, rather than in a "meeting room." This configuration has some real advantages. For example, sitting together is already progress in comparison to the absence of a meeting. Comfortably installed in an armchair, is it not more difficult to raise your voice than sitting in a chair or, especially, if standing? A meeting in the "dining room," in order to share a meal, is equally favorable, because eating a meal allows one to distance oneself from the conflict. A wise boss, playing the role of an informal mediator between two colleagues in a quarrel, is well advised to invite them to lunch. Suddenly the tension at the place of "business" (*negotium* in Latin) diminishes in a space of "leisure" (*otium*), where conversation becomes possible. Mediation, in its essence, is first the re-connection, or even creation, of relationships between the parties, and the space suitable for this goal needs to be carefully thought through by the mediator.

Sometimes, in order to accommodate advisers or lawyers, mediators add chairs around the table, between each party and the mediator – or behind each party. By putting these advisers "on the periphery," the mediator continues to orient the conversation toward the parties, who remain at the center of attention. Further, it is possible that the mediator will have a computer and/or video projector next to them. Our experience is that at certain moments, the capacity to use a laptop and projecting the meeting notes on a screen help the parties to understand and be clear about the key points that have come up and the corresponding elements in the agreement and even gives them the feeling that they are moving forward together by working on the same text. This approach also favors the immediate production of meeting reports, the agreement, and the action plan immediately published for each party.

If the mediation session will be held in a meeting room, it is important to take into account the fact that the mediation often hosts more than two parties. In more complex situations of multi-party dialogues – examples are environmental mediation or mediation workshops to bring belligerents together in Burundi or in the Democratic Republic of Congo, which two of the co-authors facilitated in teams – it could be a good idea to arrive the day before to make sure the room is set up adequately (Colson and Lempereur 2011; Lempereur 2021).

Room arrangement for mediation in the Democratic Republic of the Congo

In the conference center in Kinshasa where the meeting took place, the venue was organized from the start like … an old-fashioned classroom. In the foreground, mediators were supposed to preside over a raised platform, where padded armchairs awaited them; the participants had to sit in rows like students and were not even given a table on which to take notes. Arrival the day before allowed for rearranging the room to make it more convivial and respectful, with a U-shape arrangement so that the participants, each one being able to see each other, would be at equidistance from the mediation team – and at the same height, with the same chairs and tables as the participants. Mediators were thus "with" the parties, empowered by being on equal footing. A projector and a screen, visible to all, were also added.

After having arranged the room to be ready to welcome the parties, the mediator needs to be clear about when the mediation officially starts and may even want to step out of the room until both parties arrive. It is better that the parties enter the mediation space at the same time, reducing the probability that the mediator is found with one but without the other, thus creating the risk that party who is late feels a certain unease when seeing the mediator in the presence of the other, or that the party who arrived first loses patience regarding the "tardiness" of the other. In this spirit, it is suitable to not enter the mediation room before all parties have arrived, even if it means chatting in the antechamber with the first arriving party, around a coffee, for example.

*

Beyond the principles and the problem, the mediator needs to delve into another essential dimension: the process. How, concretely, is the mediation going to begin and then proceed? Putting into place a comprehensive plan of process guidelines helps to keep the sessions as relaxed as possible – from the moment of exploring the past to the search for possible solutions for a better future – as explored in depth in the following chapters. In many ways, the mediator prepares to be a calm "eye in the storm" (Lempereur and Willer 2016).

CHAPTER 5
THE PORTAL
Set the Stage *Before* Problem-Solving

From now on, the parties are ready to undertake mediation and agree to meet one another in the presence of one or several mediator(s). The parties might still be somehow skeptical about what mediation can bring to them, but they see some advantages of trying this Alternative Dispute Resolution (ADR) mode.

In order to alleviate the remaining doubts in the parties' minds, the mediator needs to effectively structure the process and the session(s) from the beginning to the end (Moore 2014). They organize the *beginning game* (Chapter 5) as well as the two phases of the *middle game* on problem-solving (Chapters 6 and 7) in order to come up with a potentially workable agreement and a renewed relationship that the *end game* can celebrate (Lempereur 2015c; Lempereur, Pekar, and Cecchi-Dimeglio 2015).

In that respect, the introduction of a mediation session is crucial: on the one hand, it establishes an atmosphere that is conducive to trust with everyone present; on the other hand, it aims at organizing the entire process. The mediator's objective need not yet turn to the heart of the matter. Many mediations break down because the mediator fails to recognize early on the importance of establishing relationships and of organizing the process. How to help the mediator clearly structure this fundamentally important introductory stage of mediation is the objective of this chapter. The opening serves as a guide for the parties, so that they better anticipate predictable phases of *their* mediation.

The PORTAL to introduce mediation

P	for	Presentations
O	for	Objectives
R	for	Rules of Engagement
T	for	Time and Stages
A	for	Agreement to Mediate
L	for	Launch!

P for Presentations

After having greeted the parties, the mediators present themselves, then invite the parties to do the same.

The Mediator Welcomes the Parties

The meeting room needs to be comfortable for the parties. The mediator greets the parties with a smile as soon as they arrive. When greeting them – if possible, by name – the mediator establishes eye contact. Learning the parties' names beforehand is helpful: parties are often grateful to be immediately "recognized" in this way. Certainly, it is easier for 2 parties than for 12: the more parties, the more you may want to prepare a tentative seating plan.

When the parties enter the meeting room, the mediator needs to manage unexpected attendees. Normally, the question of whether or not additional protagonists (lawyers, advisers, family members, etc.) will be present would have been settled during pre-mediation (Chapter 4). Nevertheless, it is not impossible that, during the first session, a party will unexpectedly invite some person(s) to the room or even to the mediation table. The mediator needs to manage this situation before starting the meeting. On the one hand, courtesy requires respecting what has been settled upon beforehand in the agreement to mediate. On the other hand, if a party is suddenly accompanied by someone else, this may indicate, even unconsciously, a doubt regarding the impartiality of the process. At the very least, the mediator needs to obtain the agreement of all parties regarding this unexpected attendee; alternatively, the mediator can invite the unexpected guests to remain outside the meeting room for possible consultation during a break. The mediator specifies that mediation is driven by the parties' priorities: lawyers or advisers are not supposed to take over the process. This reminder allows everyone to agree on one of the formulas proposed in Chapter 4 concerning the place and role of advisers.

Meetings between high-ranking officials naturally raise the question about including their entourage – assistants, security officers. The mediator can insist that "witnesses" without any specific contribution stay outside the physical space where the mediation takes place, so that they do not bother the parties nor obstruct the process and its confidentiality.

Mediators faced ... with bodyguards

During a reconciliation workshop in Burundi facilitated by one of the authors, bodyguards equipped with machine guns were positioned behind high-ranking participants. The mediator negotiated the exit of the bodyguards from the room into the hall so that they could *protect the venue, for the benefit of all.*" In another meeting, which included an entire high command, the question of carrying arms in the session was raised; only handguns were accepted, as symbols of status and rank of the officers – a compromise that only partially reassured the facilitators.

In these first moments, the mediator demonstrate the same courtesy toward all parties in order to illustrate the mediator's proximity to each person, in accordance with the principle of multi-partiality presented in Chapter 3.

The mediator needs to immediately illustrate that their presence serves all parties. All sides receive the same consideration, notably through questions, gestures, and expressions. The mediator then invites the parties to sit and put themselves at ease.

○ Hello Ma'am, hello Sir *(The mediator shakes the hand of each of the parties)*. I am Catherine, your mediator. Please take a seat, put yourself at ease *(pause, smile)*. I am happy to meet you and thank you for coming to this meeting.

Banal politeness? No, by speaking and acting kindly, the mediator already sets up a communication and behavior pattern. Embroiled in the conflict that pits one against one another, the parties often have a broken relationship without any cordiality between them. To pass over this opening politeness and immediately launch into the depths of the subject without establishing an appropriate tone or ambience would encourage prolongation of the conflictual dynamic.

The Mediator Presents Themselves

Will the mediator say a little or a lot about themselves? If, during pre-mediation, the parties already had the opportunity to meet their mediator or to hear about them, it is not really necessary for the mediator to provide more information. The mediator is not there to talk about themselves. A simple reminder will suffice:

○ As you know, I am also an IT engineer *(or health worker, or jurist, or parent of a student, or screenwriter, etc.)*. So, I, too, have had the experience of ..., etc. But every case is different, and I wish to hear how you experienced what happened, in order for the two of you to potentially seek a solution that works for both.

If, on the other hand, the parties are meeting the mediator for the first time, it is important to devote a few minutes to this presentation, because "first impressions" matter. The content of this presentation is guided by the stakes discussed in Chapter 4 regarding the choice of the mediator, who needs to be accepted by the parties and establish their legitimacy with them, reassuring both sides of the value of their experience and their ability to drive the process. The mediator may decide to invoke some of their personal experiences so as to be able to connect to the parties – but to all of them in a balanced way! By doing so, the mediator underlines their sensitivity to the particular stakes of the conflict, with which they are familiar. However, some mediators may prefer to not invoke their own experience in order to appear the most neutral possible.

Introducing oneself: Underlining familiarity with the apparent mediation stakes, without making it the only issue

- Mediators who are former or practicing lawyers will better understand the legal intricacies of a sub-leasing of a commercial lease and of a sub-tenant no longer paying the rent while refusing to vacate the place and arguing that jobs are at stake.

- Mediators with a medical background better understand the difficulties as well as the consequences of a surgery.

- Mediators trained in labor law evaluate to what extent this employee had the legal right to be absent for 10 days due to a death in their family.

Let us emphasize that the mediator is not meant to be a technical expert: they do not have to decide or even guide a mediation on the basis of the expertise they have, or be inspired by one cultural, religious, or moral dimension. It is for this reason that in highly technical cases, both the judge and the mediator, by agreement with the parties, sometimes resort to a subject matter expert. This is done not so that the expert decides, but so that the expert can shed light, via their expertise, on a particular aspect of the problem. The mediator can mobilize different approaches to grasp the multidimensional nature of a conflict to facilitate the parties' search for an equitable solution. When the mediator shares such or such relevant experience, it often immediately inspires and increases confidence in the parties.

Point of vigilance: "I can understand" versus "I know best for you"

Talking about one's own experiences as a mediator does not mean expanding on one's specialty and expertise. Doing otherwise, the mediator may create a double illusion:

- *For the mediator, themselves:* "I know, therefore I know what is good for the parties, and I am going to find them a good solution." If the mediator is also an expert in a particular field, they need to show self-restraint, and may use their expertise as a last resort, and only if they are solicited explicitly by the parties as an adviser or arbitrator.

- *For the parties:* The mediator can make the parties believe that the mediator knows better than the parties, even if the mediator may not know anything yet, or very little about many other dimensions of the disagreement (animosity from prior altercations, potential promises, family links or amicable break-ups, information retention, bad faith, accidents, mishaps, etc.).

The Mediator Invites the Parties to Present Themselves

Two scenarios exist:

- *The parties already know each other* – If the parties have a prior relationship, even if it is strained, what follows takes on less importance. This presentation is thus especially destined for the mediator, especially if the latter did not already meet the parties during pre-mediation. Nevertheless, through their presentation, each party "establishes their identity" in relation to the other while the mediator demonstrates particular sensitivity to what is said.

- *The parties do not know each other* – It is the case, for example, when a business (or a public body) is in conflict with a consumer (or user), or when a representative (lawyer, partner, parent, etc.) physically intervenes in the place of a party (sick, unavailable, traveling, etc.).

In the latter case, the presentation of each party is essential. It is not about describing one's civil status, but really asserting, in the presence of the mediator and the other party, one's identity as a person (or as an organization representative). As a stakeholder in a dispute, personal identities have been questioned, misunderstood, or even ridiculed. Furthermore, each party can suffer from not having succeeded in directly resolving the conflict and having to resort to a third party. Weakened, this identity is seeking recognition, even restoration. If the mediator forgets this aspect, a party may risk feeling denied or devalued, and might be tempted at a later stage to ask for more than is reasonable in order to be recognized.

This is why, by asking questions that help the parties to situate themselves in a context, the mediator invites each of the parties to say more, to go further than the platitudes behind which they sometimes hide.

○ *[To both parties:]* Now that we are sitting comfortably, it would be interesting for each one of you to explain in detail your job before evoking what brings you here.
[To one party:] Would you like to go first? Could you please present yourself and describe what your role is in the company and what you do specifically?
[To the other party:] And you?

This introduction focusing on the people dimension establishes an initial, relaxed climate in the hope that it will influence the whole process in a positive fashion. Oftentimes, this conviviality needs to be built: the parties are uncomfortable, not knowing whether they will attack each other or be attacked. The mediator anticipates their discomfort, not taking offense at it and especially not letting themselves be taken over by the parties' mood, whether it is anger or fear. Patience, the ability to smile serenely, and paying empathetic attention to the sometimes toxic emotions of parties are important assets for the mediator, from the beginning until the end of the process.

In the same spirit, anything the mediator can do to lighten the atmosphere and to create a safe space is welcome: an authentic smile; a brief moment of silence in the conversation; a calm gesture. Such details help establish the sincerity of an exchange that the mediator learns to adopt, while being true to themselves at the same time. For example, smiling is not systematic; the worst would be to fake a smile because one is uncomfortable. It is about establishing the genuine and benevolent connection with the parties, about being authentic.

If necessary, the mediator makes a reference at this stage to an absentee who holds a stake in the outcome, and therefore is concerned by the upcoming process. The mediator thus brings parties to reflect on the big picture and the possible consequences of the mediation outcome. Notably, this concerns, for example, children in a divorce, residents likely to suffer the consequences of an agreement with a factory about trash evacuation by underground canals, or managers of an association who would refuse an agreement concluded "behind their backs," or the populations when parties are belligerents in a civil war.

Last name or first name? Formal or informal language?

When addressing people, many languages, such as French or German, distinguish a formal *you* (*vous, Sie*), and an informal *you* (*tu, Du*). This proves to be tricky for the mediator, who might hesitate between the two approaches, either from the beginning of the mediation process or at some point later on.

English spares this difficulty – to a certain extent, as the choice remains between using last names (*"Dr. Webb"*) or first names (*"Jordan"*). There are no rules, except a relevant adaptation to the context, while keeping in mind the objective of putting parties at ease and treating them similarly. One of the authors quasi-systematically uses first names, including with higher-level personalities. This is not done immediately, but in the process of mediation, by "deliberately making a mistake," switching to the first name like a Freudian slip, establishing it as a self-evident fact of closeness, strengthening the links around the table. If done artfully, this simple choice of words changes the tone of the conversation.

The mediator, however, needs to remain alert: they can invite informality without forgetting that certain people feel respected, safe, and therefore at ease, with more formality. One solution for the mediator is to indicate how they hope to be called by the parties: *"If you want, you can call me*

Pauline," and ask them how they would like to be called: *"Madam,"* *"Mrs. Dominguez,"* or *"Stephanie."* This micro-agreement from the start might, of course, evolve during the mediation process, as parties warm up.

In the same spirit, in co-mediation, facilitators sometimes have an interest in referring to each other informally in front of the parties. This inter-mediator conviviality, clearly different from a formality that maintains a distance between people, models a dynamic of proximity and thus might benefit the parties. If co-mediators, beyond their status and differences, bear witness to reciprocal closeness and sympathy, there is a stronger chance that the parties will also be inspired by it to find a means of coming together. In 1988, for example, seven mediators intervened in the French overseas territory New Caledonia, then stricken by acute civil unrest over the issue of independence. This "Mission of Dialogue" driven by famous personalities chose the informal *"tu"* and the use of first names.

Sometimes, parties are so nervous that the mediator can hardly avoid letting them vent upfront and "file their complaint," before having presented the rules and the framework. Emotions can erupt unexpectedly. Restating the concerns that the parties blurted out during an emotional outburst, the mediator demonstrates their ability to take what has been said into consideration, while also explaining the need to take time to truly understand and deal with them. The mediator can then propose the rules of the process (*cf.* R for Rules below). When the mediator meets the parties privately beforehand, the risk of an abrupt start when the parties are finally together is limited, because each will have had a chance to already confide in the mediator.

The objective of these introductory presentations is to (re)establish a relationship: putting parties in a rapport with the mediator and putting them (back) in contact with one another. In a way, the golden rule is: "relationship before anything else." It is not yet about "mutual recognition" at this stage – it is still too early – but at the very least a recognition of each person, and the creation of potential trust between the mediator and parties, with everyone present. Then comes the moment to clarify the objectives of the meeting.

O for Objectives

Mediators will usefully distinguish the objectives of mediation in general – the spirit of mediation – from the particular objectives of this mediation – which the parties are expecting.

The Mediator Explains the Spirit of Mediation

At the beginning of the mediation process, the mediator specifies what mediation is – its objectives, principles, and limits – and what it is not (Chapter 2). Sometimes, but not always, these aspects can be explained in pre-mediation (Chapter 4). If one of the parties has already been informed about the mediation, so much the better: the mediator would then simply ask them for a little patience. In any case, this explanation is necessary in order to reduce the risks of misunderstanding or disappointed expectations. Also, it is always useful to summarize, in a few words, what the essence of mediation is.

What mediation is … a useful reminder

Mediation…

- is *a facilitation of negotiation between parties* with the aim of seeking a mutually satisfying agreement to their conflict; if necessary, it aims also to re-establish valuable relationships for the future;

- is *a voluntary process*, with parties keeping control over the final decision and always free to leave;

- is *a confidential process*, that the mediator and the parties need to commit to;

- can, at the request of the parties or the mediator, *include breaks*, allowing for reflection, consultation, rest, etc.;

- can include *private meetings* between a party and the mediator, at the request of one or the other;

- is composed of *a sequence of stages* that will be explained.

These features are guaranteed by the mediator who, for their part, is independent in relation to the parties, neutral in terms of the problem, and impartial when it comes to the process.

The mediator then explains *what mediation is not*. It is neither a space for pleading, nor arbitration, nor litigation. The parties need not transform mediation into a joust where they present arguments as if they were trying to convince a judge. Contrary to an arbitration or a litigation, mediation is an informal process where the third party is not responsible for determining who is ultimately right or wrong. The parties might be informed by their attorneys of what the law says on the legal aspect of the problem, but no one other than the parties has the authority to decide.

Introductory remarks, in the form of the personal commitment of the mediator, can be quite helpful.

○ My action as mediator is guided by the principles of independence, neutrality, and impartiality. I will protect the confidentiality of our exchanges, I will respect the law, and I will facilitate your search for equitable solutions. I am at your service, but the ultimate decision is yours. I will not impose any decision on you.

Finally, the mediator discusses what would happen if the mediation does not result in a solution agreed upon by the parties. This possibility is envisaged from the get-go, because it underlines the fact that if parties remain in control of accepting or refusing any solution, they need to be aware of the consequences of a refusal. It is up to them to measure the risks incurred in the case of a deadlock or extreme positions taken during the process. Two cases stand out.

- *When it is a legal question:* A judge will be brought in to decide the case. Parties in mediation "bargain in the shadow of" litigation, which is a Damocles' sword hanging over their heads (Mnookin and Kornhauser 1979).

- *When it is a non-legal question:* Unsuccessful mediation might lead to dramatic consequences. The mediator will recall the burden of an unresolved problem, with risks of blockage, deterioration, escalation, or even resort to violence, all with long-term consequences on the relationship.

The Mediator Explains Their Role

After having introduced the mediation objectives in general, the mediator explains how they personally view their role. Of course, the mediator will invest all their energy in the mediation process. Even if the result is the exclusive responsibility of the parties, the mediator's obligation is to put all the means at their disposal. At the same time, each mediator undertakes their mission with their own personal style – and it is preferable this way.

Our colleague Stephen Goldberg, Professor of Law Emeritus at Northwestern University and a mediator himself, has underlined the multiplicity of successful (and unsuccessful) mediation styles (Goldberg 2005; Goldberg and Shaw 2007). These differences from one mediator to another, each including their own repertoire, guarantee flexibility and a dynamic adaptation to circumstances.

It is not only important that the mediator is aware of the way in which they operate but also that they are able to express it clearly so that the parties know what to expect. In particular, during the mediation preparation (Chapter 4), the mediator needs to reflect on three important choices of method.

Which Level of Intervention?

The mediator is not simply concerned with the problems at stake (the substance of the conflict) but also can smooth the way for the relationship between the parties and facilitate the process. We suggest immediately clarifying that the mediator's intervention manages people, problems, and the process throughout the mediation, or sequentially. To sum up:

o As the mediator, my involvement consists of helping you find together an amicable and sustainable solution to the *problems* at the roots of your conflict.

o I will also consider the *people* involved, which means you, your wishes and emotions, keeping in mind the importance of relationships and communication. That is why I invite you to say what is in your heart; we will tackle what you divulge in confidence.

o Finally, my role is that of facilitator of a negotiation *process* between you. I will suggest working methods to move toward a solution to your conflict. This solution will be yours, but I commit as the mediator to do everything I can to open paths for you that lead toward satisfactory solutions.

Which Session Formats?

Alongside joint sessions, the mediator might decide to organize private sessions. We suggest privileging the joint meeting, both for the quality and quantity of exchanges, but allowing for private meetings if necessary. In sum, "meetings in threes, and sometimes in pairs." Whatever approach the mediator favors, they need to announce it during the introduction phase, to avoid surprising the parties later. If, all of a sudden, without any mention of it beforehand, the mediator interrupts the session and invites each of the parties to a private meeting, they risk losing some capital of trust accumulated up to then.

o As much as possible, if you agree, we will remain together in session. However, if during the mediation one of you feels the need to speak with me in private, please let me know. I may also ask for a private meeting with each one of you. If I meet one of you, automatically, for the sake of balance, I will meet the other party alone as well, unless that party declines my invitation.

Finally, it is better to avoid having a party wait while mediators discuss in private with the other side; one thus reduces frustration or suspicion of partiality. The lunch break is a perfect time to set up the private meetings: by suspending the joint session between noon and 2 pm, for example, the mediator can meet with one of the parties from 12:00 until 12:30, and then the other from 1:30 until 2 pm. Some "private, informal meetings" can also take place with one party after the end of a joint session, and with the other just before the next joint session, or in the meantime by telephone with one and the other. It is useful to introduce these possibilities from the start. The purpose of all these early details is to avoid surprising anyone later on.

Which Approach to Problem-Solving?

It is equally important for the mediator to indicate their style of intervention when it comes to problem-solving. According to the distinction proposed in Chapter 2, the mediator can choose to be either a "facilitator" or an "adviser," while also playing the role of an "idea provider." Wearing the "adviser" hat, the mediator will put their opinion forward on what they view as the best solution. While acting as a "facilitator" on the other hand, the mediator will abstain from proposing any solution, even if the parties do not think of one themselves: the mediator is thus purely a process facilitator. Finally, as "idea provider," the mediator will first invite the parties to imagine their own solutions, to which the mediator will add other ideas, especially if the parties have not thought of any themselves. Once again, whatever the method the mediator chooses to adopt, it is important to clearly explain it to the parties before the mediation begins. Thus, the mediator's "mission order" is cleared with and by the parties, even if it means modifying it along the way in agreement with them.

This prerequisite seems important to us so that the parties, understanding well the mediator's work, can wisely mobilize their skills.

○ As I indicated, as your mediator, I will pay attention to problems at stake, people and process. I will favor joint sessions and do everything I can for you to find by yourselves the solutions to your problems. My role will be that of a facilitator, and I will provide ideas only if you ask me, and if you both agree.

This approach emphasizes the participation and empowerment of parties who play an active role in the search for solutions. In contrast, in a more traditional approach, the mediator as well as parties often pushed in favor of the adviser model, in which the mediator plays the predominant role (Lempereur 1998b). This well-known evaluative model is instinctive; it suffices to go on social media or to arrive at the office to hear a multitude of experts, more or less aware of the problem and well intentioned, explain how X and Y *should* go about resolving their conflict. We might like giving advice, expressing opinions, and volunteering opinions for others. But do we like others' advice? Do we accept being told what we are supposed to do? No, of course not, and it is the same for parties in conflict.

Our bet is the following. At first sight, it may be more difficult for the mediator to lead a dialogue where they limit their communication tools to probing questions and active listening; but in the long run, the mediator increases the chances that parties listen to each other, mutually understand and recognize one another, as well as give birth to a more sustainable reconciliation through the co-development of their solutions. This approach, however much it necessitates some self-restraint on behalf of the mediator, proves to be more efficient and to yield more ownership of the solutions and therefore produces a better implementation of the agreement.

The Mediator Invites the Parties to Specify Their Expectations

Mediation serves the objective that the parties themselves assign to it. The earlier these expectations are understood, the better. The mediator will often take advantage of pre-mediation to start figuring out the parties' expectations, for example, merging two businesses or keeping them distinct, maintaining neighborly relationships, etc. To a general objective (like divorce or separation), many particular objectives can be added (custody of the children, vacation time, division of assets, residence, etc.).

These objectives for the most part have been mentioned in pre-mediation. But the following also happens:

- The objectives have evolved since the moment when the decision was made, since new facts that the mediator was not aware of are presented.

- Other objectives remain masked by the main stakes. In a criminal mediation case, the announced purpose was to define a fair compensation, but two other purposes emerged: obtaining apologies and getting the other to promise that they will renounce similar behaviors (*"That my case serves as a lesson and that it does not happen to others"*).

The mediator invites the parties to be clear about what they expect from the mediation: "What do you wish to happen at the end of our meeting? In an ideal world, what would you like this mediation to achieve?" Such simple sentences may give rise to smiles, but they could let parties express, deeply, what success looks like from their point of view. Such questions are less relevant in contexts of acute tension, when each party's preference – at this introductory stage, at least – would be that the other have nothing at all, be punished, etc. But a moment will come, once the painful past has been worked through, when it will be necessary to figure out the expectations to satisfy (Chapter 6).

By gathering the objectives of each party, the mediator demonstrates once more their attention to each person. The mediator articulates some common purposes that the parties will explore together, while also acknowledging some potential contradictory ones. The entire mediation process and the next stages are there to allow some reciprocal explanation and understanding (Friedman and Himmelstein 2009).

Sometimes, as surprising as it is, the parties discover shared interests! For example, in a divorce case, the parties will agree that they both want the children to be happy, to get a solution within a month, to prefer discretion so as not to upset the family, and to avoid litigation. Once this common ground is clarified upfront, the mediation can focus on the points of disagreement.

Mentioning commonalities and differences in the introduction has disadvantages and advantages:

- *Disadvantages* – When parties experience a conflict with much animosity, they barely want to be "like the other." Reminding them of points of similarity rarely fits their current motivation. Their intimate conviction, at this stage, is more about affirming their difference. Attempting to demonstrate the contrary might generate a defensive reaction and mistrust.

- *Advantages* – The common goal is reflected fundamentally by the parties' very presence in mediation. It might be helpful to focus their attention on both their common and different motivations, stressing both what brings them here and keeps them apart. There are few risks attached to announcing commonalities in general terms. Sometimes, one party is aware that the other party has suffered. Frequently in conflict situations, one party deems the other at fault while excusing oneself (and inversely), whereas often both parties have suffered. In order to reduce the risks of the aforementioned disadvantages, it may be wise to only mention the similarities between the parties later in the course of mediation after having explored each party's point of view.

By appreciating the situation on a case-by-case basis, the mediator will thus choose to underline, or not, these similarities during the presentation of the overall mediation objectives.

○ You are both irritated, and it was hard for you to control your language. Both of you feel that it is "the other" who started the whole fight. Is that right? If I understand well, deep down, *both of you* need that:

  ○ the difficulties that each of you have experienced be taken into consideration;

  ○ the other understand what made you act the way you did;

  ○ your problems be resolved;

  ○ your family not suffer.

Once the mediation objective is determined, or in any case outlined, it is necessary to define the rules that will preside over the upcoming joint work.

R for Rules of Engagement

Guidelines are essential to guarantee fruitful communication and to differentiate the upcoming mediation from direct, contentious negotiation. Some mediators announce the rules at the outset, to be able to refer to them later if necessary. Others, facing impatient parties, leave the presentation of these rules of functioning for later. By doing the latter, the parties are able to first express themselves, which helps them understand the need for rules. The mediator will then invite parties to agree to a series of rules, thus establishing a communication contract for the duration of the mediation. When necessary, we will be referring to some of these major principles of mediation that have already been detailed in Chapter 3.

Building on a large number of mediations, here is a set of guidelines to facilitate the mediation process. The mediator introduces them, and then confirms the understanding and agreement of the parties. There are four essential ground rules: no interruption, mutual respect, confidentiality, and the willingness to enter into a binding agreement. Let us clarify each of them.

No Interruption

The mediator encourages the parties to exchange views by alternating, i.e. listening to one another in turn without interrupting the other. This first rule has the advantage of clarity: its transgression is easily observable. In practice, it is not always easy for parties not to interrupt each other, precisely because of the emotional charge of the conversation: *"How could I remain silent, when I hear what the other dares to say?"* Confirming the rule early on, before there is even any interruption yet, is better than proposing it later in the conversation at a moment of vehement interruption. Suggesting it then is likely to appear as a violation of the impartiality principle. If this rule is announced from the very beginning, it becomes possible to refer to it later, since it has been already accepted by both parties.

○ I propose four simple ground rules to you. The first one is that of no interruption. It is possible that the exchanges between you will become heated at certain moments; it may become difficult for one or both of you to hear something without immediately reacting. I will ask you to resist the urge to interrupt in these difficult moments, and let the other side speak until the end. Later, when it is your turn to speak, I will ensure that you can also express yourself without interruption. To guarantee the balance in the speaking time, I alone will take the initiative to interrupt one to let the other carry on. Are we all in agreement on this first rule?

On this occasion, the mediator explains their own role in the management of communication. The mediator will pose many probing questions, not to judge or challenge what they hear, but to achieve a deeper comprehension and overcome potential misunderstandings. They also will be able to, from time to time, reformulate what has been said in order to summarize what has been learned during the exchanges.

Mutual Respect

Through this second rule, the mediator asks the parties to respect one another. It is in their mutual interest: not only does each one expect to be respected, but also the search for solutions requires the capacity to exchange without insults.

○ I would like to bring up a second request, that of mutual respect. Each one of us here expects to be respected. Let us take care of it together. Each one of you will be able to say all that you have on your mind, as long as it describes how you experienced the situation and it doesn't attack the other side. Courtesy will be our collective good.

A way of supporting this mutual respect is to invite parties to use "I"-messages. Starting sentences with "I" or "we," rather than "you," allows one to talk about oneself and one's emotions without falling into an accusation, attribution of intentions, or personal attack against the other side. This simple language shift helps to create dialogue in a conflict context. It is easier to listen to someone using "I" to explain how they were personally impacted, than hearing them attack "you," especially in public – in front of mediators and, if applicable, other participants.

Depending on the situation, more explicit clarifications are useful: no personal attacks, no insults, and, of course, no threats or intimations of physical violence. This courtesy and safety rule, although essential, is however not as clear in practice for mediators as the no-interruption rule. Respect in one party's eyes may be perceived as disrespect by another. Raising one's voice or waving one's hands may seem natural to some, but aggressive to others. The transgression of this rule is thus more subjective; the mediator will need to be vigilant on their personal interpretation of "respect." As they need to ensure that a session is not transformed into a rat race, their perception of respect is revised in the light of the cultures and personalities of each party. If the mediator judges it useful to introduce this rule for better communication, they will benefit from presenting it with precision early on, in a way that precludes being accused of partiality later.

Confidentiality

The importance of confidentiality for mediation exchanges has already been explained in detail (Chapter 3). Confidentiality protects the mediation space and constitutes the third rule to share with parties.

○ **Confidentiality is the third rule to which I ask you to adhere. Exchanges during mediation sessions are protected by the seal of confidentiality and thus may not be shared outside our sessions. This rule also applies to me as the mediator. That is the condition for us to be able to tell each other everything. Do we all agree on this rule?**

To reiterate, without this rule, and out of fear that divulged information be held against oneself later (for example, in court), a party may find that sharing deeply held information is too risky – thus potentially preventing an amicable resolution of the conflict. Naturally, if they wish so, parties may decide to shelve this obligation. They can decide together (possibly by a common document written at the end of the session) about the elements that may be communicated to the outside world, for example, to the media or to colleagues, to avoid rumors and unauthorized disclosure of information out of context.

Willingness to Enter into a Binding Agreement

In mediation, parties remain free to not reach an agreement, and that is perfectly fine. But if they do reach an agreement on anything – be it only the date of a new session – they commit to executing it. For the mediation to be effective, it is critical that parties accept, from the very beginning, the principle to commit to follow through with jointly made agreements. This assures that no one loses their time. By definition in mediation, there is agreement only if all parties want it; they want it because they find it in their interest; and precisely because they find it in their interest, they will execute it willingly.

○ A final rule, to which I ask you to adhere, concerns any points of agreement that you might find together. By definition, the final decision belongs to you, and I will not force anything. But if you reach any agreement on any issue, it is necessary for each one of you to solemnly commit, here and now, to execute the elements of that agreement. Can we consider that you will implement, in good faith, the content of any agreement you would arrive at?

Naturally, this final rule is subject to special cases or nuances. For example, it is possible that a party acting as an authorized representative needs a principal's ratification before accepting the agreement. A suspension of session can suffice. In other cases, it may mean that the authorized representative has only the capacity to make recommendations to their principal, who will make the final decision on whether or not to accept the agreement.

The Mediator Gets the Parties to Agree on All the Rules

These four rules pave the way for a smooth and successful mediation. Some mediators *impose* them on parties in their introduction. From our experience, it is better to *share* them with the parties and obtain each party's individual commitment to respect them. In general, parties will give consent without any difficulty, and therefore apply more easily what they willingly chose. It is also easier, later on, if necessary, for the mediator to remind the parties that they all had agreed to these rules.

Should one or both parties consider it important, nothing prevents modifying some rules. For example, one party might wish some accommodation to the no-interruption rule: *"I want to be able to interrupt if Mr. H. says something incorrect from my point of view, so that I can rectify it."* Or about confidentiality: *"I have nothing to hide and I want to be able to talk to the team about what is said here."* From our point of view, some amendments to this body of rules do not pose a major problem, as long as everyone, including the mediator, agrees to the adjustments. The rules are negotiated, then agreed upon: *"Exceptional interruption, with rectification wished on such or such a fact,"* or perhaps *"Confidentiality limited by a collective decision, at the end of the mediation session, on the content of what will be said by each one to the team or to the media, in order to reduce rumors."*

If challenged by a refusal by either party, or both, to accept the ground rules or to implement them during mediation, the mediator might feel obliged to inform the parties that, under such conditions, it seems difficult for them to pursue their mission. It is up to the parties, then, to take their responsibilities while considering, lucidly, their situation in the absence of an amicable agreement. Their choice is either to reject the perspective of any agreement in mediation, or to admit to common rules that will govern the process.

T for Time and Stages

The mediation PORTAL is quasi-open from now on: it remains for the mediator to describe the path on which to travel. Over *Time*, a sequence of *Stages* will unfold, structuring the actual mediation (Lempereur 1998a).

Time

Time management constitutes a key requirement in mediation. The parties, like the mediator, need to organize their availability in order to allow the mediation to succeed. Nothing is more frustrating than a mediation session that is interrupted, due to a lack of time, especially when major progress seemed near.

In general, the time allowed for mediation has been addressed during the pre-mediation phase (Chapter 4). The introduction to mediation also consists of revisiting the time frame or schedules. Here, the mediator needs to probe the margins of flexibility available to the parties.

○ Can you please confirm that you have three hours in front of you/the day/until 5 pm?

○ If we need a little more time, until what time can you stay?

○ Before adjourning this session, can we specify the day and time of the next meeting?

There is no ideal duration for a mediation session. In general, a period of time that is "too short" (less than an hour) does not allow for getting into the substance. On the other hand, when it is "too long" a moment comes where fatigue and weariness prevent the parties – and mediators! – from efficiently moving forward. The mediator will sense the mood around the table and suggest, wisely, a prolongation, a brief pause, or an adjournment in the session.

Coordinating agendas can prove to be complex, especially if there are many parties – and possible advisers – around the table. That is why it is better, from the beginning, to schedule several plenary sessions. It is always possible to cancel some meetings, once an agreement has been found. The parties will be pleased at having succeeded before the expected deadline. On the other hand, finding an additional date convenient for everyone can be difficult in the short term; if suspended for too long, the mediation may lose steam. That is also why certain institutions fix maximum delays for mediation: in France, for instance, it is three months for a court-ordered mediation. Only in exceptional situations can this delay be extended.

Stages

The purpose is not to carve in stone a strict sequence of stages, but to reassure parties as to the ability of the mediator to orient exchanges toward success. The mediator plays the role of the tour guide, announcing the various stages of a journey and making sure the passengers understand the map. The mediator gives a brief description of the two major stages we identified in the Introduction of this book.

○ Let me suggest two overall stages. The first goes from the past toward the present. It will allow each one of you to share from your perspective what happened. This exploration of the past supposes mutual listening. It won't always be easy, but this stage will help each one of you to feel and understand – even if you disagree – what is truly important for the other. It sheds light on what drove you here and what you are expecting.

In this first stage, we will be brought to understand the problem:

o *first,* identify the points at stake (concerns, worries, difficulties, etc.);

o *then,* explore these points in depth;

o *finally,* recognize together the different perceptions, so that each one of you feels understood.

We will take all the time we need to reach this reciprocal, in-depth understanding of the problem. Then we will move to the second major stage.

This first stage is handled in Chapter 6. Its purpose is to ensure a better understanding of the problems experienced by each party, their feelings, interests, and needs. It aims at identifying the more profound motivations and achieving a reciprocal recognition of identities.

o The second stage moves from the present toward the future. Starting from a mutual understanding of needs, you will imagine all the possible solutions, so that you can structure an agreement, to which you can commit.

To respond to your needs, we will:

o *first,* imagine and list all the possible solutions;

o *then,* evaluate those that you could retain, weighing their pros and cons;

o *finally,* choose, among those, the adequate solutions that can satisfy you and that you can accept.

If no solution is found at the mediation table, we will evaluate the consequences one last time, and you will decide if we are to go our separate ways, or if you want to still give yourselves more time for reflection.

Chapter 7 will handle this second stage. All of the resources of the imagination will be solicited. In fact, too many conflicts can mentally lock up the parties in polarized positions: selling/keeping, staying/leaving, etc. Yet, in practice, some creative options respond better to the needs of one another: a piece of property can be built/shared at leisure over time; its space can be divided; the choice of materials or finances can be adjusted, etc. A multitude of creativity techniques, enabling value creation, exist: Chapter 7 will explore them. We will also review different ways of selecting the most adequate solutions and weighing the needs in an agreement – as compared to the absence of any agreement. If there is an agreement, its formalization will also be necessary.

The speed of the transition from the first stage to the second will depend on the complexity of the conflict, its ripeness, the willingness and availability of the parties, and many other contextual factors. If a mediation requires several sessions, every new one will be introduced, connected to the previous one (by summarizing the potential accomplishments), and by questioning parties on what happened since; its specific objective will be outlined in the progression of the two stages (and their steps). It will end with a summary of new accomplishments, and, if necessary, a new meeting date.

A for Agreement to Mediate

The introduction ends somehow in a more or less formal manner by obtaining a final commitment from all the parties to these common rules and the joint process, to an *agreement to mediate*, a framework agreement (Lempereur 2003d). The mediator concludes by asking the parties two clear questions on the rules and the general principle of mediation and waits until they get a genuine YES.

○ **1) Do you agree to follow the principles and ground rules we just evoked?**

○ **2) Do you agree to undertake this mediation?**

○ **Madam? … Yes, thank you. Sir? … Yes, thank you.**

○ **Well, from now on, we have an agreement to mediate between us, that allows us to move forward and will guide us throughout the mediation.**

Such a framework agreement is thus built, which, before addressing the problems, sets boundaries for the way both the parties and the mediator will proceed. In good faith, and hopefully without too many hidden motives, parties express their common willingness to enter mediation and to adhere to its explicit principles. They may not know if this particular mediation will succeed; but they agree, willingly, to try. If any of the principles are violated, it might suffice for the mediator to recall this initial commitment.

This agreement to engage in mediation already constitutes some rapprochement between the parties. Although they thought they agreed on nothing, and that everything opposed them, the parties at least came to agree on a process to move forward on their dispute. Common ground has been created. Of course, there is no commitment yet on the substantive problems, but, nonchalantly, the mediator has already obtained a series of micro-agreements. Parties rediscover the other, share something improbable together, even just some small, trivial rules of process methods. That is the mediation miracle: transforming small bits of agreements, little by little, *peace by peace*, into an agreement on everything, by engaging the parties in a *logic of accordance*.

Agreement between Greenpeace and Monsanto

One of the authors facilitated a meeting between environmental activists and corporate representatives – notably from Greenpeace on one side and from Monsanto on the other. In appearance, it seemed unlikely that this meeting would produce any agreement at all. Yet, at the end of an evening (focusing on the relationship between people) and then a day (to establish the process), a framework agreement was at least brought about. If one had asked participants before the meeting if they thought they would be able to reach any agreement on the smallest matter, the answer would have been unanimously negative. How surprised they were at the end of their first day of work that they had already been able to find common ground on *how* to work together!

Mediation: A result of successive agreements

Mediation, even with parties grappling with the biggest of disagreements, can move forward by small, successive consolidations:

1. *Agreement on the principle of mediation*, on the act of coming to the table (acquired in pre-mediation).

---

2. *Agreement to mediate on the spirit, ground rules, and time* of mediation (acquired during the introduction).

3. *Agreement on the agenda:* What needs to be discussed (acquired during the introduction or during the stage "from past to present" developed in the next chapter).

4. *Agreement on different perceptions,* with the joint identification of disagreements and of different reasoning/cultures/feelings.

5. *Agreement on different needs,* recognized from now on.

6. *Agreement on solutions,* in response to identified needs.

7. *Agreement on producing a written commitment.*

8. Possible *agreement on a follow-up* to mediation.

If agreements 5-6-7 mark the final achievement on the objective of mediation in substantial terms and if agreements 3-4 prepare them, one need not neglect the symbolic value of obtaining an agreement on points 1–2, the introduction being more developed and thus more important than a mere presentation because it is here where collaboration between the parties and the mediator starts taking root.

L for Launch!

This introduction is now almost done. Parties know what to expect. The mediator can now engage into the substance of the mediation, i.e. the examination of the conflict and hopefully its resolution.

○ **Let me thank both you for agreeing on how we are going to work together. Unless there is a last process issue you would like to raise, I suggest we get down to work!**

The stakes of this introduction are that now the parties – who earlier had often ignored what was going to happen, and sometimes imagined that the mediator was some kind of arbitrator who would decide at the end of the process – have a clear and distinct idea about the path they will travel. Naturally, as in any voyage, unforeseen events can happen, but, at least, each party has some points of reference that will guide them down the path. Table 5.1 summarizes this essential introduction.

TABLE 5.1 Summary: Mediators Open a PORTAL

Steps	Objectives	Methods	Principles
		P for Presentations	
1.1. The mediator welcomes the parties	• Establish first contact • Manage unexpected attendees • Create a courteous climate	• Set up a pleasant space before the meeting • Share first and last names • Always search for a balance between the parties, and between them and the mediator • Negotiate with parties the presence of advisers and the family	• Impartiality • Neutrality • Conviviality • Confidentiality • Fairness • Security
1.2 The mediator presents themselves	• Establish legitimacy • Be "accepted" by the parties	• Find good points of contact between the parties and the mediator • Reassure the parties about the mediator's general experience and, if necessary, about their particular expertise	• Impartiality • Neutrality • Trust

Steps	Objectives	Methods	Principles
1.3 The mediator invites parties to present themselves	• (Re)establish contact between the parties • Recognition of the parties	• Alternate presentations • Immediate consideration for parties • Open and benevolent questions, active listening	• Impartiality or multi-partiality • Trust • Conviviality

O for Objectives

Steps	Objectives	Methods	Principles
2.1 The mediator explains the objective of mediation	• Avoid the parties' misunderstanding and disappointed expectations	• Short definition of mediation (*what it is*) and its principles • Contrast with other conflict resolution modes of intervention (*what it is not*) • Explanation of what will happen if the mediation does not produce a solution agreed upon by parties	• Parties' self-determination • Mediator's commitment concerning only the means and not the results • Impartiality, neutrality, fairness, respect for the law

(*continued*)

TABLE 5.1 (Continued)

Steps	Objectives	O for Objectives		Principles
		Methods		

2.2 The mediator explains their role	• Clarify with parties the way in which they conceive the mediator's role	Explanation of the chosen model among:
		• *Three levels of intervention:*
		  – Problems
		  – People
		  – Process
		
		• *Three session formats:*
		  – Only private meetings
		  – Only joint sessions
		  – Mixed system
		
		• *Three ways to look for solutions:*
		  – Adviser
		  – Facilitator
		  – Provider of ideas
				• Confidentiality
				• Efficiency
				• Credibility
				• Trust
				• Impartiality
				• Neutrality
				• Empowerment

Steps	Objectives	Methods	Principles
2.3 The mediator invites the parties to specify their expectations		• Outline the stakes of this mediation	• Results of exchanges in pre-mediation • Open questioning • Shedding light on expectations and common interests	• Impartiality • Neutrality • Empowerment

R for Rules of Engagement

Steps	Objectives	Methods	Principles

3. The mediator sets basic rules	• Facilitate communication
	• Facilitate mediation proceedings
	• Prevent conflicts with either of the parties
		• Explanations of four basic rules:
		  – *No interruption*
		  – *Mutual respect*
		  – *Confidentiality*
		  – *Willingness to enter into a binding decision*
			• Communication
			• Confidentiality
			• Parties' self-determination
			• Binding agreements
			• Anticipation of possible incidents

(*continued*)

TABLE 5.1 (Continued)

T for Times and Stages

Steps	Objectives	Methods	Principles
4. The mediator organizes the timing	• Have sufficient time • Not lose any time	• Reminder of the planned calendar from pre-mediation, if necessary • Probe the margins of operation	• Structured process • Anticipation • Micro-agreements

5. The mediator summarizes the future stages of mediation proceedings	• Inform the parties about the path to come	Explanation of the *two major stages*:
		• From the past to the present:
		  – Identify points to negotiate
		  – Deal with them in depth
		  – Mutually recognize one another
		• From the present to the future:
		  – Imagine possible solutions
		  – Evaluate
		  – Decide
			• Structured process
			• Credibility
			• Trust
			• Shared knowledge about the path

Steps	Objectives	Methods	Principles
6. The mediator obtains the agreement of the parties	• Create an initial agreement between parties • Circumvent in advance an accusation of partiality in the case of a later call to order	• Final validation of the general willingness to commit to mediation • Eventual writing of a framework agreement • Potential signature on a document confirming the process methods which will be used	• Autonomy of parties • Empowerment • Commitment and micro-agreements

L for Launch!

Steps	Objectives	Methods	Principles
7. The mediator launches the mediation	• Engage with the substance of the mediation	• Congratulate parties for having achieved an agreement to mediate • Keep up this positive momentum	• All the aforementioned principles

Despite all these precautions, the mediator may still miss out on elements that are of concern to the parties, before entering into the heart of the matter. Hence the necessity, at the end of the introduction, to leave *time for questions*, to which the mediator will provide responses. Maybe the mediator makes a reference to a supplementary rule, particularly adapted to these specific parties or this case? Even better: in this way, the agreement is consolidated on the process, the true foundation that offers the mediator a solid base from which to launch the mediation per se. The following chapters will analyze this.

CHAPTER 6
THE PAST TOWARD THE PRESENT

Grasp the Problems
Before Seeking Mutual Recognition

After the parties have agreed to move ahead with mediation and abide by its principles (Chapters 2 and 3), prepared for their meeting (Chapter 4), and established a framework agreement to mediate with common ground rules (Chapter 5), they are ready to work on the problems. To find solutions to the dispute that pits them against each other, the parties need to first explore their conflictual past, which prevents them from coming together in the present. If each side understands what created the problem and the underlying needs of each other, they increase the chance of finding solutions in the next stage (Chapter 7).

At any given moment, how did each party perceive imbalance, rupture, and tension? By allowing both parties to talk this through with the help of a facilitator, the mediation sheds light on the past and on the needs and requests of each side, bringing them fully into the present moment. From the start, it is quite common for the parties to see the situation only in binary terms: to divorce/not to divorce; to quit/to stay in the company; to obtain a reparation/to not concede it; to ask for the organization of elections/to refuse them; to occupy a territory forever/to obtain its immediate evacuation, etc. Once the needs and deep motivations of all the parties are better understood by each other, a broader spectrum of solutions becomes possible.

As indicated in the previous chapter, this first significant stage concerning the problem includes *three moves*. Although each move is set up to occur in sequential order, it is essential to take into account the ebbs and flows of exchanges. Sometimes it will be necessary to glide back and forth between the different moves to make sure no stone is left unturned. What is important is that the mediator helps the parties deeply explore each one.

- *First move: Identification of the problems or points to negotiate.* Which issues need to be addressed? It is important to establish, to the extent possible, a list of recurring "hot topics" that are useful to explore.

- *Second move: Deepening the analysis of these problems to discover the underlying motivations and needs.* Why are these topics so important? Engaging in quality listening while asking probing questions will help a mediator to uncover – within the limit of what each party confides – what lies hidden beneath outer appearances.

- *Third move: Mutual understanding.* Does each party understand why these points are so important to the other? Here, it is essential for the mediator to emphasize that "understanding" does not mean "agreeing." Once the parties have mutually understood and recognized each other, this first stage comes to a close, successfully moving from the past toward the present.

Two fundamental tools guide this mediation stage: listening and questioning. In this chapter, we will present some examples of how to actively listen and also examples of some pertinent questions to ask. Finally, we include a framework of analysis that will serve mediators during this major stage, as well as throughout the entire process.

First Move: Identify the Problems to Negotiate

During this first major move, the mediator engages with the parties and invites them to express the problems from their perspective. In order to guide this exchange, the mediator can draw inspiration from typical mediation approaches, but no matter which approach is chosen, asking the right questions will be crucial for the success of the mediation.

Engage the Parties in a Dialogue

Who should speak first? This question may appear trivial at first, because in any case each party will talk in turn. And yet …

- If X rather than Y is invited to speak first, there is the risk of the mediator being perceived as favoring a party, even if it is not the mediator's intention.

- The parties may perceive the one who speaks first as winning a power position and thus obtaining a first symbolic victory. The risk here is that an early asymmetry may unwittingly be created between the parties.

- For some, speaking first is an advantage because it anchors the entire story favorably for the speaker. This is called the anchor bias. It creates a first impression of what the facts are, which sticks, and which the other will feel obliged to respond to, instead of narrating their own story.

- For others, it may be a disadvantage to begin the discussion because hearing the other's story may help them twist the situation, enabling them to adapt their own speech and fine-tune their arguments to maximize the persuasiveness of their own story.

- Finally, the mediator might think that they will not be influenced by the first story they hear and be equally receptive to a new story told by the second party. But is this truly the case? The mediator needs to remain vigilant about anchoring biases and also needs to learn to remain in listening mode without being judgmental about whatever any party tells them first, never considering whatever one hears as the *only* version of reality.

Based on the above, what matters for the mediator is not to be perceived by a party as preferring X or Y. Here are some possible ways of circumventing this risk:

- *"Who would like to start?"* (followed by a silent pause, leaving the choice to whoever wants to initiate the exchange). Here, the mediator emphasizes that they are at the disposal of both parties. Let us note that the phrase "would like" invites both parties to help each other begin to negotiate the problem together. In this sense, this expression differs from other possible candidate sentences such as *"Who would rather start?,"* which risks pitting the parties against each other. The "who is going to be the first" becomes a "who is going to win against the other by being the first to speak," perpetuating the conflict that we are trying to resolve.

- *"I propose that one of you starts ... You?* (accompanied by a glance at one party); *Or you?* (accompanied by a glance at the other party)."* If both parties intervene at the same time, the mediator can add, very simply: *"You both apparently have a lot of things to say. Great! Could you reach agreement on who really wants to start?"* It is already a "mini-agreement" that the mediator invites the parties to put in place.

- *One speaking first rather than the other for a good reason: "I propose that Mr. X, who solicited this mediation first, starts."* Granting the privilege of speaking first to whoever called for the meeting corresponds to legal reasoning. One needs to immediately add: *"As soon as Mr. X has finished, you will be able, Ms. Y, to tell us how you experienced this situation from your point of view."* Whatever the justification used to grant the privilege of speaking first ("Ladies first," "Those having greater seniority," etc.), it is important for the mediator to makes this explicit in order to maintain the perception of impartiality and trust in the parties' eyes.

- *The floor to one, asking for the agreement of the other:* In order to mitigate the risks of the previous formula, certain mediators – who invite one of the parties to start or the one party who spontaneously speaks first – immediately add, looking at the other party: *"Mr. X, do you agree that Ms. Y can start?"* Usually, if the mediator echoes this courtesy of marking the identity of the one starting as well as the one who has not yet spoken, the latter will acquiesce. When – though this is rare – both parties want to talk first, the debate is quickly resolved if mediators explain that they will be granted equal attention – even a random choice can be made.

- *The random draw:* The mediator takes out a coin and tosses it: heads or tails. They let fate decide in order to demonstrate, sometimes with humor, that they do not have a preference.

Conduct a Mediation: The Action Plan

Once the question of "who starts" is settled, the mediator can employ different approaches to help the parties uncoil the thread that links the past to the present. Here are the main ones.

The History of the Relationship, from the Origins to the Present

○ **For how long have you known each other? How did you meet? For how long have your organizations collaborated? How did your relationship unfold since you first met each other? What led you (employer) to hire Ms. Smith 10 years ago? And, you (employee), what motivated you to work for the company? How has that evolved since?**

This historically sensitive approach – valid for a family, commercial, social, or international conflict – proceeds by alternating the expression of the parties, each of whom narrates, in turn, a part of their shared story. The mediator stimulates this dialogue by turning toward the other party at the end of each sequence: *"So, what happened next?"* The mediator notes, as they go along, the points of potential agreement and disagreement in the account of reality as each party remembers it subjectively. Thus, each party is brought to recall

- what led them to become familiar with each other, their early mutual respect and a positive balance that may have existed at the beginning between them; and,

- what later brought about problems, disagreements, and conflicts.

The motivation underlying this method is to make step-by-step progress, together, with the parties, toward identifying how each contributed, at a given moment, to the conflict. How did the conflict start, grow, and evolve until the present day? The chronological structure allows each person to see clearly where and when feelings or values were bruised, giving rise to dissatisfaction. This echoes what Larry Susskind calls "joint fact-finding" (Matsuura and Schenk 2016). This method is used in two ways:

- *By dating it back to the start of problems:* Here, the mediator wishes to focus rather quickly on the problems the parties want to fix.

- *By dating it back to the very start of the relationship:* The intention here is to make the parties relive their "good moments," before coming to the litany of problems. Often, both positive and negative episodes have occurred in the history of the relationship. Whether we talk about relationships within a family, at work, or between states, the past includes peaceful times that are good to remember.

  o You have known each other since … Can you remember when you first met? The first time that you heard about the other? Can you also recall when the problems subsequently arose? Let us sort things out:

  o Please list everything *positive* that has happened (was pleasant, functioned well, etc.).

  o Then, list everything that posed a problem (was difficult, is still heavy today, needs reparation, etc.).

The History of the Conflict, From the Origins to the Present

  o When and how did the difficulties start? Can you date the beginning of the problems? What happened subsequently and what do you want now?

This approach does not start with the relationship between people, but with the perceived problems. Often, each party has their own perception of when the problems started. Psycho-sociologist Watzlawick (Watzlawick, Bavelas, and Jackson 1967) called this "the punctuation" of events, where each person marks the period where the phrase – that is to say, phase – began – i.e. when the conflict started.

The List of Problems

This approach invites parties to immediately describe the issues, but without necessarily following a strict historic order.

○ What would be useful to talk about here so that you will ultimately feel satisfied? Could you summarize, in a few sentences, the issues or problems you have to discuss so that we understand each other?

This approach – where parties start immediately with their vision of what the problems are – results in a list of "problems" to negotiate. Sometimes parties are asked to put this in writing separately in order to be more aware of the facts and their effects on the current situation.

○ Could each of you take a few minutes for reflection? Here is a piece of paper and a pencil. Please note the events that created problems. The first event, the second, etc. You can, of course, if there are a lot of items, select those that seem the most significant to you.

From these points, the mediator then builds, with the parties, an *agenda* that is composed of different lines of reasoning:

- *Chronology:* By negotiating the problems, in the order in which they were mentioned by the parties, without, however, trying to rank the points, which can often become a source of disagreement between the parties.

- *Urgency:* Dealing with the most pressing issues first and keeping time for the rest.

- *"Crescendo," going from the least to the most difficult:* In the hope of obtaining "bits of agreement" on easy points, thereby contributing to reestablishing the trust and the relationship, which will be useful in the treatment of the more delicate points later on.

- *"Decrescendo," going from the most to the least difficult:* In the hope of showing the parties that the mediation concentrates on what is most significant, and that once the most challenging issues are settled, the rest will follow rapidly and painlessly.

This problem-based approach can be combined with the two history-based approaches we mentioned earlier. The mediator can propose to establish a genealogy of the most important problems. This combined approach is best adapted to people or organizations with long-standing relationships where many different facts and perceptions may have affected the parties, but it can also be used for short-term relationships characterized by only one major contention.

The Return to Spontaneous Exchanges Between the Parties

○ Both of you, no doubt, have things to say to each other, some questions to ask one another … put yourself at ease in order to do so. Keep in mind the guidelines of mutual respect we have agreed upon. During the exchanges, my only role will be to facilitate a constructive conversation.

This approach does not follow a pre-established plan, but places the parties in the driving seat of the conflict and, ultimately, of the process of resolution. The mediator remains present as an attentive observer, guarantor of courtesy, restating and reflecting like a mirror what the parties say. The mediator identifies themes that have been raised spontaneously, possible contradictions, and possible paths forward.

○ Please share, from your point of view, what happened. Express, in turn, what is on your mind. You are the best expert in your life (of your work ...); I am not. Afterward I will ask: did the other know, feel, and understand all of that? We will engage in this clarification for as long as necessary.

Three remarks can be made about this model:

- If the parties spontaneously return to their past, they relive what remains "hypersensitive" to them and what preoccupies them. In some cases, they can get so heated up that they forget the mediator's presence, for better or worse.

- This approach requires patience on the part of the mediator, who might lose part of their capacity to structure the discussion. The mediator will prefer to let the content emerge through detours and back-and-forth excursions between the present and the future. Problems are identified that the parties had no idea about, but which they want to broach. This approach may take more time but might positively impact the relationship between the parties and even help them to mend their broken past.

- This "transformative" model of mediation (Bush and Folger 2004) increases the parties' control and responsibility. Here, under the watchful eye of the mediator, the parties generally reflect on the relevance of the arguments they present.

Other Approaches ... to Be Determined

A particular situation may dictate a specific approach, but parties and mediators are not limited to any of them. Any party or mediator may propose their own approach, or a combination thereof.

Whatever approach ends up being used, these first moments are key: the carefully chosen words (*"the problems you have in mind that need to be discussed"*) and the way a mediator unveils an approach will impact the mediation process and its results.

Some Open Questions to Figure Out the Sensitive Points for Each Party

Whatever the selected plan, the idea is to discuss what the parties want to talk about. Which aspect does each want to emphasize? What other angle(s) can the mediator also shed light on? The mediator's task is to identify issues to put on the table. For a book, it would be to establish the table of contents; for a meeting, it would be the agenda. For a mediation, it is the list of sensitive points that each person wishes to address.

In order to identify these points, the mediator will start by asking open questions, so that the parties avoid focusing on a single dimension of the conflict. How much time and energy mediators spend on this open questioning depends on how much they know the parties or about their problems. Here, the mediator tries to grasp three moments of the conflict: the present, the past, and the future.

○ *The present* – What is it about? I am listening to you … Can you tell me, in a few minutes, the essence of what you need right now?

○ *The past* – Could you describe what happened, the events that led you here today? What problems arose for you? From your perspective, what other elements could have influenced what happened? Can you describe the context (the atmosphere in the neighborhood, company, family, etc.)? What other people in the family, close or distant, could have influenced what happened?

○ *The desired future* – Starting from what happened, what are your expectations? What would you like? What would you wish for at the end of these meetings, to be satisfied? What does success look like for you?

It is also with the future in mind, as parties contemplate it here and now, that the journey from the past to the present unfolds. What *current* desire is expressed in the fact that each party remembers such or such event from the past? By listening to the responses to these open questions, the mediator can grasp, without assumptions, how each party situates, dates, poses, and sometimes repeats what this mediation is about.

At this stage, the mediator can remember to use mostly *"wh" questions*, rather than *"yes/no" questions*, as in the technique of criminal investigation that Quintilian developed: "who did it, what was it, where, who else, why, how and when?"

Quintilian's Hexameter, or seven open, useful questions for mediators

Who?	Who is concerned by this situation?
What?	What is it about? What is the problem?
Where?	Where did it happen? Is the problem linked to a specific place?
Who else?	Who else was involved? Any other stakeholders?
Why?	What was the intention of each person, their objectives?
How?	How did one arrive at the current situation?
When?	When did the problem appear? What have been difficult moments?

Put a List of Points on a Flip Chart

At the end of this identification move, the mediator summarizes the list of points to address by making them clear to all, either on a flip chart, for example, on a word processing document projected on a screen for everybody to see, or simply on a sheet of paper. The mediator ensures that the vocabulary used is sufficiently neutral to announce a claim, reproach, or grievance without using hurtful terms: the mediator can reframe, for example, "false accounts" into "statement of accounts."

The inscription of points on a common support constitutes in itself a mediation. Each party sees, by looking at the flip chart or screen or sheet, that their points of concern have been carefully noted and will be discussed. This approach reduces the risk that a party who hears a concern of the other party will believe that their own concern has been dismissed. Let us take two examples of lists: one from a family dispute (#1) and another from a corporate dispute (#2):

List #1:	List #2:
• Children's domicile	• Reasons for late delivery
• Visitation rights	• Quality of products
• Child support	• Payment delays
• Follow-up at school	• Rules for future orders

"Are there other points to add to the list?" Before closing this phase, it is useful to use silence to allow parties to reflect and verify, as a preventive measure, that no other sticky point has been forgotten. Such a pause reduces the risk that at the moment when an agreement seems in sight, one party, all of a sudden, signals: *"Yes, except that we did not talk about …,"* endangering the progress that had been achieved so far.

If Necessary, Prioritize the Problems

Once the different problems are identified, the mediator might ask the parties to order them, for a triple clarification:

- *For the party who formulated these points:* Increasing awareness of priorities.

- *For the party who listens:* The possible discovery of the other side's priorities. For example, one party may imagine that the other wants to terminate the contract and regain their autonomy, whereas in fact they want to maintain the contract but use other sales techniques. Likewise, nation 1 may fear that nation 2 is rearming itself in order to launch an invasion of nation 1, whereas, in fact, nation 2 simply wants to protect itself against an invasion by nation 3.

- *For the mediator:* Similarly, sometimes the mediator discovers that the parties' priorities are different from what the mediator had initially thought.

How to introduce a potentially delicate question smoothly

Sometimes the parties might ask themselves why the mediator asks a particular question and feel uncomfortable about it. They may react defensively with: *"What is the point of asking me this?"* or *"Why me? Ask the other party!"* If the mediator anticipates this reaction, they may want to forestall the problem by preceding a potentially difficult question with a mollifying sentence such as: *"The question that I would like to ask you may seem indiscreet. Sorry in advance."* Or: *"Before asking you this question, just a reminder that what is said here between us remains entirely confidential."* Or: *"My goal here is to better understand the situation and its possible evolution"* or *"To make it easier for the other party to go in your direction, why don't you share your difficulties?"* Of course, if the mediator forgets this "smooth" introduction, they can always respond by using some of these arguments, or a variation thereof, after the parties have reacted defensively.

In the course of this first move of identification, the mediator avoids orienting the remarks in one direction or another: the parties themselves can underscore better than anyone else what troubles them most and what issues they wish to raise. When none of the parties wants to add any new elements, the moment has come to look at the most important points in depth. The mediator may look at their notes, and focus on

- something that was *evoked only vaguely* ("some difficulties," "the situation changed ...") and requires in-depth understanding;

- something known and clear to one party, but *unknown and obscure* for the other;

- something that caused *strong emotions* for one party or both (discomfort, fear, anger, disgust, contempt, sadness, desire for vengeance, indignation, shame, etc.);

- some *attribution of intention* to one party from the other (with a possible impact, but maybe another intention).

Before beginning an in-depth exploration of each identified problem – the second move – the mediator will summarize what has already been said in order to mitigate the risk that parties raise the same issues again.

Second Move: Uncover Motivations

A more targeted questioning to examine the identified points in depth will help draw out, beyond positions, the deep-seated motivations of the parties. To succeed in this work, the mediator's mastery of the art of questioning and listening is essential, and to support it, we will suggest several levels of analysis.

Why an In-Depth Examination?

The solutions proposed in mediation will be satisfying only if they respond to the true needs of the parties: to their deep-seated motivations, sometimes

buried by months or years of antagonism. The nature and dynamic of conflicts produce extreme requests, which sometimes do not reflect the actual
needs. The mediator's mission is to help the parties go beyond their starting
positions in order to allow exchanges on the basis of their deep motivations.

Matignon agreements on New Caledonia

New Caledonia is a French overseas territory, an island in the Pacific
Ocean, where there are two major groups, the indigenous Kanaks
and the Caldoches, who are of French descent. The former sought
independence from France, whereas the latter refused it. Major clashes,
causing casualties on both sides, put the island on the brink of civil
war in the 1980s, and the French Prime Minister at the time, Michel
Rocard, sent in Spring 1988 a mission of mediators to New Caledonia.
Jean-Marie Tjibaou, leader of the independentist party Kanak and
Socialist National Liberation Front (FLNKS), faced Jacques Lafleur,
leader of the pro-French party Rally for Caledonia in the Republic
(RPCR). Between the two camps, agreement seemed inconceivable.

The key to dialogue went beyond the binary positions (for or against
independence) to identify the motivations of each party. For example,
Christian Blanc, one of the mediators, asked Jean-Marie Tjibaou: *"Have
a dream: describe the independent New Caledonia to me."* To this invitation, simple and complex at the same time, the leader of FLNKS, himself a
former priest, responded: *"A dream like Martin Luther King?"* and started
describing the needs that independence would allow to better satisfy: the
recognition of the Kanak identity – by way of a flag and the teaching
of indigenous languages; economic development shared more equitably
between the two communities – notably nickel extraction; tourism that is
more respectful of the cultural and natural heritage of the island; a route
to make the North province accessible, etc.

All these needs were included in the mediation, which was successful and
resulted in the Matignon Agreements on 26 June 1988, in Paris.

The move to deepen one's understanding means staying longer with the
problems at stake, clarifying what they are, thereby serving the goal of

problem-solving through a deeper diagnostic. As the mediator and parties dig deeper, they find the root causes of conflict on which to work, so that future solutions will be durable, thus preventing a recurrence of the problems.

This move also makes new arguments emerge, more personal and intimate ones that are often linked to emotions and personal or cultural values that have been bruised during the conflict. During this stage of deepening one's understanding, it may be discovered that there are other protagonists, absent up to now, who need to be associated with the mediation process. Depending on the specific case, the mediator might solicit them, suspend mediation, and/or commit to a specific approach to include their perspective.

The reasons *why* deepening one's understanding is important are simple to formulate and to comprehend, but *how* to do it is more delicate. In this respect, mediators use two major tools: questioning and listening.

The Art of Questioning

The art of questioning does not mean "subjecting the parties to questions," as an investigator of the Inquisition would, but helping the parties, subtly, to express their deep-seated motivations (Miles 2013; Pohlmann and Thomas 2015). The mediator has a palette of questions of varying types. For each question they ask, the mediator will ensure that they raise the most pertinent ones and remain silent after each question is asked, rather than overwhelming the parties with a barrage of questions.

Different Types of Questions

First, there are the *questions to avoid*, because they jeopardize the impartiality of the mediator or alienate them from the parties:

- *Guilt-tripping questions:* "How were you able to say/do such a thing?"

- *Loaded questions:* "When did you finally start taking these claims seriously?" — implying that for a long time a party has not taken it as such.

- *Infantilizing questions:* "Would you make a small effort?"

- *Harmful questions:* "Is it too much asking that you say …?"

- *Leading questions:* "But is it not necessary to respect the precautionary principle?" – barely leaving no other choice than a "yes."

- *Overly complex questions:* "Given the Supreme Court precedents in this matter, and also the current trends of legal doctrine on the Frye Test, which kind of expert opinion would qualify as admissible scientific evidence in your case?" – the mediator needs to avoid technical jargon that parties may be unfamiliar with.

What are *fruitful questions* that promote in-depth understanding?

- *"Why"* (and, to a lesser extent, *"how many?"*) – Such questions contribute to the clarification and also the quantification of certain points:

  o **Why are these people concerned? How many people are involved? Why at this place? Are other places concerned and, if yes, how many? Why at this moment? How many times did it occur?**

- *Motivation-based questions* – These questions clarify the desires, needs, motivations, interests, and values that underlie positions or claims.

  o **What would this request satisfy for you? Why is it important for you? What bothers you about this approach? What do you fear losing?**

- *Clarification questions* – The mediator refers to something that a party mentioned and asks them to elaborate on it in order to get more detail and nuance.

  o **You said: "One should have more means." Can you expand on this? You indicated that it was not at all easy. Why was it not easy? (Facing a very quiet party) I noticed that you are staying silent: would you care to discuss how what was said resonates in you?**

- *Hypotheses, closed questions, or multiple-choice questions* – The mediator makes suggestions, helping a party react or formulate their ideas, or guides their reflection. Questioning is more pointed, so that the parties focus on a precise point.

  ○ **I sense you are upset; do you wish to talk about it?**
  Do you refuse to pay this amount because you have a budget issue or because you disagree with the requested amount?
  By saying this is unacceptable, are you referring to the contentious behavior or the proposal being made?

- *Validation questions* – The mediator confirms and records a progress of understanding, a deepening of each point.

  ○ **Is that correct? Do you agree?**
  Is their explanation satisfactory for you?

From Contradiction to Explanation

By employing probing questions and by reformulating, the mediator moves from a posture of debate with ongoing contradictions (attack, response, counterattack, etc.) toward what looks more and more like a conversation with mutual explanations. The mediator, as they dig deeper, ensures that each party gives the best attention to the other's viewpoint. Here are some examples when the mediator needs to accompany the parties to promote understanding.

- From *evaluation* to *observation* – It is about re-focusing on what was seen, heard, and imagined without evaluation or judgment. Thus, *"Robert works too slowly, he is poorly qualified to be a senior biologist"* becomes *"Robert spent eight more hours than what was expected in the estimate."*

  ○ **Can you give a specific example?**
  Describe to us, in a very factual way, how this incident occurred?

- From *opinion* to *perception* – Rather than expressing some accusatory judgment about the other party ("YOU are like this"), parties are asked to express the feelings they had in that situation by using the "I-message" ("I feel …").

  ○ **How did you experience this situation?**
  How did that make you feel?

- From *impact* to *intent* – The distinction between intent and impact has already been emphasized in the chapter on mediation preparation (Chapter 4; Stone, Patton, and Heen 1999). Expressing how certain actions or words impact people sometimes helps in the expression of the real underlying intentions. Most often, a gradual gap appears between what one wanted to do, what one eventually did, what today one thinks one has done in the past, what the other concluded at that time, and what the other remembers today.

  ○ **What was your intention at that time?**
  What did you imagine at that time?
  Why did you react like this?

Listen in Mediation

Probing questions, as we just explored, as well as active listening aid in problem-solving. Yet listening is more complicated than it seems. Listening *how, to whom,* and *to what* creates many struggles (Salzer, Simonet, and Soudée 2004).

Listening How?

Let us be reminded of four styles of listening to avoid (Lempereur and Colson, ed. by Pekar, 2010):

- *Impassive listening* – If the mediator is overly concerned about impartiality, there is a risk that they will remain so withdrawn from the conversation that they show no signs of emotion, as if they were not interested in what the parties are saying.

- *Distracted listening* – Preoccupied by all their tasks (showing, at the same time, interest in one party and the other; keeping an eye on the process flow and the ticking clock, and also remembering all the other mediation files in the dock), the mediator does not manage to concentrate on what one of the parties is expressing to them here and now, and it is showing. It looks as though the mediator is daydreaming.

- *Reactive listening* – The mediator does not succeed in preventing themselves from passing judgment, and belittles what a party is telling them.

- *Directive listening* – The mediator controls the exchanges excessively, to the extent that parties feel as though they are under investigation.

Rather, the mediator should favor the technique of *active listening* by drawing inspiration from the following principles.

Ten principles for active listening

1. *Listen with all signs of attention*: Do nothing that is a source of distraction, maintain eye contact, smile, punctuate remarks with nods, etc.

2. *Take in all remarks carefully*, with benevolence, an open mind, and non-judgmentally, i.e. without criticism.

3. *Give equal attention to nonverbal communication* such as gestures, facial expressions, and body language, where intimate emotions are expressed (Lempereur and Willer 2016).

4. *Take notes*, if necessary, both for future use and to demonstrate that each party's remarks are valued.

5. *Reformulate*, which means putting in your own words what a party just said, in order to demonstrate to them through your own words that you have understood them and grasped their points.

6. *After reformulating*, invite the party to correct what might have been misunderstood, in order to nip in the bud, then and there, a potential misunderstanding.

7. *Pay attention* to what you may not have grasped during your first attempts at listening.

---

8. *Ask clarification questions* in order to invite the party, if necessary, to complete or specify their views.

9. *Get the party's concurrence* regarding your understanding of their views.

10. *Close the listening phase* on this point by asking the parties if they wish to add anything and also by thanking them.

Listening *to Whom?*

The mediator, of course, first listens to the parties around the table. But in addition to this "local" dimension, the mediator often needs to add a "global" dimension to listening that goes beyond the parties. Restricting the conflict to only the interpersonal dimension limits the understanding and imagination of the parties, each one making the other party guilty for the conflict, and, therefore, solely responsible for identifying a future solution. In mediation, *global listening* looks in depth at the problem. Beyond the individual, the *ego* in Greek, a mnemonic chart extends the conscience to *I.G.O.S.* so that mediators listen to the following:

- *The I* – The *Individual* as self.

- *The G* – Besides the I, the mediator needs to be aware of the *Groups* to which individuals belong: a family, a village, a neighborhood, a social group, a team.

- *The O* – Further, the parties belong to *Organizations* in which they play a role and which impose rules on them or, at least, influence them: the company and its organizational chart, the union or the political party and its charter; the association and its statutes; the university and its academic rules, etc.

- *The S* – Finally, the *Systems* to which individuals belong: political, legal, cultural, technological, customary, and traditional systems; customs, dos and don'ts, the affirmation of some desires and prohibition of others, all influencers of decision-making processes.

Questioning and listening across the I.G.O.S. chart proves to be enlightening for all. Sometimes, a party realizes that "the other" is not the source of all the problems but is rather under the influence of rules or processes imposed by an organization or a system. A more *structural solution,* though it takes longer, will integrate changes within organizations or systems to avoid the recurrence of the same "interpersonal" problem over and over.

Frequent conflicts over noise in a housing project

At the *individual* level, some solutions exist: placing felt pads under the furniture, putting in a carpet instead of hardwood floors, temporary or permanent reduction of noise volume of electronics, moving out, etc. However, during a mediation on this subject in a housing project, the root cause of the noise was recognized as being related to the *System* – i.e., building constructions without soundproofing, considered normal at the time of construction. As a result, the Housing Project Committee, an *Organization*, itself dismayed by the repetitive complaints and the quarrels within the neighborhood about the noise problems, decided to soundproof the entire building, and make sure that subsequent constructions included soundproofing. The exploration of the *past* allowed, in the *present* time of mediation, a transfer of a neighbors' problem (the noise), from the parties involved to an organization that could address an economic problem (financing soundproofing) for which it had found both a "systemic" response and an "organizational" structural solution for the future.

Frequent conflicts between detached-house neighbors

In a residential neighborhood, with few parking spaces, neighbors squeeze their vehicles one against the other – blocking exits of homes and causing multiple conflicts. Following a mediation, two neighbors decided together to refer the issue to the mayor, who soon set up a nearby vacant space as a parking lot.

Listening *to What?*

Listening and memory are selective. Each of us chooses, consciously or not, to remember only some parts of a conversation. Neither the mediator nor the parties escape this psychological bias (Natale and Hantas 1982; Saunders 2012). To protect them from it – at least partly – and still stay within the logic of probing, we invite mediators to use many *frameworks of analysis*, which will help them retrace this past that resonates with the present. These seven frameworks help both the mediator and the parties to grasp the complexity of a conflict.

Framework 1 – Subject Changes

During a contentious dialogue, when parties do not like what they hear, they are spontaneously tempted to interrupt the other, or even when they let them speak, to redirect the exchanges toward another subject, that shows them in a more favorable "light" – where they appear to be more in the "right." During this probing move, these verbal diversions might become significant, and the mediator needs to listen to keywords, translating these subject changes. They will note such shifts and recall them as they reformulate, ensuring that all the points emerge, and not uniquely those that, in a power struggle, one party emphasizes more than another party.

In the following examples, *italicized keywords* signal subject changes from one party to the other. It is up to the mediator to be vigilant and capture them in order to deepen the content of each subject, without, at this stage, clarifying any of them yet. On each point, the mediator will coordinate exchanges to extract points of agreement and disagreement, with the parties *exchanging views with each other on each point,* without any change of subject at this time.

Condominium issues involving three parties
(P.: property management company; X.: Ms. X., owner; Y.: Mr. Y, owner)
P.   It is going to be necessary to *do safety work* on the elevator doors.
X.   We *already did* work on the elevator two years ago.
Y. *(to X.)* *You are always against* doing any work.
X.   I said that we already did the work. I want to *know why we must restart.*

Y.   If *the property management company tells* you we must, it is because it is necessary.

X.   Yes, so that it gets paid *a commission* on this work.

P.   If I propose it, it is for *you, as co-owners, to decide*, because in the final analysis, you are responsible for it. I can only make recommendations.

X.   I say *no*, I do not see why there would be new work.

Y.   I say *yes* because I trust the property management company.

P.   There is *a new law* that imposes a new, automatic closure within three years.

X.   It is thus *not* a question of carrying them out *immediately*.

Y.   If we don't do it now, it will never happen, and we will pay *a fine*.

X.   I respect the law, but I am *not that rich* and *currently* do not wish to finance this work.

Firing

(HR: the personnel manager; S: Mr. S, sales representative)

HR.   Listen, *the demand* for cigarettes is *decreasing*, so we *can no longer assign five representatives* for Spain, but only four. You had *the worst results last year*. A client complained that you had *arrived drunk* at a meeting. Do you remember? We are *going to have to let you go*.

S.   *Last month*, I had the *best results* of anyone on the team.

HR.   I told you that arriving *drunk* at a client meeting is unacceptable. You only had a warning, but you should have been fired.

S.   I am 32; I have *two children* who are 3 and 7.

HR.   The company *no longer has the means* to pay you.

S.   When I got this job only a year ago, I started producing *better results than others* who have been there for at least five years.

HR.   We apply the *"last come, first go"* rule.

S.   *I do not understand.*

HR.   You made *a professional mistake*, and you were the last recruit. You will be the first to go. That is all.

Delivery

(client C.; supplier S.)

C.   You *did not deliver* on 15 November *as expected*. We *lost a million* euros. The items were not in our stores for Christmas.

S.   There was *a factory strike* in France. We received nothing.

C.   You *promised* to deliver on 15 November.

S.   This was an *emergency situation, out of our control*.

C.   You should have *informed us before*. We would have tried to find another supplier.

S.   We *did not know* that a strike was going to happen.

C.   You owe us a million euros in *damages*. And we are only counting damages, not the interest.

S.   These are shared *risks*.

C.   You owe us a million euros in damages – period.

S.   You are *exaggerating*.

C.   What does *the contract* say?

S.   But, didn't you hear me, this was an emergency situation that was out of our control!

Faced with this lack of mutual listening, mediators are necessary "deepeners" so that parties are really able to understand one another with respect to the underlying motivations emphasized by each of the italicized keywords. Deep down, this framework suggests, *first and foremost*, spotting and isolating different ingredients of the conflict, and *second*, examining them in depth separately, before discussing how they might fit together: decompose to recompose, or deconstruct to reconstruct.

Framework 2 – Chronology of Events in the Conflict

Earlier, we mentioned the usefulness of a chronological approach in order to identify the problems. Reused here, the same method helps each party to become aware of the role they may have played in conflict escalation as in its de-escalation.

Framework 3 – What and How

The "what" refers to the *substance of the conflict* (encroachment on a territory, defective work, late delivery, etc.). It is not the only source of conflict. The mediator needs to be attentive to keywords demonstrating that deep down there is also the "how," referring to how the conflict aspects were communicated or handled (*"We are neighbors … and they sent us registered mail!"* or *"They did not even ask us for our opinion,"* or *"You think that at least they would have apologized.*") So many aspects of both substance and form need to be uncovered and then acknowledged by both parties.

Framework 4 – The Motivation of the Motivation, or the "Why of the Why"

"Why is it important for you to want that?" These successive questions on motivations shed light on other unsaid arguments, including scorned cultural or personal values, feelings or emotions that were not reported in the early identification move. It is about asking, tirelessly and as often as possible, the question of "why?" to arrive at the root causes of the conflict, on which the remedial actions will be based. If we do not take the time to dig deeper in mediation, neither the mediator nor the parties themselves will be able to grasp the essential knots of the conflict.

For example, in the following real-life dialogue, the mediator (M.) researches, beneath the surface, the "why of the why," exploring the motivations of the parents (P.) who refuse to meet the young woman whom their son has just married.

The impossible marriage

P.   We don't want to meet the wife of our son.

M.   *Why?*

P.   Because she is neither from our country nor belongs to our religion.

M.   *Why* is it important for you that she is from your country and has the same religion as you?

B.   It is not so important that she is not of our religion. In our family, some people have already married people of other religions.

M.   And *why* is it so important that she is from your country?

B.   It is not so much that she is not from our country, but that she is from country A.

M.   And why does the fact that she is from country A upset you so much?

B.   Do you know what people from country A did to us during the war, 40 years ago?

M.   Please say more.

B. In my village, I saw my four brothers and my three sisters, as well as 15 other inhabitants, of which three were women, arrested by soldiers from country A, taken to the village square and tortured in front of us so that they would reveal where the other villagers were hidden. After two days, other soldiers arrived. They prevented us from caring for our wounded, feeding them, and giving them water. We saw them die in front of us. I cannot accept that my son married a young girl from there, even 40 years afterward. I will never see her! It is not possible!

The point identified in the first sentence – *"We do not want to meet the wife of our son"* – suggested an interpersonal relationship issue. The series of "whys?" drew out other possible causes: *"She is not of our religion," "She is not from our country," "She is from country A."* We finally discover that the problem to be worked on for reconciliation is neither the character of the young woman, nor her religion, nor her nationality. The problem is that some people from country A have, in the past, inflicted grievous suffering on the family of this young man's parents, which scarred their memory forever. Grasping this deep-seated motivation will call for a disassociation, in the father's mind, between his daughter-in-law and the painful past, possibly via a family meeting including acknowledgment of past suffering, a possible apology or request for pardon, i.e. a symbolic separation between the suffering of the older generation and the future prospects of the next generation.

Framework 5 – Needs-Values-Feelings

This framework that builds on Nonviolent Communication developed by Rosenberg (2003) allows for reattaching the fact(s) to their effects: what emotions have been felt, what values are found to be affected, what needs have been neglected.

- *Needs* – These are the most important motivations that a party has been deprived of by the conflict (recognition, moral support, visibility in an organization, autonomy, material compensation, etc.).

- *Values* – They are linked to ethical, moral, or legal principles and to the opinions and beliefs that a party holds (maintaining a relationship, respect of the contract, honesty, cost-effectiveness, etc.) and which, in their eyes, are not being respected.

- *Feelings* (fear, anger, sadness, rancor, joy, shame) – We can distinguish between past feelings (those experienced at the moment of the conflict) and current feelings at the time of mediation (feelings expressed and listened to in the here and now, which the passage of time has not dissipated). Reliving the distressful emotions of the past, however hard it may be, can make parties feel relieved and more available. Here again, the right questions are key: *"What did you experience at that moment?"* (past); *"What do you feel now?"* (present).

  o For each event that posed a problem for you, I propose that you:

    ■ describe the *event* (for example: on that day at noon, you, without informing me, etc.);

    ■ add what it did to you: your *perceptions* (and the possible feelings you had);

    ■ analyze what you think about it: the *values* (principles, rules) it evoked; what made you judge that it was good or bad (fair or unfair, ethical or not, legal or not, equitable or not, allowed or prohibited, acceptable or not), given what you believe in;

    ■ finally, formulate what you would have *needed* at that moment, and still need today.

These three keywords – needs, values, and feelings – will guide as much the mediator's listening of the parties' words (where events are tainted by emotions, values, and needs, whether they are expressed or not) as the mediator's questioning to bring them out in the open.

Framework 6 – The Multidimensionality of a Conflict

Many dimensions, of variable importance, affect conflicts. Identifying them, then exploring their respective weights for the parties, helps deepen the present needs, and lead to more relevant solutions. An analysis of 8,000 conflicts revealed repetitive causes that can guide the listening of mediators and put them on the road to discovering needs and solutions (Salzer 2004; Salzer and Stimec 2015). In the following box, 15 conflict dimensions are summarized by key adjectives.

Looking in depth at 15 typical conflict dimensions

1. *Technical* – Are there differences in techniques or in methods of construction?

2. *Historical* – Does the disagreement relate to another past conflict that was either poorly resolved or left unresolved and which bears on the present conflict?

3. *Personal* – Are there exchanges (words, actions) that infringed on one party's sense of self, identity, dignity, or honor?

4. *Economic* – Is there some imbalance perceived as inequitable between what both are going to have, receive, give, or take?

5. *Symbolic* – What does this apparent conflict symbolize? "Teach a lesson" or "make an example" of the other party to prevent the recurrence of a similar situation, etc.?

6. *Emotional* – Are there emotions embedded in the conflict (anger, fear, etc.), in one party or both?

7. *Coercive* – Were some arguments or actions based on force or threats ("I can fire you," "We can go on strike")?

8. *Legal* – Is there ignorance or are there contradictions in terms of legal analysis (laws, legal precedent, ruling)?

9. *Spatial* – Is there a perception of overlap or encroachment on the territory of the other, physical or symbolic?

10. *Temporal* – Is there a different perception of the time in conflict (too short or too long, tension about the past or projection toward the future)?

11. *Institutional* – Are there discrepancies stemming from the structures of the organization, notably in the distribution of power and responsibilities?

12. *Cultural* – Are there differences in opinions, values, personal judgments, beliefs, or lifestyles?

13. *Informational* – Does one party have information that the other party does not? Is there disagreement on the facts?

---

14. *Interpretive* – Have diverging interpretations of words, gestures, actions, and silences triggered or amplified the conflict?

15. *Escalatory* – Is interaction between the parties characterized by a pattern of systematic adversarial mechanisms (attack-attack, attack-defense, scapegoat, vicious cycle, etc.) that feed the conflict?

Once some of these sensitive points have been identified for each party, it would be an interesting exercise to verify if all the parties assign the same value to them. The conflict may seem, for example, more "economic" and "technical" for one party, and more "emotional" and "long-standing" for another party. When a large number of dimensions are involved, parties may want to evaluate the degree of importance of each dimension: *"What is the most important dimension for you? And for you?"* Parties could be asked to rank them from 1 to 5, to come up with priorities.

Again, underlying each prioritized dimension are needs to explore and to satisfy. For example, in one specific conflict between neighbors, the "technical" and "legal" needs may require fence modifications integrating these two dimensions (resorting to an expert surveyor for tracing the boundaries of two parcels by referring to the deeded lands). But in another conflict between neighbors, the "personal" need (for apologies) and "cultural" need (discretion and privacy for the other) may prevail, and the mediator might need to quickly wrap up the legal and technical dimensions.

Framework 7 – Differences and Similarities

One of the essential results of active, in-depth listening is that it gradually detects

- *the points of agreement:* everything that brings the parties together;

- *the points of disagreement:* everything that keeps them apart.

The mediator will distill these points of similarities and differences, without fearing areas of disagreement. Little by little, by mutual exploration, the mediator will help the parties transform the points of disagreement into points of understanding: parties may not agree on the past, but each one (better) understands what happened to the other. Therefore, the third move (mutual understanding) takes place within the phase of going from the past to the present.

Third Move: Seek Mutual Understanding

However difficult a conflict, it is a deep understanding of the blocking points and the corresponding needs that guides us toward the solutions. This understanding not only serves the mediator, but, above all, the parties themselves. Because the solution will emanate from them, each party has an interest in understanding what is difficult for the other, what the other needs, and what will satisfy both parties in the future. It is only when each party agrees to try to really understand the other that mediation can become truly fruitful and prepare the ground for a more efficient search for future solutions. Such is the spirit of the third and final move of this first major phase in problem-solving.

Before Reciprocal Recognition

At this stage, an essential distinction that has already been mentioned needs to be reiterated so that it stays fixed in the minds of the parties:

"Understanding does not mean agreement."

This simple sentence summarizes the objective of this major phase of traveling from the past to the present. "Understanding the other does not belittle me or deny me." Recognizing the other does not signify that I have abandoned myself. Understanding the other widens my perspectives. Nobody renounces who they are, but each person makes an opening up to the other. Understanding the other is "to carry within oneself" what the other experiences. It is to internalize the fact that the other is different from me; to give up on demanding, implicitly, that the other be entirely like me, all the while recognizing that they are also human like me. It is to recognize their identity. The word "identity" incidentally exemplifies the contradiction experienced in conflict and in mediation. Identity refers to the "identical," to what makes us similar; at the same time, it refers to the "singular," to what makes us different. Mediation calls on the commonality in each person to recognize the other's difference, their singular essence.

Hopefully, at this stage of deepening, each party grasps their own needs and the other's: the stakes are thus to bring each party to bear witness, with sincerity, to their understanding and recognition of the other and their needs. This transition allows a smooth passage from the present to the future. In fact, the question is how to "move" to the future without somehow denying the past? Experience shows that this reciprocal recognition of what happened constitutes a powerful motivator to let go of the past and to recompose, rebuild an acceptable and more satisfying balance with the other than what was the case before the conflict.

It is up to the mediator to invite each party to express to the other – with words or gestures – that they understand and recognize the other's narrative. The objective is to get each party to say to the other: "I understand what you say and what happened to you, even if (on such a point) I disagree with you." So, how do we get there?

Asking a Question to Each Party

The mediator prepares the ground for mutual recognition by posing a question to each party in order to verify that they accurately "heard" what happened to the other.

○ **I would like to put a question to each of you to explore what you heard and understood about the problems that you face, Ms. X, as well as the problems that you face, Mr. Y.**

The act of naming each person models reciprocity. Recognizing the other becomes more acceptable because everyone knows, in advance, that they will also be recognized by the other in the patient minuet that mediators choreograph. However, an attempt by the mediator to get recognition from only one party is destined to fail, if there is no immediate gesture of reciprocity toward the other party. The mediator who directly turns toward one party and says: *"Do you understand, Sir, that for Madam, etc."* rarely succeeds in getting recognition. This method can actually generate resistance: one party will have the feeling that it is only they who must hear, understand, and make efforts. In this case, because they ignore the fact that the mediator will solicit the other party as well, immediately afterward, they will often say: *"Why me? Why should I have to understand her, when she doesn't need to understand me? In addition to saying things that weaken my positions, why should I also have to understand her reasons, when she does not have to understand mine?"*

If each person knows *in advance* that the other will have to understand them as well, each one will commit, more easily, to the effort of mutual recognition. Mediation functions much better when it is established on the basis of such reciprocity. This notion illustrates the "multi-partiality" concept presented in Chapter 3, as the mediator accompanies, successively, one party *and* the other. This move thus requires some skills from the mediator, in order to establish and maintain the reciprocal understanding that lies at the heart of the mediation plan, especially when parties do not arrive there spontaneously.

The Invitation to Mutual Recognition

The question that the mediator will ask each party to ensure that each of them properly understands the other's point of view can refer to a specific element, or all the elements that were studied in depth in the previous move: facts, emotions, values, and needs. It is up to the mediator to seize the moment and determine the scope of this mutual recognition by the parties. Will it be only about some specific aspects of the case? Will they aim for the recognition of facts, or rather feelings, or even values, etc.? Whatever the choice, it is useful to connect facts to emotions, experienced or shaken values, which stem from specific needs.

To invite mutual recognition of one by the other, the mediator recalls:

- what *facts* have been admitted during the in-depth exploration (for example: that one treated the other "as incapable" in public, even though they both worked in the same company for five years and were both recognized as competent);

- that these facts produced some *emotions* (for example: shame, bitterness, anger);

- that these facts have, then, hurt some fundamental *values* (for example: professional conscience, love for work done well, the principle according to which criticism requires explanations);

- that consequently some *needs* – past, present, or future – to be satisfied (for example: with respect to the past, one party wishes the other to offer an apology now for using the term "incapable"; with respect to the future, they wish that such general, negative terms are never again used and, if there's an error, that it should be specified and that there should be a priori agreement to help fix it).

Depending on the specific cases, the people involved, and the urgency and gravity of what happened, the needs may concern more the past, present (immediate urgency), future, or both, and even all three. The recognition of the other person's identity involves understanding what time period is important to them. In the following examples, when mutual understanding concludes the stage "from the past to the present," the mediator (M) addresses the parties, in pendulum fashion, by looking at them alternately.

Family Mediation: The Runaway Son

M. Now that each one of you has explained what happened, I would like to ask each one of you to explore your understanding of what happened to the other.

M. *(To the runaway son)* Did you understand that your parents, because you did not return to the house at all one night *(recognized fact)*, were apprehensive about what could have happened to you *(emotion)* and went to the police station *(recognized fact)* — not to file a complaint against you, but to ask for help *(need)* in finding you?

M. *(To the parents)* To you, as parents, I would like to ask if you understand that your son said he has suffered *(emotion)* from the daily quarrels and insults between the two of you *(recognized facts)* and that, according to him, he needed to get away for a couple of days *(need)*?

Community Mediation: Neighbor Spills Paint on Flowers

M. I would like to ask you to verify if you heard and understood what each one of you said about what happened.

M. *(To the neighbor who spilled the tub of paint in the garden from one side while painting the shared wall)* For you, Mr. H, can you imagine what your neighbor felt *(emotion)* when she saw the patch of rare flowers that she had nurtured for five years, drowned under gray paint *(recognized fact)*? Did you understand her when she said she "hurt" inside, for her flowers? Can you imagine the sadness and anger that she could have felt *(emotion)*?

M. *(To the neighbor whose flowers have been destroyed)* And you, Ms. P, do you understand that it is when he was falling back that Mr. H, by grabbing the ladder where he was painting, inadvertently spilled the tub of paint *(fact)*? Did you also hear him say here that he was ready to apologize to you and compensate for the damage *(values)* before you lost your temper *(emotion)* and addressed him in the harshest terms *(recognized fact)*?

Mediation at the Workplace

After a two-hour meeting with Mrs. F, the new financial director of a small company, and the bookkeeper, Mr. B, who was fired after 12 years of work for the business:

M. *(To Mrs. F)* Can you understand that for Mr. B, the thought that he could be fired for an error produced insomnia for weeks *(emotion)*? Do you see why he is wondering about being called a bad bookkeeper, when the errors he was accused of making were errors that he had been making for 12 years, which he always rectified after checking the amounts at the end of the year and for which he was never reprimanded before *(recognized facts)*? Do you understand, even if you do not agree about letting these errors pass, that Mr. B experiences the fact that he was fired as an injustice *(value)* for some errors for which no one ever reproached him – until you arrived?

M.   (*To Mr. B*) Did you understand that the new director, in the business for three months, considered that although you addressed the errors at the end of the fiscal year, this was too late? That, from her perspective, these observations – recorded as they were before her arrival at the company – signaled a lack of professional efficiency (*value*)? That she thought that the sending of three certified letters asking you to put an end to these errors (*recognized fact*) would suffice (*value: obedience to the hierarchy*)? You do not approve of her behavior and think that she should have first talked to you and shared her methods (*values: information, explanation before punishment*). But do you understand that, from her point of view, she was worried (*emotion*) about the incorrect amounts, and the fact that you spend 20% of your work time rectifying your own errors?

As observed earlier, recognizing the other can be based on the perception of partly shared facts, but diverging on "what that did to us": emotions, values, needs, etc. This process is more readily accepted if one does not include "agreement" at this stage, but confines oneself to verifying that both have understood what happened to the other.

Hastening this request for recognition without establishing its coherence can cost much time and reinforce oppositions connected to dignity, honor, and "losing face," and it can even amplify the tensions. All the prior work of reformulation is not just procedural, but it also needs a sound basis in reality. In our last example, a mediator might think they could gain time with a quick "general" synthesis:

o   (*To the bookkeeper*) **Do you understand that these errors bothered the director?**

o   (*To the financial director*) **Do you understand that the bookkeeper, having always worked in this way, was surprised and affected by this firing?**

But in conflictual situations, "general ideas" of synthesis are dismissed by defensive reactions if they are not grounded in substantive details. Our defensive reflexes can be easily triggered and often perceived as aggression by the other side. When the bookkeeper hears "*Do you understand that these errors bothered the director?"* (a sentence that is only centered on the other's conclusion), it spontaneously triggers an instinctive reaction: *"But I rigorously corrected all of them for 12 years!"* He forgets everything that was said during the deepening move about the director's perspective and hears only an accusation. Even unconsciously, each person returns to their "own planet," resumes their own single story, and forgets that of the other. Yet, it is the mediator's mission and responsibility to attempt to broaden the perspective of both parties so that each one, having acquired a shared vision of the situation, can begin an efficient exploration of possible solutions in response to the needs of each party. Hence the importance of a specific and precise – yet concise – question, detailing, for each point, the coherence of the motivations announced by the other side.

It is useful to run through the series of events with significant details in order to shed light on the internal consistency experienced by each person, and the effects that each action had on them. Indeed, in our experience, it is not because a party expresses, explains, and even repeats something that the other retains it – which is to say, perceives, hears, understands, memorizes, integrates, considers, imagines, and feels it. Often, while one party talks, the other, while listening, is also preparing their own arguments and possible responses. Human communication, especially in a contentious context, instead of being based on what is common – even if the word *communication* gives us that illusion – functions via separate monologues. The mediator transforms these parallel voices (and routes) into a dialogue, into a shared demand for recognition integrating as much information as possible toward a shared vision of recomposition in the present of the complexity and diversity of the past.

This mutual understanding constitutes a first victory for all the parties. This feeling of finally being genuinely heard and understood by the other offers the best foundation for building the second major stage of problem-solving in mediation, the one that will turn toward the future and search for the best possible realistic and sustainable solutions. Even if no mutual understanding is created at this stage, it may be useful to restate some key points with different words, explaining again, until each side understands the other better.

Lacking this mutual understanding, the movement to the next stage of seeking solutions is not impossible, of course, but it will be more challenging.

*

This first major stage in problem-solving is henceforth completed: the parties, with the mediator's support, have identified the points of disagreement and then explored the most important ones in depth, in order to shed light on the needs and motivations of both. On this basis, a potential, mutual understanding is established. A commitment to the search for solutions is the objective of the following stage and chapter. It is important to note that the parties' motivations are not rigidly fixed; they will still evolve, from the start of the mediation until its end. The mediator thus needs to remain vigilant and always re-validate their understanding of the parties' dynamic needs, knowing in addition that in an identical situation, some people will express their needs differently. In the previous example concerning the bookkeeper:

- the *first need* of the bookkeeper would be to receive apologies: the need for reparation;

- the *second need* would be that someone explains his error to him, that is all: the need for explanation;

- the *third need* would be a negotiated departure from the company, because he became ill and could not adapt to the character of his new boss: the need for separation;

- the *fourth need* would be to continue working but with the director committing to no longer use devaluing terms (the need for a commitment to respect) and to show him how to successfully operate the next time: the need for training;

- the *n*-th *need* of the bookkeeper would be a new need or a combination of the different needs mentioned above.

At the end of this chapter, although we deliberately concentrated on the mediator, let us emphasize that their moves are undertaken to serve the parties' empowerment. A risk that threatens the mediator (which Chapter 8 will return to) consists of claiming ownership of the problem and projecting, onto the parties their own understanding of their needs. Certainly, the mediator can mention frequent motivations in this type of situation from their own experience, even tossing some ideas in the air; but it is up to the parties to find them relevant or not.

Even if we do not find responses to the needs of all at this stage, and even if there may not be an agreement regarding the past, this first phase, by inviting each person to step into the other's shoes, often creates a different relationship between the parties, during and after the mediation. After a deep reflection on what has happened, the parties sometimes find a direct agreement together, the mediation corresponding to a particular moment of reciprocal explanation in the evolution of their history. The agreement is a fruit ripened by the respectful dialogue that mediation facilitated.

CHAPTER 7
THE PRESENT TOWARD THE FUTURE
Generate Possible Solutions
Before Potentially Committing

We have two ears and one mouth so that we can listen twice as much as we speak, according to Epictetus. It is not always easy to listen – especially when something coming from the other side challenges us. The best mediators are, before anything else, communication acrobats. They help transform two people who want to scream at each other into persons who eventually listen and succeed in speaking in turn. This is the first challenge that the previous chapter tackled. The parties finally *hear* one another. They open up to the idea and possibility of speaking to each other. *Conflict often obliterates listening; mediation helps restore it.*

We have two eyes in front of our face and none behind. This second natural observation pushes us to look in front of us and envision what we can create together. But in a conflict situation, it is difficult for us to not look at, and therefore get stuck in, the past. We keep focusing on what others could have done differently – and *we accuse them* (accuser's bias). And for what we ourselves were not able to do differently – *we excuse ourselves* (excuser's bias) (Allred 2000). Mediation, as the previous chapter proves, looks at the past in order to purge a poor track record of objectivity, as much as possible in all its dimensions, to break free from simplistic interpretations, and to succeed in stepping back, opening new perspectives, creating a new space together, and coexisting peacefully with one another. However, the mediator needs to sense the moment when the eyes have sufficiently looked backward and need to shift to start looking forward. The mediator can help the parties to start hearing one another about the future, envisioning and hopefully reaching agreement. This is the objective of this chapter. *Conflict obliterates the future; mediation often helps restore it.*

In this stage (from the present to the future), mediation is less about bringing the parties to agree on the past – they will most often retain contrasting views about what happened based on their respective perceptions – than about the search for a workable agreement in the future. This second major stage of problem-solving in mediation involves *three moves*:

- The first move: *Invent solutions.*
- The second move: *Evaluate solutions.*
- The third move: *Decide.*

First Move: Invent as Many Solutions as Possible

○ Alex and Lou, let's take a moment to summarize where we are. You each have had the opportunity to express yourself regarding what happened. You also looked in depth at the problems to negotiate and took the time to better understand each other's viewpoints. I now invite you to reflect together on some possible solutions. There might be hurdles on our way; some solutions may be satisfying to one, but not to the other, and vice versa. But as we go, ideas will emerge that you might both agree on.

Despite the good intent of moving forward, the risk still exists of being too hasty and, while searching for adequate solutions to the needs (in qualitative terms), confusing them with the first ideas that come to mind, before even having attempted to explore a large number of paths together (in quantitative terms). To avoid this short circuit, the mediator can propose three types of strategies:

- *Creativity:* Push the parties to think out of the box through brainstorming.

- *Value creation:* Encourage the parties in a less spontaneous manner by asking questions to create value.

- *Offering ideas:* Help the parties in the case of an impasse by providing suggestions.

Strategy #1: Creativity and Brainstorming

Brainstorming is a method which the mediator proposes to improve the *quality* of solutions through a *quantitative* method, by searching for as many solutions as possible. To make a smooth transition to brainstorming, the mediator needs to explain this technique to the parties. It is a good idea to get the parties to explicitly agree on the rules of this method.

o At this stage, the time is ripe to advance toward the identification of possible solutions. It is useful to do so through a technique you might know, called 'brainstorming.' The objective, here, is to imagine multiple ways of satisfying the needs that you both have shared. As we engage in brainstorming, could we agree on the following three rules?

1. Each one of you *actively participates* in the search for solutions and suggests as many ideas as possible, even those that seem far-fetched or difficult to implement.

2. I ask you *not to critique the ideas* that the other puts on the table, in order to let creativity flow. At times, it will not be easy, but, at this stage, let us avoid evaluating the soundness of any ideas.

3. For the same reason, please *do not feel committed*, either by what you or the other says. Brainstorming is not yet the moment for decision-making.

o Do you agree to commit to this brainstorm and apply these three rules? Yes, Alex? Yes, Lou? Ok, let's proceed, then.

It is important that the parties explicitly (either by body language or verbally) indicate their agreement, for two reasons. First, such a micro-agreement reinforces the *logic of accordance*: despite their disagreements, the parties are capable of committing to process rules. Although it is not yet an agreement on the substance of their conflict, it is already an agreement on how to approach it. Second, if a party does not respect the brainstorming rules, the mediator (M), without making it appear as a reprimand directed to a specific party, can gently recall the original agreement reached on this point. Let us pick up the example of the mediation between Alex (A) and Lou (L).

Who will have custody of the kids?

Alex   "I propose to have full custody of our two children."

Lou   "Or I could keep them every other week at the very least."

A.   "And why not full custody? How dare you? What are you saying? You can't even cook!"

Mediator   "Do not forget our agreement to put as many ideas as possible on the table. At this stage, even if it is difficult, it is best not to react. Once we have many ideas on the table, both of you will have ample opportunity to evaluate them. Certain options will be eliminated; others will be sharpened or modified. Alex, does it suit you if we proceed in this way, in two phases?"

A.   "Fine, if you say so. But admit that what you are asking me is almost impossible."

M.   "Thank you, Alex. Of course, this is not easy, but we are getting there. Let us go back to our brainstorming; you reflected on the different possibilities for the custody of your two children. Any other ideas?"

L.   "Maybe instead of joint or full custody, we could imagine increased visitation rights that would allow me to see the kids more often."

A.   "We could imagine that you would come to pick them up in the morning to bring them to school. I would go to pick them up in the afternoon, and you could see them every other weekend."

L.   "Or I could see them at least every Sunday and every other Saturday."

M.   "Any other ideas on this point? No? We have, if I counted well, seven ideas: 1) Alex's full custody, 2) joint custody, 3) Lou's full custody, 4) Alex's custody accompanied by extensive visitation rights, 5) Alex's custody with an agreement related to driving the children to school, 6) potentially with Lou for every other weekend or 7) every Sunday and every other Saturday. Bravo! There is now a lot on our plate to discuss."

In this excerpt, we notice how Alex "wavered" when she heard Lou's first idea and started criticizing it. The mediator will not hesitate to reframe and delay action, all the while drawing the parties' attention to the fact that the purpose of the brainstorming agreement is to separate the invention of ideas from their evaluation. The mediator also recognizes the difficulty of the approach and then takes up the flow of ideas. Throughout, they ask the same questions: "Any other ideas? Anything else you could do?" Finally, they summarize the different options, including the one that Alex dismissed.

Analogous Universes and the SCAMPER Method

If parties enjoy creativity games, the mediator can reinforce the power of imagination by using these two complementary techniques. As in brainstorming, the rules of no criticism and no commitment also apply here. The mediator will resort to these techniques to further open the range of possible solutions, and even to lighten the parties' moods.

Imagine a criminal mediation case and the need for one party to get reparation for the damage caused by graffiti on a house wall. The technique of *analogous universes* makes parties reflect on the way in which a concept – in this case, reparation – is applied in other contexts (i.e., universes). After thus having kindled their imagination and curiosity, the parties then return to their "real" universe.

A graffitied wall – detour by an analogous universe

Mediator (M.)	"How does the reparation proceed at home, for example, when your clothes get torn?"
Graffiti Artist (G.)	"My mother knows how to re-sew the clothes. But my father had warned me that if I did this again, he would require me to re-sew my clothes myself."
Owner of the damaged wall (O.)	"My father made my brother and me apologize and promise to be less negligent in the future."
M.	"Any other ideas?"

G.   "One day, my father asked me to break my piggybank to replace an article of clothing that I had damaged in a fight with my brother."

O.   "When I broke my glasses, my father made me wear my old pair for three days."

Looping back to the starting universe while transposing

M.   "Here is a series of interesting ideas; how do they translate into our situation with the graffiti on the wall?"

G.   "At my age, I cannot ask my mother to correct my errors; but I could repaint the wall myself and ask for advice from a friend who is a construction painter. I could also apologize and promise to no longer draw graffiti on walls unless I have the authorization to do so."

This technique of analogous universes invites parties to step away from the object of their disagreement and take a detour through a "place of memory or experience" without any risk of commitment. It is *first* about putting parties at ease, in a safe place where the stakes are limited, and *second*, about pushing them outside of their comfort zone to where the stakes are high.

For example, in the Burundian and Congolese contexts, some reconciliation workshops (Lempereur 2007, 2009b, 2021; Colson and Lempereur 2011) used role-playing exercises. These simulations put participants in analogous universes, which were different from their immediate everyday life. Participants drew lessons from them that they could then apply to their own world in crisis. This detour offered a powerful experience that spurred the problem-solving abilities of the participants.

SIMSOC in Burundi

The participants in a reconciliation workshop in Burundi – senior military and political leaders, including current and past heads of state and government – have been involved in a role-playing exercise called SIMSOC (for "Simulated Society") developed by William Gamson (2000). This game features a simulated society that includes four regions: green (the richest), red (very poor, with neither means of subsistence nor employment), yellow, and blue (two middle-class regions). Each participant is assigned a different role, including being unemployed, wealthy, working class, trade union member, etc. They behave as any individual would, with their personal and collective objectives as a member of a society or a group. All the participants involved in this workshop adopted insightful behaviors, in particular to overcome the tensions and conflicts within this alternate society. They then analyzed their interactions together in a debriefing, notably emphasizing the need for better communication among the members of a real society and for more equitable resource allocation in order to reduce the risks of recurrent conflicts. Participants then had no problem applying the lessons learned from this analogous universe to the Burundian society, by imagining realistic solutions and personal commitments to implement them (Wolpe et al. 2004; Lempereur 2021).

The *SCAMPER Method* (Eberle 2008) *(Substitute, Combine, Adapt, Modify, Put to another use, Eliminate, Reverse)* starts from a word or a concept, and modifies, decomposes, completes, and furthermore recomposes, increases, shrinks, moves it, etc. It can be repeated *ad infinitum* on multiple fronts:

- *Time* (when? – yesterday, today, tomorrow; definitive or temporary; for a day or a month, etc.)

- *Space* (where? – my place, the other's place, a friend's place; elsewhere; in a virtual space; big or small; the whole and the part, etc.)

- *Protagonists* (who? with whom? – alone, two, many; authorities; generations, young and old; cultures; etc.)

- *Materials* (with what? how? – sustainable or consumed; in its components, with new or stronger materials, etc.)

- *Rules of application* (what rules? – professional, ethical, legal, international, etc.)

- *Finances* (who pays? – both, one, the state, the city, the insurance company, the bank, the polluter, the troublemaker, etc.)

To reuse the example of the "graffitied wall," the mediator stimulates the parties' imaginations by applying this SCAMPER method through questioning oriented toward a particular previous category to increase, shrink, recompose, add, etc.

The graffitied wall – the SCAMPER method

Mediator	"In our story, there is a 'wall,' a 'graffitied painting.' How could we rearrange that in terms of space for an original reparation? Concerning the wall, for example?"
Graffiti Artist	"I could graffiti the rest of the wall with motifs chosen by the owner."
Owner	"Or he could redo the entire wall for me and not only the damaged part; or paint a wall in the bedroom of my adolescent daughter, who dreams of a wall graffitied by a professional."
G.	"Or you leave me a part of the wall and I create a tag from a common agreement, and we frame it like a painting."
M.	"And in our town, who could help us?"
O.	"Maybe we could organize a competition for the best tag in town, inviting artists, sociologists, neighbors, associations, the mayor."
G.	"On this occasion, we could suggest graffitiing the sidewalks with washable paint; or organizing a major exhibit of miniature graffitied walls."

If the mediator senses that the parties are not yet ready for brainstorming or these two other creativity techniques, they can forgo the specific term "brainstorming," and invite parties "to imagine the largest number of possible solutions that can respond to both of your needs." Steve Goldberg, a specialist in labor mediation, together with others, has questioned the ability of proceeding by brainstorming in the heat of the moment. We imagine that some people under a lot of stress are not always keen on creativity sessions. It is illusory to think the parties will gladly commit to it, or even that the parties will conduct these sessions as patiently and extensively as brainstorm necessitates. It is thus possible that after brainstorming, parties have not yet identified all the useful options for the resolution of their problems. This is why we introduce two complementary paths.

Strategy #2: Techniques of Value Creation and Directed Questioning

Inventing solutions is certainly a matter of creativity, but creativity is not a synonym for "creative genius." Practical techniques can be used that yield promising ideas, techniques that do not require innate creative skills that a party may or may not have and for which brainstorming would be the ultimate tool. Often, to lighten the mood, we sometimes say that we are not all Picassos of mediation, whether we are referring to the parties or to the mediator!

Brainstorming is a powerful technique that generates many ideas. This is why we encourage it, but it can be complemented by employing value creation techniques developed by negotiation theories. Such techniques can be learned and mobilized by the mediator as a specific skill set. Mediation is not only a psychology or an art; it also includes some specific, technical knowledge.

Before getting into the details of the second strategy of value creation techniques, it is important for us to distinguish it from the other strategies mentioned in this section. Value creation techniques contrast with brainstorming and other creative techniques in the sense that the mediator goes further than asking open, general questions: they ask *precise questions* that, without necessarily orienting the response in one direction or another, enable the parties to identify more satisfactory solutions.

In the third path, which we will discuss later, the mediator will provide ideas, which may come from either creative techniques (strategy 1) or from value creation techniques (strategy 2). It seems necessary for us to be precise about this second strategy because it is often omitted, and even unknown, with mediators transitioning instinctively from the first path to the third, as if they had to make up for a party's lack of creativity. Yet, mediators have another responsibility: leveraging value creation techniques, not so much to test their own talent, but to help parties benefit from a more directed questioning.

Building on our previous work (Lempereur and Colson, ed. Pekar, 2010), we also put value creation before its distribution – which helps parties make choices among various solutions – a step that falls under our next move of evaluation. Too often, in a conflict, protagonists use a *zero-sum logic* to evaluate the situation – an amount to recover, a position to fill, a territory to regain – where a gain for one side is a loss for another, and where, ultimately, there can be only one winner – "us" or "them," but never *both*. Yet, before dividing the proverbial pie, we need to try to expand it first, envisioning opportunities offered by initial cooperation and its corollary, the lever of value creation. Value creation differs significantly from an approach founded mainly on competition or the immediate distribution of value. To grasp it, the mediator needs to familiarize themselves with the following approaches and keep a checklist, at least in their mind.

Create Value by Leveraging Differences

Value creation involves *using differences in preferences between parties to better satisfy both*, enabling them to escape pointless and prolonged contradictions. Parties can reveal preferences about different types of issues, and the mediator can invite them to imagine new solutions. Some people adapt to risk, others do not. Some people like a particular object, but others do not. Some people are in a rush, whereas others can wait.

Differences in Time Preferences

Without realizing it, it was Alex's idea that with Lou, both of them alternately drive their children to school – Lou in the morning, and Alex in the afternoon. Maybe the school is on the way to Lou's office and thus driving the kids in the morning was actually convenient? On the other hand, for Alex, it is a detour. Thus, if Lou is in charge of the children in the morning, this formula actually enables Alex to gain time, arriving at work earlier and leaving earlier to pick up the kids. Maybe Lou works late and picking up the kids is inconvenient. Here, taking into account the different preferences of each party generates value-creating opportunities that suit both sides. The fact that each parent ends up taking care of their "better" half of driving the children to, or from, school satisfies both. It becomes a "win-win" solution, even better, a "satisfaction-satisfaction" one. Lou can see his kids daily in this new arrangement.

Differences in Value

What represents a high value for one party can hold less for another. This highlighted difference is another source of value creation.

Two homes to share in a divorce

Alex and Lou have two homes: one was their main residence before the divorce; the other was their seaside apartment, which they used on weekends and during vacations. As the two head toward full custody for Alex and visitation rights for Lou during a good part of the weekends or during a month of vacation, it might seem logical to develop a solution with the main residence for Alex and the seaside apartment for Lou. The "subjective value" of each residence, i.e. how they feel about it, differs from one party to the other (Curhan, Elfenbein, and Eisenkraft 2010).

How can the mediator empower parties to discover such solutions? The fact that there are two residences will appear quickly during the diagnosis part of the conversation, the first step of problem-solving. During this phase, the mediator can ask questions like:

○ **When do you usually use the secondary residence? Where is it located? Is it a family home?**

By eliciting who uses the home and for what purpose, mediators can infer which of the two parties, if either, is more attached to it, and if it can constitute the future main residence of one party and a property for the other. Next, during the search for solutions, the mediator can find it useful to ask pointed questions (even yes/no questions) like:

○ **If either of you had visitation rights, would you want to visit the kids in this house? Is it possible for a weekend? Taking into account the age of the children, is it a permanent vacation destination? Etc.**

It is not difficult for the parties to discover the optimal solution for the properties in these circumstances. The fruit may fall naturally from the tree:

○ **Taking into account what you both shared, what would be a possible solution for the seaside apartment?**

We can also bring differences into play in relation to risks or resources.

Differences in Risk Preferences

Some people are more risk-seeking than others, in general or in specific circumstances. The mediator can use such differences to better satisfy the parties.

A spouse fearing for her future earnings in divorce

Divorce mediation reveals that a spouse stayed at home to take care of the children and is now worried about her future income. She fears no longer being able to meet her needs. This situation pushes her to ask for a significant amount of alimony for herself and her children. On the other hand, she would like to start working again, but is not certain that her professional skills are up to date. For his part, the husband fears having to pay an exorbitant alimony for his entire life. It seems like a distributive dilemma: whether the amount is high or low, one spouse wins and the other loses.

Yet, a mediator who understands risk management can well discern some innovative ideas for both parties. The mediator can orient the discussion toward mutually beneficial solutions.

Mediator	"If I understood you well, Jackie, you would like to start working again, but you are not certain that you could easily find a job. You would need to update your professional skills, which would facilitate your job search. Is this correct? Did I miss anything?"
Jackie	"Absolutely. Through continuing education, I could more easily find a job, and then I would not need as much external support. The idea of depending on my ex-husband hardly delights me. By the way, I never did like depending on him financially, especially since I had gone to the university, just as he did."
M.	"Therefore, you would wish to refresh your skills and be self-sufficient again. And you, Henry, if I am not mistaken, you are not enthusiastic about the idea of supporting your spouse for a very long time? What do you think of Jackie's idea to return to school?"
Henry	"That would increase her chances to quickly find a job again."
M.	"What suggestions do you have on helping Jackie get this extra training?"
H.	"Well, if Jackie takes some courses, that will cost extra money and will require some of her time. Maybe I could pay more child support while she is studying, to cover her costs, but also take care of the children during the evenings when she is in class? Then, after she is reemployed, I could pay less in child support."
M.	"Thank you, Henry. Jackie, any other ideas?"
J.	"In fact, I remember, Henry, you know the head of continuing education at this prominent business school … Perhaps she could serve as my adviser?"
H.	"You are right, I will be happy to introduce you to her."

The previous illustration shows how the mediator can facilitate the emergence of solutions that are far more promising, by integrating differences. The mediator raises the difference in risks (revenue losses for one; indefinite payment for the other), and they help resolve it through a solution over time that reduces the risk for one (studies, leading to increased job opportunities) and for the other (taking more risks at the start, with the expectation that payments will decrease afterward). During this process, the "win-win" solution is born where one spouse's success becomes key to the other's too: Jackie's ability to become self-sufficient is, in fact, in Henry's interest. The soon-to-be divorced spouses could even complexify their formula, by adding that if Jackie, after her studies, finds employment over a certain threshold, child support will be further reduced. The mediator could also bring up the idea of contracting an "insurance covering the risk of loss of employment" for Henry and his future ex-spouse, etc.

Differences in Resources

The previous example ends with Jackie's idea, that Henry knows a "go-to person" who could help and "coach" her. Maybe a neighbor can look after the children when Henry cannot do so, etc.? Each party has different resources, related to their expertise, profession, family, network, property, and time. These productive differences suggest solutions that rely on what one party endows and the other does not, leading to mutually beneficial exchanges: "*I can make you benefit from this resource, while you can offer me another one, etc.*"

The previous examples demonstrate that creativity cannot be imposed but can be worked on as long as the key areas to promote it are identified. Here, the mediator becomes like the conductor of an orchestra, knowing how to activate the right instrument when the time comes, because they know the score. Let us review some of the other strategies at their disposal.

Create Economies of Scale and Scope

Each time that we *share activities*, namely by combining formerly separate activities, we benefit from economies of scale. Each time that we *enlarge the range of someone's activity* while reducing the costs formerly related to the multiplicity of actors involved, or of actors to manage, we create economies of scope.

For example, when two people decide to live together, they benefit from all the advantages of marital economies of scale: *one* rent, *one* home insurance, *one* refrigerator, *one* apartment and *one* car for vacation, *one* inspection of children's report cards, etc. During a divorce or a conflict, most of these synergies disappear, putting pressure on time and resources. Single parents often face this situation. On the contrary, there is an economy of scope for the former spouse, because the parent in charge of child custody from now on has to do all the daily duties and thus allowing the other to manage as they wish the face-to-face time with the children.

It is undeniable that finding solutions through mediation concerning economies of scale is not simple. Likewise, business partners whose relationship has soured no longer have the initial drive to search for economies of scale together.

However, it is possible to imagine economies of scale, for example, by making sure that children go to the dentist together at least once a year, or to the hairdresser once a month. Divorced parents can also decide that instead of one child playing football and the other horseback riding, they both will from now on practice tennis at the same time, of course, as long as they enjoy this sport.

Some *economies of scope* can be discovered by identifying the activities near the place where each of the spouses lives. Thus, we can imagine that the children's dentist, hairdresser, and tennis court are near where the father now lives, whereas the children's school, doctor, pharmacy, and horseback riding lessons are closer to the mother's home. When custody is entrusted to one or the other parent, it is possible to consolidate the children's activities appropriately. Each time, the idea is to reduce useless trips, and, thus, the time and cost of transportation.

Creating this type of economy, in the form of effort reduction for both sides, keeps *transaction costs* under control. It is, in fact, less about value creation than cost reduction. This approach significantly curtails the weight of small transactions – each time, daily, that we make mini-decisions together – because the rules concerning them have been determined during the mediation process.

A final example to illustrate this subject applies to the mediation process in general, because its transaction costs are "more economical" than other avenues. For example, if parties succeed in coming to an agreement through mediation, they will not have to go to court and spend a considerable amount of money on lawyers' fees. So, here, *mediation itself presents an economy of scale:* parties share the mediation costs, which, in most cases, are much less onerous than two lawyers' fees.

Other economies of scope are possible when exploring all possible solutions that the mediator needs to unearth, because they often constitute the essence of an agreement. For example, if in the case of a divorce, the parties succeed in not only negotiating obvious questions (custody, allocation of properties, child support), *but also* other questions that emerge from taking needs into account (satisfaction of the preferences of each person and mobilization of differences, allocation of activities, rationalization of agendas, etc.), mediation will have increased the scope of the agreement. This point is crucial: if mediation detects hidden points and resolves them, it will have resolved more points than the conflict suggested at the start. This is one of the strengths of mediation. It is like motorists who go to the gas station and discover that the station offers more than gas – the newspaper and morning donut, coffee, some wood for the barbecue, etc. They are happy about it, because they will not have to go to the supermarket just for the wood, or to the newsstand just for the newspaper. Mediation, in its essence, if it works well, develops economies of scope and often delivers more than what we expect of it from the start.

Value creation techniques, without resolving everything, succeed in rationalizing a good number of activities. They renew a positive, creative force, in contrast to the negativity and opposition that characterized relations before mediation. The mediator needs to integrate value creation methods in order to prepare "rewarding" questioning. In doing so, they help the parties to overcome certain routines which have become blinding, suboptimal, even destructive of value. Value creation is a fundamental tool that relates to the essence of mediation: it focuses on resolving the problems and at the same time preparing the future in such a way that the problems do not recur.

Avoid the Recurrence of Conflict

One conflict can hide another, one apparent problem being the cause of a series of problems. In sum, a conflict is an epiphenomenon, and if it is not deeply treated, it will flare up once again, sometimes even more strongly than before. The mediator thus needs to be aware that a simple, *short-term ruling on conflict* could be a mirage and should rather aim for *a long-term resolution*.

Disintegration of the former Yugoslavia

Numerous mediations took place to attempt to end the crisis resulting from the collapse of Yugoslavia at the start of the final decade of the twentieth century. Lord Carrington, the first mediator, had pleaded for a global solution to the conflict in the whole former territory of Yugoslavia, but his opinion was not heeded. His successors/mediators substituted it for a ruling on a case-by-case basis for each former republic, without tackling the problem of relations between all the former republics and its diverse populations. Following this, Slovenia and Croatia announced their independence in 1992 without being concerned about the essential question of minorities or disputed territories. They also preferred not to "rule" on an overly complicated point about a mini-Yugoslavia that constituted Bosnia. The conflict, whose deep causes had not been taken into account, resumed, notably in multiethnic enclaves, and the war in Bosnia broke out with horrors. To put an end to it, numerous mediation attempts followed, and it was only in 1995 that the Dayton Agreement ended the war, at least in Bosnia. However, a major question remained unresolved: how to protect the minorities within a Yugoslav federation reduced to Serbia and Montenegro? Hence the tensions between the

Albanian majority of Kosovo and its Serbian minority erupted into a new, useless, deadly war, requiring a new agreement, etc. This historical example shows that it is important for the mediator to guard against superficial or incomplete outcomes that have not addressed the problem in a comprehensive manner in all its dimensions.

After a thorough multi-analysis of a conflict (Chapter 6), the mediator needs to help the parties resolve it in such a manner that all its parts are addressed. In mediation, the phase "from the past to the present" needs to feed the objective of the subsequent phase "from the present to the future" in such a way that inadequate solutions, apparent interests, and obvious points are set aside, but hidden needs and essential points for the parties are explored; this maximizes the chance for sustainable resolution. We do not pretend that this task is easy, but it merits an attempt.

Conflict between a key shareholder and the managing partner

A mediator is called in for a problem within a company – an apparent disagreement about communication between a major shareholder and the managing partner – and contributes to resolving it for some time. Yet, by working toward only a superficial reconciliation on a specific point between the two protagonists, the conditions for a resumption of conflict remain. If the parties do not try hard to treat the underlying causes of the conflict, new conflicts will emerge again. To avoid this, the mediator will have to make evident, for example, that business development is slowed down by a governance system and decision-making processes under which a key shareholder has the capacity to block decisions and to prevent the managing partner from running the company. The mediator needs to ask whether or not there is an interest for these two people to continue working together under such conditions. The mediator sometimes acts as a surgeon; their help with a full diagnostic sometimes pushes the parties to consider a parting of ways as a possible option rather than giving simply a placebo, separation rather than reconciliation.

Behind appearances, the mediator, as a catalyst of solutions in decision-making, reveals the forest beyond the tree, *knows how to recognize and make the parties recognize the generic character* of problems, beyond the appearances of a specific problem (Lempereur 2012a). The mediator pushes the parties toward a *structural analysis*. If the mediator notices repetitive behaviors by the parties, even successive agreements whose execution or inexecution drives increased conflict between them, they question this recurrent, problematic situation that far from reinforcing the relationship between parties distances one from the other. In sum, the mediator does not fear certain radical solutions to break the vicious cycle: "conflict–mediation–agreement–conflict–mediation–agreement–conflict–etc."

Belgium or centrifugal mediations

Since the 1960s, Belgium offers a rather ominous example of negotiations facilitated by a succession of mediators who have not yet succeeded in resolving "the Belgium problem" – i.e. ongoing tensions between the two main communities, Flemish- and French-speaking, from the north and the south of the country, respectively. Whatever constitutional rearrangements parties agree to in order to reallocate power and resources among the various governments at the national, community, and regional levels, the conflict rebounds. The parties start arguing again on new political issues and an adequate balance of power. Over time, the proposed solutions gave increasingly more power to language-based institutions, but did not bridge the identity divide between the Flemish- and French-speaking communities. Paradoxically, further centrifugal devolution of power only widened the gap between people from the north and south of Belgium. Each constitutional reform put the patient under a sedative but did not cure the Belgian illness, instead rendering it chronic and possibly incurable.

It is often following an error of diagnosis, a failure to rigorously analyze the problem in the phase "from the past to the present," that the potential of value creation is limited to circumstantial treatment of the case in the here and now. It is an inherent risk of *"problem-centered"* mediation in contrast to *"relationship-centered" mediation,* which also works on the people dimension, in order to secure a tension-free future.

- The former, *"problem-centered" mediation,* relates to the short term. It is attached to the consequences of the conflict, resolving obvious problems, without always envisioning that the relationship is also at stake. Basically, it might create less value, resulting in a smaller common denominator and a bad compromise that displeases everyone.

- The second, *"relationship-centered" or "transformative" mediation,* aims to ensure a more long-term change in actors and in the system. It remodels organizations with new principles, defining policies and processes. It puts into place mechanisms for monitoring disagreements, systems of alert to prevent escalation and avoid the return to similar conflicts. It is attached to redefining relationships between the parties, even to recognizing their inability to continue working together.

A mediation mission in a collective bargaining dispute

Too often, social crises in France have triggered long and difficult strikes, which most often "ended" through exhaustion, but whose root causes were rarely examined in depth. After the conflict, a simplistic one-sided analysis by each party often denounced "the other," whether it was management or a union, for being responsible for the deterioration of social dialogue (Colson et al. 2015). Mediators called to intervene in a specific collective bargaining conflict are often tempted to limit their action to "the object of the conflict," especially if this is their mission. However, it can be useful to develop a more holistic vision and larger ambitions with the parties on these occasions. Together, the parties and the mediator can take seriously the condition of success, namely, an active partnership between all the representatives at the table. The parties are persuaded to reflect on the implementation of a more solid social dialogue in the future for the prevention of recurrent tensions, but also to serenely handle future conflicts, in a spirit of respect and mutual listening.

In addition to the temporary and fragile resolution of an isolated mission, the mediator therefore considers the conflict that is entrusted to them as an opportunity to transform the enemies of yesterday into true "partners" for tomorrow. A conflict, which mediation manages well, constitutes a springboard for a new start to relations.

Dispute system design to prevent and resolve conflicts

Collective labor partners, following a strike, for example, are persuaded to rethink and restructure their relations by putting into place a real *system* (Ury, Brett, and Goldberg 1993; Euwema 2019) to not only more effectively prevent conflicts but also to resolve them better and faster if they recur. This system favors dialogue and foresees *timely* negotiation beforehand to prevent minor tensions from degenerating and the climate from worsening. And if the negotiation fails, mediation still remains the ultimate intervention mode "before" a social movement, such as a strike. Strikes would no more be considered as the first reflex, but as a final resort, because a strong and renewed trust between protagonists, around the spaces defined by dialogue, would render it quasi-obsolete.

Such conflict prevention and resolution systems are practiced in many countries. They may even become obligatory, following an "agreement regarding the system governing the relations" between the employer and the unions. This is the case in Poland and in Spain, for example. Let us note that in England, individual labor disputes first pass through an independent body of conciliation, ACAS, which resolves 75% of the cases; the remaining cases are settled in labor courts. By comparison, France has experienced an under-utilization of mediation mechanisms for individual labor disputes.

Multiple examples demonstrate the potential of solutions that cover a broad spectrum, relevant not only for individuals but also for groups, organizations, and systems. For this, the mediator draws on the widened analysis

"IGOS" (individuals, groups, organizations, systems) that we proposed in Chapter 6. Such solutions, activated by this third strategy of value creation or by other strategies mentioned before, can of course be *discovered* more or less spontaneously by the parties. However, sometimes even the mediator's art of questioning does not suffice to discover them. Hence, the mediator needs to proceed through the phase of providing ideas, the third strategy explored here.

Strategy #3: Suggest Solutions in Case of Impasse

Despite all the previous efforts, let us suppose that it is neither clear that solutions have been found to all the problems nor that all impasses are overcome. It is possible that certain points have produced fruitful exchanges, that the protagonists are *"fertile in expedience,"* to use the beautiful expression of the eighteenth-century French diplomat François de Callières (2002), but that other points remain unresolved, putting the mediation in danger of partial or complete failure.

Despite precise questions on the mediator's part, the parties remain unable to find even a minimally promising concrete solution on important points and are ready to give up. It is also possible that the trust between them is not yet strong enough to get them past some blocking points. In general, confronted with these heavy and more and more pressing difficulties, the parties will be grateful to a mediator for all the help up until now, but probably hope, more or less secretively, that the mediator will "pull the solution out of a hat."

If the mediator is willing to take an active role in mentioning possible solutions, the parties risk losing less face. The solution itself is also easier to accept because the idea came from an outsider and not from "the other." If the mediator is not willing to intervene in this fashion, the parties can take the initiative and more or less directly solicit the mediator's involvement. Let us imagine that one party asks: *"Taking everything we heard into account, what would you do in our place on this point, as a mediator?"* Faced with such a question, the mediator can return it to the parties, in four possible ways:

- *Option 1: Reflection* toward the party who asks the question – The mediator returns the question toward party 1: *"What I would do is less important than what you would do. Exactly what would you do about this point?"*

- *Option 2: Deflection* toward the other party – The mediator passes the question to party 2: *"You* (looking at party 1) *ask the question to me; but maybe we should ask it to the other party? Exactly* (looking at party 2) *what would you do about this point?"*

- *Option 3: Omni-flection* – The mediator returns the question to both parties: *"You ask the question to me; but will you allow me to ask it to you both? Exactly what would you do about this point?"*

- *Option 4: Extra-flection* – The mediator returns the questions toward a third party, real or imaginary: *"You ask the question to me; how do you think that your children/a judge/a friend/your constituency would respond to this question?"*

The four options mentioned above allow the mediator to elude the question "for a while," but for how much time? If a party insists that they want to hear the mediator's view, opinion, or ideas, the mediator can quickly become trapped in an untenable situation. The mediator is faced not only with their responsibility, but also with the *dilemma of being a solicited mediator:*

- On the one hand, not giving their opinion allows the mediator to preserve neutrality and impartiality, but risks mediation failure and disappointing the parties, who question the usefulness of the whole process.

- On the other hand, succumbing to the temptation of responding to the solicitations of the parties, even anticipating them by giving ideas, increases the risk of no longer appearing neutral and impartial to one of the parties or to both.

It is not simple for a mediator to handle this dilemma. In fact, it is a turning point in the mediation. Up to now, during the entire phase "from the present to the future," the mediator has stayed focused on the process and empowered the parties, enabling them to formulate their own solutions to their problem. During all this time, the mediator may have had many ideas in mind, but remained quiet. Here, the mediator is being asked to change that posture, focus in depth on the *problem,* and propose solutions. Because it is a turning point, the mediator needs to negotiate it well. Care must be exercised in order to not commit a *faux pas.*

Receive Express Validation of the Mandate by Both Parties

o *The mediator returning the question to both parties:* I have been asked to give my opinion on the merits of the case. Before I respond, I would like to know if the request from one party is shared by both of you. Does each one of you truly want me to suggest some ideas on this point?

After both parties agree to the principle of the mediator sharing ideas, some supplementary advice is worth remembering.

Recall the Principle of Self-Determination in Mediation

o I am honored that you would like my ideas on this point. You recall that I am not an arbitrator and that my opinion is only my opinion; it doesn't constitute 'the' response to the problem. You may find it useful or not and, in any case, the solution you come up with, whether or not it is based on what I say, requires your agreement. Mediation is a voluntary process, and no one can impose their solutions on you.

Present Many Solutions, Opinions, or Ideas

The entire phase of solution exploration is driven by a concern to not confine the parties to the first solution or only one solution. This phase aims to push the parties to think otherwise, beyond what seems obvious, and diversely, beyond a single idea, beyond their starting position (Lempereur 2003c). The objective for each party is to integrate the other into their decision-making process. If the parties are encouraged to think inclusively beyond themselves, the mediator is advised to do the same. Likewise, proposing many ideas rather than one demonstrates that the mediator is not the holder of *the* only good idea. Further, the mediator models the search for multiple solutions without appearing linked to one party or the other. Multiple techniques related to creativity and to value creation play an important role here.

- ○ **You asked me for my opinion on the value of the vehicle at the moment of the accident. It is evident that an expert could decide this, but it seems already possible to conceive of many ways to calculate it. There is the Blue Book value, or the part exchange value, or the prices noted in specialized car magazines, etc.**

As we mentioned, if the parties are short on ideas, either the mediator gives an opinion (*mediator as adviser*) with the strong conviction that the recommended solution is more equitable than the other solutions, or they only propose some solutions that stem from their imagination or from their experience (*mediator as ideas provider*). In the latter case, the mediator does not pretend that their ideas are better than those of the parties. They wonder aloud, in the presence of the parties, about the merits of a particular solution. Mediator Bill Wilmot (Wilmot and Yarbrough 1996) insists that if he has to suggest solutions to the parties, he never proposes only one, but always at least three. Being exposed to a plurality of solutions, parties understand that the mediator does not have *the* only good one.

Justify Solutions

It is also important for the mediator to show, as much as possible, that any suggested ideas are not the expression of their authority, but elements within easy reach, "rediscovered" in all simplicity, through available criteria.

- ○ **Apart from the different criteria that exist to assess the value of the vehicle, one evidently needs to take into consideration several other factors: the age of the vehicle, mileage, general state, the four new tires, and other factors that I may have omitted.**

The mediator as adviser may give a legal opinion, but this interpretation of the law is tempered by fairness. Whatever the law says, the mediator examines if it applies properly to this specific situation, i.e. if it is equitable, and if it is not, the mediator may propose a different opinion. In any case, they need to justify whatever opinion they give. Even mediators as idea providers need to justify the solutions that they offer.

It is important to anchor any ideas in a responsible framework that can be explained and justified to anyone outside of the mediation. Any solutions may be linked to *reference points* that do not simply depend on the parties' will or whim, but that are rather verifiable and objective, being based on *independent legitimacy*. These can be articles of law, precedents, a compensation increase corresponding to the cost of the damage suffered, or a price responding to the market value. The use of such criteria avoids the risk of power asymmetry and facilitates a responsible approach founded on commonly held principles.

However, a solution sometimes also rests on the *subjectivity of the needs* of a party, which emerge from the explanations developed in the preceding phase ("past to the present").

The children's return from school

A mother fears for the safety of her children as they walk down a busy street on their way home from school. Yet children from other families come home from school on their own. The mediator will take subjective and objective criteria into consideration at the same time if called upon to suggest a solution. In this example, the mediator can propose a progressive approach to safety, first by having the children accompanied and then by granting them full autonomy once they know the itinerary well.

This dual justification, objective or subjective, is equally useful for corporate conflicts.

An antibacterial component desired by a client

A company, displeased with its food product deliveries, demands that its supplier should furnish an antibacterial component that is neither legally requested nor required by other clients. The mediator takes this exceptional request into account for the future by a price adjustment and a full exoneration of past mistakes.

When negotiation fails to generate ideas, mediation compensates by anchoring, according to the case, the solutions in *"objective," commonly held principles*. If *"subjective" principles* are used for anchoring, they are explained to, and recognized by, the other party, who accepts that these needs have to be taken into account. This strategy, if it does not cause abuse – caprice, affirmation of more subjectivity than necessary – constitutes an essential benefit of mediation. It is the fruit of *the exchange of subjective perceptions* in the presence of an outsider. These more singular *recognized, subjective needs* add to the rational and objective solutions.

Invite the Parties to Elaborate on Proposed Solutions

o   I imagine that the solutions I mentioned evoke reactions in you, make you imagine other solutions, or allow you to refine the proposition. Mary, how does it resonate with you?

Sometimes the expression of ideas by the mediator produces a triggering effect in the parties, who suddenly feel exhilarated and start suggesting solutions that they had not envisioned before.

When there is an impasse in the search for solutions, the use of *private meetings* also offers opportunities for progress. Before proposing solutions, the mediator may wish to take each party aside to ask them if they have not imagined other solutions not publicly mentioned from fear of ridicule, defiance, or for any other reason. If any such idea emerges out of this private meeting, the mediator needs to ask the party for the authorization to mention it, even if it means taking on "responsibility," if the party lacks assertiveness. During these individual conversations, the mediator can also offer some ideas, inviting each party to consider and refine them, so that if later on the mediator decides to propose these ideas to both parties, each party is familiar with them and will thus receive them positively.

In the previous phase ("from the past to the present") and at the end of this first exercise of coming up with some solutions, normally, the parties, with the support of the mediator, would have identified a multiplicity of options on diverse problems. It is now time to strengthen the list of options and transition from a gamut of ideas to a prioritized list. Some ideas will be dropped thanks to the justification criteria. Others will be maintained because they respond to the deep-seated motivations of both parties, etc. This is the object of the following move: evaluation.

Second Move: Evaluate Solutions

After the parties have explored the largest possible number of options, they need to evaluate them so that a shared solution emerges. The mediator needs to explain at this stage:

- that the parties will try hard together to find solutions with which they can live and that they agree to implement;

- and that if none of these solutions are feasible, parties can still resort to solutions away from the mediation table.

According to Peter Drucker (2006), there is a good and a bad compromise. If there is a half a loaf of bread, it is still bread. However, in Solomon's story, "a baby cut in half" is no longer a child at all. Why is it like this? Because in a proper decision-making process, when the boundaries of what works are examined, it is necessary to evaluate the solutions in light of existing justifications, for example, to make it work for both parties or to avoid stripping Peter to dress Paul and vice versa.

The purpose is not to simply try to agree for the pleasure of agreeing, because contrary to the usual proverb, it is not always the case that *"a bad settlement is better than a good judgement."* When the parties examine the solutions they came up with, the usual theoretical negotiation framework applies, namely, that "solutions at the mediation table" need to be better than "solutions away from the table." That is to say that each party will gain more, or at least as much, from a mediated solution than from another solution, like going to court.

For example, returning for a moment to our divorce mediation case, none of the spouses has an interest in accepting a mediated custody agreement that is less advantageous than what a judge would give them. The mediator needs to encourage the parties to come up with an agreement that creates more value than their best solution away from mediation. Except for extraordinary circumstances related to child protection, a court will not deprive any parent of the right to spend time with their children. A court decision would come up with a configuration that either entrusts full custody of the children to one parent while giving visitation rights to the other or decide on joint custody. The amicable agreement needs to do better than what the strict application of the law would produce, or at least as well. Are there other clauses that would work better for each of the parties? The solution that alternates picking up the children at school, for example, creates more value than a narrow definition of custody and visitation rights. A mediated agreement that the two parents co-construct also integrates the children's interests and will be more beneficial than a solution concocted by a judge and imposed on everyone.

In a selection process among multiple solutions, there are often two steps: excluding the extremes and ranking the remaining solutions.

Dual Request for the Exclusion of Extremes

Each party is asked to rule out solutions that, in their eyes, *they cannot accept.* The mediator invites the party in question to justify why these solutions are unacceptable. This first request poses few difficulties, because it is easy for a party to distance themselves from solutions beyond their red lines, and that, in general, correspond to extreme positions stated by the other, like sole custody without visitation rights.

Similarly, each party is invited to pay special attention to solutions that *the other party cannot accept*. Here we are dealing with solutions that one party has suggested and that the other finds unacceptable. It is important that the party who has suggested the solution understand why the other cannot easily acquiesce. This second request requires a sustained effort at empathy vis-à-vis the other; it is more challenging, because it supposes the abandonment of some wishes or dreams. In 2006, the late Giorgos Vassiliou, former president of Cyprus, told one of the authors that parties need to let go of some of their *desires* (efkteon, εkteon) to focus on what is *possible* (efikto, Ευφικτο).

This dual request, especially the second, is better understood and achievable in private meetings.

Occupied territories

Negotiation expert Roger Fisher, who one day met Egyptian President Gamal Abdel Nasser, asked him what solution Israeli Prime Minister Golda Meir needed, from his viewpoint, to implement a quick return to peace between the two countries. Nasser indicated that *"she should simply leave the occupied territories"* as the solution. Fisher then pushed the questioning further: *"And let us imagine that Golda Meir does what you propose, Mr. President, what would happen to her?"* Nasser immediately erupted in laughter and with a big hand gesture, concluded: *"I see what you mean; if she did what I asked her to do, she would have many problems at home …"*

In the secrecy of private meetings, it is easier for a party to realize that one of "their" solutions, while often claimed to please public opinion, is unacceptable from the other side's perspective. In Nasser's case, if Meir accepted it, she would lose face and probably power. In the evaluation stage, the mediator sometimes needs to *push the parties to put themselves in the other side's shoes*. This enables them to realize the sheer unreasonableness of their proposed solution. Of course, it takes the confidence of a Roger Fisher to speak so candidly (almost brazenly) to someone like President Nasser. The broader learning point – especially when mediating between powerful individuals – is that the mediator needs enough personal character and professional gravitas not only to demonstrate empathetic understanding but also to ask probing questions, and "speak truth to power."

Rank All Solutions to Move toward One Solution

After the extreme solutions are shown to be impractical comes the challenging task of classifying the remaining array of solutions. There are multiple strategies to choose from. The mediator needs to call on different methods, like listing the pros and cons of each solution, a cost-benefit analysis, etc. In this bottleneck situation, the mediator guides the parties toward the best solutions. When there is no obvious best solution, no *Eureka* moment, this path is full of pitfalls, trial and error, fumbling, and failures. Everyone's patience is put to the test.

At this stage, tensions are likely, because, unlike in the previous phase, the mediator needs to help parties to distribute, divide, choose, and exclude. Before starting, the mediator usefully indicates that these tensions are normal in the life of a conflict, its negotiation, and its resolution. The idea is to encourage the parties to consider them as challenges to be overcome by intelligence and imagination.

What are the different strategies that the mediator can follow in order to overcome a possible deadlock at this stage? Some of these are as follows:

- *Strategy 1:* Ask a party to *explain* where the idea comes from – for example, this amount.

- *Strategy 2:* Inquire with the party about the *justification criteria* for a solution, whether these criteria are of an objective or subjective nature (just as we mentioned for a mediator's solutions).

- *Strategy 3:* Reopen *directed questioning* to mobilize value-creating solutions that are likely to fit in the gap between two solutions, each desired by one of the parties.

- *Strategy 4:* Suggest *unilateral concession*, with the person who takes the initiative, often priming the pump of reciprocity, inspiring the other party to do the same.

- *Strategy 5:* Initiate a *give-and-take moment*, which is to say a concession against another concession.

- *Strategy 6:* Consider an appropriate *compensation* to alleviate the pain of a difficult solution, helping a party to accept it.

- *Strategy 7:* Suggest the necessity of *external/systemic/organizational guarantees* to reassure both parties.

- *Strategy 8:* Invite the parties to identify the *reasons for the impasse*, by returning to what is truly important for each one. "*I do not want to concede this point, which hurt me too much in the past.*" This return to the past-present phase puts the emphasis back, in this case, on a symbolic request, to which the mediator apparently did not pay enough attention. This request "can be resolved" now in the present-future phase, for example, by a mark of recognition that the party responsible for the impact can express through:

  - a (public or private) *apology*;

  - a recognition of unintentional *errors*;

  - an expression of *regret* for the impact caused;

  - a *withdrawal of* expressed *words*;

  - an announcement of *positive things* that one party recognizes in the other.

- *Strategy 9:* Skip to *another point*, to reexamine the impasse later, once progress has been achieved on other items.

- *Strategy 10:* Use the *private meeting* to question a party on their room for maneuver or for possible effort (e.g., "*what would be a number that would seem acceptable to you?*"), or to discover a new solution (e.g., "*if the husband's new partner does not want him to give money to his former spouse, could she agree to give it to the children?"*).

- *Strategy 11*: Suggest a return to the respective *principals* (or clients), to release the straitjacket of the mandate and expand red lines.

- *Strategy 12:* Invite the intervention of *other stakeholders*, such as the children, whose opinion sometimes contributes to the progress of a situation.

- *Strategy 13:* Call for *fairness* or *best practices* in society, to elucidate what possible choices judges or experts make, for example, by questioning parties on the average amount for child support in the region where the mediation is taking place.

- *Strategy 14:* Move from mediation to *conciliation*: propose a package that seems balanced and equitable; and which integrates diverse strategies of value creation, leveraging time and risk differences, economies of scale and scope, financing, guarantees, reparations, stakeholders, etc.

- *Strategy 15:* Mention the possibility of *arbitration* to resolve the impasse points (e.g., by an arbitrator employed by the same professional association in charge of appointing the mediator).

- *Strategy 16:* Remind the parties of the possible existence of *a deadline*: *"We have three months for this mediation to succeed. Unfortunately, if we do not have an agreement tomorrow, I will have to halt my mission."*

- *Strategy 17*: Hand in a *mirror to the parties about their disagreement*, acknowledge that if we continue on this path, we head toward failure: *"We have been deadlocked on this point for two days, and, despite shuttling between you two, no solution has emerged. Do you suggest we stop the mediation?"*

- *Strategy 18:* If necessary, be ready to propose *solutions away from mediation*. If a prolonged impasse persists at this stage, i.e. if the parties are unable to hear one another on some negotiated solutions, the mediator can make them explore together or separately the path they intend to take in the event that the mediation fails. Explicitly taking into account the possibility of mediation failure is often an indispensable reality test for the deadlocked parties, who may each overestimate the quality of their solutions away from the mediation table. Often, when these alternatives are explicitly discussed and examined in their full details, their luster often dissipates. For example, a potential judicial decision might, prima facie, appeal to the parties, until they contemplate the cost in lawyers' fees, the length of the procedure, and the uncertainty of the ultimate decision (see Chapter 8 for an in-depth discussion).

In most cases, at the end of this second move of the present-future phase, the parties have discovered that certain solutions, among the multitude of options imagined in the first move, could be agreed upon by both. They gain a glimpse of a solution or a bundle of solutions that can constitute the basis of the common decision, which nevertheless still needs to be structured in order to avoid any possible misunderstanding.

Third Move: Decide – Toward a Commitment Among Parties

Once certain solutions are recognized as acceptable by both parties, it is important to start confirming points of agreement in writing.

Use Single Text, Shuttle, and Brackets

A fruitful method here is the *one-text procedure*. This method requires the mediator to ask the parties to examine a single text by making them "direct-ly" construct the clauses of a potential agreement and by letting them react in order to avoid the risk of divergent interpretations later on. A key advantage of this technique is to focus the parties' attention on the text in front of them (rather than on themselves or their notes). It also curbs the feeling of confrontation between the parties by engaging them in a joint exercise.

Sometimes, the text is created by *shuttling back and forth* between the parties. During each of the private meetings, the mediator submits a text, which each party completes, corrects, fine-tunes, and which is modified in the course of such meetings, until one text is obtained that satisfies all parties.

As a complement to the methods of a single text and of shuttling, the mediator can also use the *brackets technique* that is applied to passages of the text on which there is still divergence, and which demands fuller discussions and adjustments. The objective of the mediator is to progressively reduce the number of brackets to get a text that meets the parties' approval from beginning to end.

Get Support for the Final Draft of the Agreement

Let us underscore the advantage, during this phase, of getting expert advice during the drafting of the agreement. It is preferable for the parties to have the text in hand rather than being surprised with an unfamiliar text, increasing the risk of it being rejected. The presence of an expert during the drafting stage is also an index of quality, legality, and sustainability all at the same time. These external actors can raise points neglected by the parties, reframe others to adopt a less ambiguous formulation that is more in accordance with the law, and even add clauses to the agreement that ensure implementation without any loopholes and that protect both parties from one or the other refusing to implement the deal.

Validate the Agreement

If a *commitment* emerges, the mediator will, before anything else, make sure that the parties commit knowingly to not only *sign an agreement* today but to keep it tomorrow and to scrupulously execute its terms. The mediator contributes to testing the robustness of the settlement, by checking four validation criteria:

- *Satisfaction with the agreement:* It is measured, for example, in relation to the 10 preparation assets (see Chapter 4). A party can be considered satisfied:

  ○ *in terms of people,* if the relationship with the other party is improved; if the mandate of each person was respected, and if the interests of diverse stakeholders absent from the table have been taken into account; if all these people aspects are satisfied, we increase the chances of smooth implementation;

- ○ *in terms of problems,* if the solutions satisfy the identified motivations and needs of all parties; if they create value for both and are much better than potentially available solutions away from the mediation table; and if these agreed-upon solutions are anchored in justification criteria; if all these aspects on the problems are validated, it is likely that nothing essential has been overlooked and thus we can be confident that the conflict will not reoccur;

- ○ *in terms of process,* if the mediator managed the meetings in this commitment stage well, and also those in all the previous stages; if the rights and obligations of both parties have been well communicated and recorded in the text and if the necessary signatures have been procured; if all these aspects of the process above are well managed, we increase the chance of a successful implementation;

- *Actual authentication:* The parties are always free to refuse a solution or a compromise, but if they decide to adhere to an agreement, the mediator needs to verify one last time the sincerity of this commitment: "*The agreement is now in front of you, with all its clauses; can you confirm to me that it suits you and that you will fully implement all the clauses in good faith? Madam? – Yes. Sir? – Yes.*"

- *Feasibility:* The clauses in the final contract need to be realistic so that parties can materially implement them. To do this, the agreement includes an action plan outlining all the necessary next steps to know "who does what when." The mediator sometimes also needs to verify that the commitments are clear for both parties: "*Madam and Sir, the clauses that your agreement contains, are they really clear for each of you? Do you understand the rights and obligations that it contains? Do your commitments appear implementable to you?*" The mediator is to foresee, if necessary, monitoring mechanisms in view of the verification – by the mediator and/or the parties themselves – of proper implementation over time.

- *Sustainability:* The decision contains all the details that ensure the greatest durability over time; the different circumstances and their potential modification have been anticipated as much as possible; the clauses need to be durable and forestall a resurgence of conflict at one point or another. Even here, the mediator proceeds to make one last verification: *"Are you certain that the elements of your contract will withstand the test of time and that nothing essential has been forgotten and could weaken its implementation?"*

Summarize Commitments and Get Signatures

To avoid any misunderstanding, it is indispensable that the mediator summarizes the agreement at the end of the session. This is the occasion to verify with the parties the content of the commitments. To confer a certain solemnity on them, the mediator suggests putting them in writing and asks the parties to sign the document.

Certain parties may prefer an oral agreement (words of honor; a handshake; *it's a deal!*). But even if a written report is *just a piece of paper* to record the agreement, it recalls the exact terms detailing what the parties agreed upon. The mediator's vigilance prevents any ambiguity and any new sources of tensions.

Should the *mediator countersign* the agreement? This point is strongly debated. Some think that the mediator does not have to sign, because it is an agreement between parties. For others, the mediator signs after the words *"in the presence of …,"* as a natural witness to the contract between the parties. Finally, for others, the mediator countersigns to make official the agreement among parties.

Absence of a General Agreement

If a general commitment on all aspects of the conflict was not reached, the mediator nevertheless tries to obtain one of the following agreements, ranging from the strongest to the weakest:

- *Agreement on the points of agreement and disagreement*, noting on the one hand, substantive solutions on which the parties agree, and on the other hand, blocking points that will be addressed during the next sessions.

- *Agreement on the problems that parties have to address*, that is to say, on the progress made in the exploration of the motivations and underlying needs of the parties and the search for solutions.

- *Agreement on the process itself*, on the framework and methods to be used to support the parties on their journey to an agreement.

- *Agreement on the next meeting*, which implies choosing a specific time and date as well as a provisional agenda.

- *Agreement on the disagreement itself*, which is to say an agreement that identifies the disagreement, which constitutes the minimal contribution of the mediation process, and which did not allow for the resolution of conflict.

End of Session: Final Moments of the Mediation

In all these cases, at the end of the mediation, the mediator *congratulates the parties* for having worked together toward a mutual understanding of the conflict and an exploration of solutions – and even better still, the drafting of the settlement. The mediator *leaves the parties and invites them to congratulate one another* with the hope that their relationship has improved so that they will do so spontaneously.

*

During this process, some pitfalls may appear, and we cannot underestimate the difficulty of the exercise, as much for the mediator as for the parties. This is why the eighth and last chapter in this book explores, in detail, a large number of mediation pitfalls, as well as the ways to avoid them.

CHAPTER 8
THE PITFALLS
Question Practices *Before* Acting

Mediation is not a long, tranquil river. There will be ebbs and flows, swirls, rapids to pass, and even waterfalls to negotiate. Anticipating these obstacles and challenges is a way to protect the integrity of mediation. Awareness of certain unfortunate human instincts helps the mediator avoid risky situations. Strategies are also available to improve the likelihood of overcoming obstacles. This chapter is therefore devoted to an analysis of the most frequent difficulties encountered in mediation and a presentation of the best available antidotes. Like this book, this chapter is not meant exclusively for mediators. Parties will also note pitfalls they may fall into – sometimes unconsciously and in all good faith – that would have the effect of disturbing the fluidity of the process. For clarity of presentation, this chapter distinguishes the problems stemming from *the mediator*'s initiatives from those stemming from *the parties*' behaviors (Lempereur 1999b). Examining these critical moments will also illuminate, from a different angle, some principles and tools mentioned in the previous chapters.

This catalog of obstacles does not seek to be exhaustive. It invites the mediator to reconsider their behavior and aims to favor reflection about and a critical examination of their practices and some difficult moments they may experience (Friedman 2015). This chapter will have achieved its objectives if it increases, even marginally, the mediator's awareness concerning how parties may interpret certain behaviors and the importance of process. Conscious of these possible pitfalls, the mediator and the parties will be more likely to recognize them when the time comes.

The Mediator's Initiatives: Measuring Risky Behaviors

While managing the various steps of the process, the mediator, even with the best intentions, sometimes induces paradoxical results where they do more harm than good (Lempereur 1999b, 1999d). They let the process go off course, undermine the search for solutions, and upset the establishment of a healthy relationship between the parties. They are like doctors who administer the wrong medicine to a sick patient, without even being aware of it. To some extent, instinctive behaviors are at the core of a number of pitfalls and hence the importance of identifying them at different moments of the process. In the following list, these counterproductive reflexes are placed as much as possible in chronological order according to their potential for occurrence during the process. They can, however, emerge, randomly during exchanges and at a variety of moments. To facilitate the reader's understanding, these instinctive behaviors of mediators are expressed in the first person from a mediator's viewpoint.

Items requiring vigilance during the introduction phase

Reminder about the suggested method: PORTAL		
P	for	Presentations
O	for	Objectives
R	for	Rules of Engagement
T	for	Time and Stages
A	for	Agreement to Mediate
L	for	Launch!

Assuming That the Parties Know What Mediation Is

Instinctive behavior of the mediator – I do not believe that I need to explain to the parties what mediation is.

Probable causes of this behavior – I do not want to lose time; instead, I want the mediation to proceed as expeditiously as possible. I am sure that the parties share this desire. In any event, I assume that the parties know what mediation is about.

Risks incurred – I risk a misunderstanding with one or several of the parties, who mistake mediation for another type of conflict resolution – for instance, an expert assessment or arbitrage.

Recommendations – I recognize that by saving a little time now (not wasting time by explaining something that seems obvious to me), I may lose time later. Worse, I may face the parties' anger at having "misled" them into a "wrong" process. Taking some time now to explain mediation is a good investment. I recall what mediation is – a voluntary process of joint problem-solving – and what it is not.

Expected outcome – I clearly outline what is to be expected in mediation, emphasizing that the final decision is up to the parties to make.

Defending the Principle of Mediation

Instinctive behavior – I feel obliged to defend mediation, for example, when encountering skepticism from one of the parties.

Probable causes – I wish to overcome doubt from one (or both) of the parties as to the relevance of mediation in general, or its utility in this situation.

Incurred risks – By multiplying justifications, I risk increasing the doubts in the mind of the party I am trying to convince. Worse, they may end up feeling trapped in mediation, hardening their initial skeptical reaction to the process.

Recommendations – I take the reluctance seriously, recalling that parties retain total autonomy at any moment to resort to other modes of conflict resolution (Chapter 2).

Expected outcome – The parties participate willingly in the process and give mediation a chance to resolve their conflict.

Entertaining an Unspoken Vision of the Mediator's Role

Instinctive behavior – I do not explain how I envision my role as mediator.

Probable causes – It seems a waste of time for me to explain how I intend to do my job. These technical details concern only me. Incidentally, all mediators proceed in the same way, or each one in their own way. Therefore, it is pointless to talk about it.

Incurred risks – The parties may be surprised by my practices. They expect that I will suggest solutions – or, on the contrary, they are surprised when I do so.

Recommendations – I specify my task. I will act as a *facilitator* letting parties suggest solutions, or as an *idea provider* if it becomes necessary later, or as an *adviser* giving my opinion. I explain the possibility of resorting to private meetings. I get the parties' agreement on my proposed method.

Expected outcome – Parties understand my mediation approach, and I adjust my methods to their wishes, all the while reassuring them of mediation's core principles.

Defending Myself as a Mediator

Instinctive behavior – I feel attacked as a mediator and decide to defend myself.

Probable causes – One of the parties expresses some doubts about me personally. I find this questioning of my skills, experience, impartiality, or neutrality unfair.

Incurred risks – In defending myself, I feed the doubt of the party whom I seek to convince and who can view my reaction as a way of serving my own personal interest as mediator.

Recommendations – I recall that if parties wish to, they can resort to other modes of conflict resolution and decide to replace the mediator at any moment by someone of their choice. The mediator will perform their task only after the parties have entrusted the mission to them.

Expected outcome – By showing a certain detachment in relation to my mission as a mediator, I am more likely to ensure the parties' trust and to gain in legitimacy as a mediator.

Rushing to Solve the Problem

Instinctive behavior – I find it useless to introduce the mediation process and skip any explanation about the principles. Instead, I start addressing the substance of the conflict immediately.

Probable causes – I want to be efficient in order to finish the mediation as quickly as possible. I believe I need to leave maximum space for spontaneity and flexibility. Luck will determine and serve the process well. I will adapt myself along the way.

Incurred risks – The parties may have an inaccurate idea of the various steps that will structure the mediation process. I risk surprising them, or even disappointing them with my practices. The hare turns out to be less efficient than the turtle.

Recommendations – I choose to present a succinct plan of the process. I get the parties to approve the major steps to follow.

Expected outcome – I reduce the element of surprise for the parties, reassure them, and guide them through the mediation process, making references to it when necessary and encouraging the parties to stay on course.

Trusting Unbridled Spontaneity

Instinctive behavior – I do not establish any rules for communication between the parties, counting on the parties' spontaneous improvisation and on my ability to manage problems as they come.

Probable causes – I want to get to the core of what matters as early as possible. Needless to say, the parties know they must not interrupt one another. If necessary, I can always recall this obligation later on.

Incurred risks – When one party interrupts the other party, my involvement risks appearing partial, to the extent that I seem to favor the interrupted party.

Recommendations – I immediately announce the reasons for the non-interruption principle; I obtain its validation by parties. I then apply it consistently.

Expected outcome – Parties get acquainted with a communication style that facilitates exchanges of information and perspectives, the future of their relationship, and the resolution of their conflict.

Relying Solely on Subjective Principles

Instinctive behavior – I limit myself to asking the parties to respect one another but offer my own definition of the word "respect," without worrying about their opinions.

Probable causes – Each side knows what respect is. It is sufficiently general for the parties to understand and employ it.

Incurred risks – The rule of mutual respect is difficult to objectify, and any specification by the mediator can appear partial. The definition of respect varies from one party to the other and depends on the circumstances. The risk of divergent interpretations on what mutual respect means contributes to later disappointments.

Recommendations – I simultaneously announce the principles of non-interruption and of mutual respect. I rely on the first to define the second. I obtain the agreement of the parties on these two principles. For any potential deviation during the process, I recall the parties' prior agreement.

Expected outcome – I increase the chances that neither party feels personally targeted if I need to remind them of the rules. I simply hold them to the commitment that they made beforehand on this point.

Favoring Transparency without Insisting on Confidentiality

Instinctive behavior – I do not mention the principle of confidentiality. I also do not consider the dangers of transparency vis-à-vis external actors of one party or the other.

Probable causes – I do not want to rule too heavily on the process or prolong the introduction. Why mention this well-known principle?

Incurred risks – The parties, lacking the guarantee that what they will say will not be used against them, may hesitate to share important information, which could prevent needs from emerging and hinder the effective search for a zone of possible agreement. Further, they are caught off guard when some information leaks.

Recommendations – I explain the utility of confidentiality and confirm that the parties agree on this principle. I state that mediators are also ethically required to respect it, and that what is exchanged in mediation cannot be divulged later.

Expected outcome – I reassure the parties, build confidence, and create a favorable climate for better exchange of information, because what is shared in mediation cannot be used against one another outside mediation.

Not Getting Prior Agreement on Implementation

Instinctive behavior – I do not immediately confirm that if the parties commit to anything, they have to execute it, whatever the content of the agreement, complete or partial.

Probable causes – I do not want to put pressure on the parties at this point. I feel I can mention it in due time.

Incurred risks – The parties and the mediator risk wasting their time, due to an implicit acceptance that the mediation could be used for stalling purposes. What is the point of engaging in a process that would result in an agreement that may not be enforced?

Recommendations – I ask the parties to commit from the start that they will execute any commitment that they might make, whatever its content or informality. I record their willingness to enforce their potential agreement.

Expected outcome – I reassure each side regarding the seriousness of the other in relation to the mediation process and to the potentially accepted agreement.

Monopolizing the Process

Instinctive behavior – I show that I am the only boss aboard, and I ask parties to only talk to me, rather than to one another.

Probable causes – I have the feeling that if a part of the communication process escapes me, the parties will fall back into irreconcilable positions.

Incurred risks – Parties feel patronized and infantilized. They find me vain. I deprive them of all sense of personal responsibility. The danger is that I will end up as a stakeholder in their conflict.

Recommendations – I confine myself to my role as a mediator and facilitate direct communication among the parties. I gradually transition from an interventionist mode to a decentralized mode.

Expected outcome – I favor an open attitude by parties regarding one another, and exemplify this in my conduct.

The Mediator's Awareness during the Phase "From the Past to the Present"

Reminder of suggested moves (Chapter 6)

1. Identify the problems to negotiate
2. Grasp motivations
3. Mutually understand each other

Owning the Problem

Instinctive behavior – I immediately take over the problem in order to arrive at the solutions faster.

Probable causes – To save time, I'm always in action mode. If not, the process will go on forever. I think that thanks to my technical expertise and my understanding of the content, we will get quickly to some satisfying solutions for all.

Incurred risks – There is a risk of making assumptions about the problem (*petitio principii*), a feeling of misappropriation from the parties, a potential misreading of the problem, and a misguided approach of coming up with solutions.

Recommendations – The essence of problem-solving remains "the parties' realm," and I never stop gently reminding them of their responsibilities. I let them deal with the problem so that I can better concentrate on the process.

Expected outcome – I bring the parties to accept that they have a personal stake in contributing to a progressive resolution. The division of labor and responsibilities between us is clear for everyone.

Proceeding as if We Were in Court

Instinctive behavior – I decide – without giving any explanations – that the party who came to see me first will be the first to speak.

Probable causes – I consider the party who came to see me first as the "plaintiff" and, as is typical before a judge, that this "litigant" should "plead first." This judicial model of operation guides me throughout the mediation process.

Incurred risks – My choice may be poorly received for various reasons by the two parties: the first to speak does not necessarily understand why they are invited to open the exchange, and the second party does not appreciate being made to wait. I risk undermining my *impartiality*.

Recommendations – I ask the parties who would like to start. If both wish to begin, I conduct a random draw.

Expected outcome – As mediator, I practice impartiality vis-à-vis the parties. I show that no matter who initiated the mediation process, I remain "in the middle" of both parties, at an equidistance from each side, even for the smallest details.

Giving Too Much Attention to One of the Parties

Instinctive behavior – I let a party explain at length their view of the facts without paying attention to the other party.

Probable causes – I want to let this party present the facts without interrupting them, allowing them to clear the air. I wish to show that I am listening. The other side just needs to wait to speak.

Incurred risks – I alienate the other party and frustrate them. Even if one of the parties justifiably needs to present a long account, the other side might feel ignored.

Recommendations – In advance, I warn both parties that I might interrupt them at some point, if necessary. I establish a time limit, continue to look at the silent party, and tell them that their turn will come, granting them as much time as the other to express themselves.

Expected outcome – Each party's speaking time is balanced, and this way I prevent frustration on either side. Both parties feel fairly treated.

Talking Too Much during the Listening Phase

Instinctive behavior – I ask numerous questions about the facts to prove that I have mastered the subject matter. I participate in the fact telling, add my own interpretations and assertions, and do not stop showing that I can anticipate what will be said.

Probable causes – I want to know more about the subject matter, or at least show that I am well prepared. I want to show how much I agree on certain points with one of the parties. I wish to validate a certain number of hypotheses with them.

Incurred risks – My intentions, however laudable, can generate two unintended effects. First, I risk not giving the parties enough time to express the facts in their own words. Second, I also risk being misinterpreted: the party who is speaking may feel "grilled" and thus obligated to justify themselves, suspecting that my questions violate the impartiality principle and are aimed at orienting the debate in a biased direction.

Recommendations – Rather than making assumptions about, or preceding, a party, I follow the process step by step: I limit myself to active listening, deftly reformulating comments that may hurt the other side. I ask clarifying questions about what the party has already *said*.

Expected outcome – I get the parties to engage in active communication, using questions in a constructive and non-rhetorical way, without hints or blame.

Being Obsessed with the "Truth"

Instinctive behavior – I ask for *proof* of all the facts mentioned, as if to confirm the truth in legal or scientific terms.

Probable causes – I am motivated by legal expertise or powered by work routines that aim to reveal objective facts. By discovering *the* truth, I am convinced that we will more easily find the most satisfactory solution.

Incurred risks – I lose myself in an infinite debate on facts, the admissibility of proof, its validity, etc. Once again, I confuse mediation with a legal trial, and my concern about the truth biases the perception of the parties.

Recommendations – I refrain from legal jargon, and if a notion needs to be elucidated, I express it in an accessible manner. I ask for *clarifications* on the stated facts. In some cases, a party may, *on their own*, prove their claims to the other party. My objective, however, is less about establishing "the Truth" than about identifying the perceptions of the facts, the narratives that the parties wish to study in depth (feelings, values, needs).

Expected outcome – Without losing myself in a legal maze, I focus on an in-depth study of the parties' understanding of a situation through both the objective details of the facts and the subjective dimensions of their personal needs.

Confusing Listening with Agreement

Instinctive behavior – Without realizing it, after each party's remarks, I seem to point out that I agree with them.

Probable causes – Being attentive to one of the parties, I want to show that not only do I understand them, but that I also approve of what they are saying. My hope is to reassure them.

Incurred risks – The initial satisfaction that a party receives when they feel that I agree with them proves to be counterproductive in the long term, because this party comes to see me as a supporter of their viewpoint. The other party may see my remarks as an agreement with the other side's perspective, and therefore view me as biased and partial.

Recommendations – I use precise formulas like "*I see,*" "*I understand,*" and not "*OK,*" or "*I agree.*" I use active listening: what I restate is the perspective of the party who expressed themselves and not mine: "*From your perspective, etc.*"

Expected outcome – I demonstrate that understanding does not mean agreeing. The party who expressed themselves feels listened to by me, and the other party hears an authentic reformulation of the other's words from my mouth. My restatement without judgment models responsible communication.

Favoring Adversarial Proceedings

Instinctive behavior – Following the intervention of one party, I encourage the other side to contradict the first version of facts, to correct it, i.e. to "react."

Probable causes – I allow one of the parties to untangle the complexities of the conflict. Because the other party absolutely wants to react and can no longer listen, I yield to their impatience, and invite them to take over the discussion.

Incurred risks – A ping-pong match traps the parties in a logic of verbal confrontation, contradiction, and escalation. An impasse becomes more likely, with parties going around in circles without looking for solutions. The mediator can even contribute to it (Gino 2016).

Recommendations – I reformulate, subtly, the remarks expressed by one of the parties. Then, I welcome a complementary logic and ask the silent party to say how they see the situation from their viewpoint.

Expected outcome – I allow two versions of a situation to coexist, without settling or pointing out contradictions. I value a diversity of opinions, facts, and their effects.

Withdrawing

Instinctive behavior – I have the feeling that I am keeping score for the parties. I would like to interrupt them, but I am not sure how or when to do it. I therefore become motionless and let things happen.

Probable causes – The parties are prisoners of the past and experience difficulties in detaching themselves from it. They feel the need to express their internal hurt and to be heard, resulting in repetitive and, ultimately, fruitless statements. I do not wish to look impolite and to interfere in this fruitless conversation.

Incurred risks – My inaction leads to an impasse, and, worse, to escalation. I lose my grip on the mediation process, which henceforth lacks direction.

Recommendations – I act quickly to prevent the negotiation from degenerating, and I play my facilitator's role. I firmly interrupt a logic that goes around in circles by acknowledging the disagreement or declaring a pause. I encourage the parties' problem-solving and their request to look to the future. On the other hand, I do not fear remaining quiet if some good exchanges resume between the parties.

Expected outcome – The parties avoid a vicious circle of escalation, and thus engage in a virtuous circle of appeasement so that a constructive approach of problem-solving is put back in place.

Mistaking Positions for Solutions

Instinctive behavior – After reviewing the facts, as soon as the points of view are expressed, I wish to turn toward finding solutions, without taking the time to study these points in depth or favoring mutual recognition of identities and needs. I now want to proceed to solutions, even to agreement. I ask each party what their position is in order to resolve the conflict.

Probable causes – My impression is that the first exchanges among the parties brought the problem to maturity for a settlement and that the parties' positions will serve as springboards for solutions.

Incurred risks – This strategy that is founded on stating positions, without taking the time to study in depth the needs and motivations of each party, foreshadows an inadequate treatment of the problems, increased tension among the parties, and a deterioration of the process. The announcement of extreme, antagonistic, and incompatible positions, without recognition of the identities of each side, risks provoking an impasse and increasing relational tensions.

Recommendations – I invite the parties to undertake an explicit and in-depth search for the motivations, needs, and expectations of each party. I then check with the other party that they understand the other well, before turning to the future.

Expected outcome – I move beyond the preconceived positions toward the co-construction of a solution that parties could not have imagined before the discussion.

The Mediator's Awareness During the Phase "From the Present to the Future"

Reminder of the suggested moves (Chapter 7)

1. Invent as many solutions as possible
2. Evaluate solutions
3. Decide (toward a commitment among parties)

Linking Common Interests to Solutions

Instinctive behavior – I retain only motivations or needs shared in common by the parties.

Probable causes – I think that only the shared needs are the basis of a reconciliation and *a fortiori* of an agreement. I thus make them the heart of my plan for the search for solutions.

Incurred risks – I miss opportunities for exchanges and value creation offered by the differences and priorities of each side.

Recommendations – I explore the motivations, shared and different, and reiterate that it is by mutual recognition of all motivations that we will get a better agreement. I then focus the search for solutions on the satisfaction of the needs expressed by both parties.

Expected outcome – I favor creating value through a mutual understanding of the parties on what they share, but also on their differences.

Dreaming About the Good Solution

Instinctive behavior – I tell the parties how they can resolve their problems, and what solution they should adopt.

Probable causes – After hearing the parties, I have made up my mind. I know and what would work for them. It would be a shame to miss a solution that I can clearly see. I am apprehensive about the inability of the parties to find this good solution without my intervention. In addition, I want to demonstrate that I am a mediator for a reason.

Incurred risks – I propose an inappropriate solution to the parties, with the false belief that I know better than they do about what is good for them. One of the parties may acquiesce to my proposition, whereas the other side will find me biased.

Recommendations – Whatever my opinion, I keep quiet about it. I continue to help the parties find the solution themselves. I employ questions rather than assertions, and I mobilize creativity and value creation techniques.

Expected outcome – I avoid being presumptuous and reinforce my impartiality. I make the parties aware of their responsibilities. I maximize the probability that the solution found at the end of the process responds well to the needs of the parties, who as a result become willing to implement it.

Being Tempted to Respond to One Party's Request for a Solution

Instinctive behavior – I respond favorably to one of the parties who asks me to settle a specific point or to propose a solution, without confirming if the other party agrees.

Probable causes – One of the parties believes I am well placed, due to my expertise or my neutrality, to propose a solution. They think I can resolve the situation. It is probably their hope that I will express a solution that is advantageous to them. They are not wrong; I have some ideas about how to resolve the problem.

Incurred risks – The risks have already been stated in the previous point. I may appear partial, disappoint the party who solicited me, but also upset the other side, who will undoubtedly consider my solution as interference.

Recommendations – Though I may inquire why this party makes this request, I reiterate the parties' ability to find solutions themselves and invite them to do so. However, if both parties approve this request for aid on coming up with solutions, I participate with them in brainstorming by giving ideas. I propose many ideas, never only one. I present them as options among others, that the parties might want to validate or not. I am not offended if the parties reject my ideas.

Expected outcome – My ideas may or may not have contributed to creating a solution chosen by the parties. I have been able to maintain my impartiality and neutrality intact, all the while contributing to the search for equity.

Acting as a Deus Ex Machina

Instinctive behavior – At the end of mediation, I take the initiative to indicate to the parties how they can resolve their conflict.

Probable causes – A persistent impasse, my concern about a prospective failed mediation, and my urge to make myself useful are the reasons why I feel the need to intervene and save the mediation from failure.

Incurred risks – For the reasons already suggested, the proposed remedy can appear to be worse than the problem from the viewpoint of one or both of the parties, especially if my suggestion is overbearing and is not presented as one idea among many other ideas.

Recommendations – When the parties are entangled and unable to find the solution themselves, I, as a facilitative mediator, can be transformed into an ideas provider. However, I verify the willingness of the parties to have me play this role.

Expected outcome – The same as the previous point.

Rescuing One of the Parties

Instinctive behavior – I have a strong feeling that one of the parties is right, or, rather, that one of the parties must be supported in relation to the other, who excessively dominates the conversation. I am ready to act on this conviction through gestures or remarks, and even to correct an unbalanced disagreement.

Probable causes – A specific element (a fact, conduct, etc.) makes the balance tilt toward one of the parties. I will not let slip the chance to reestablish the balance through a solution that I find fair for the side who I think is unfairly treated.

Incurred risks – This bout of sincerity diminishes my impartial stance with the other party – the side whom I perceive to be "wrong" and/or dominant – who has the feeling that the mediator is negotiating on behalf of the other party. In fact, I am not really helping the party whom I allegedly supported, because I exonerate them of all sense of responsibility and risk being disavowed as a mediator.

Recommendations – I ask *both* parties to examine the envisioned solution and to compare it with other solutions that they perhaps would obtain away from the mediation table (e.g. in court). Whatever my impressions, I keep them to myself, and if the parties ask me for my opinion, I propose many ideas rather than only one. Potentially, I conduct a private meeting for this purpose. In the worst-case scenario, I use the "I" message to express what I think as a mediator, by adding that the parties may choose to dismiss me as mediator.

Expected outcome – I am upfront about my feelings of injustice. I let each of the parties decide what the best route is, concerning the interest in pursuing mediation or in retaining me as a mediator.

Getting an Agreement, No Matter What

Instinctive behavior – I attempt to obtain an agreement at any price. Even if one or both parties are doubtful about the utility of a solution, I do my utmost to try to get an agreement at the last minute.

Probable causes – The parties go around in circles, procrastinate, express doubts. It seems that they cannot reach an agreement despite all the efforts undertaken, except if I help them a bit. At this stage, they respect my authority, and I have gained their respect. Maybe I should push them to accept an agreement? My professional interest is significantly at stake: I want to be able to communicate that I successfully mediated this important situation. This achievement will enable me to get more rewarding mediation opportunities.

Incurred risks – I push the parties to an agreement against their will. Everyone runs the risk that such an agreement is neither implementable nor sustainable.

Recommendations – I invite parties to confirm that they have not overestimated their solutions away from the mediation table (in terms of cost, duration, risk, etc.). I acknowledge the partial agreement or the disagreement. I reiterate that mediation allowed for identifying concerns and the reasons for disagreement. I congratulate the parties for their effort. My power resides in the ability to let it go as mediator, holding myself back from imposing a solution on reluctant parties.

Expected outcome – Even in the absence of agreement, I can finish on a positive note. I admit that mediation in itself does not imply an agreement; the mediator intervenes only if it serves the motivations of the parties better than what they could obtain by other moves. I do not transform mediation into a showdown between myself and the parties.

Closing Prematurely

Instinctive behavior – Without any prior warning, I put an end to the mediation at the moment when the parties have identified common ground and finally come up with an agreement.

Probable causes – Overly happy to have terminated the mediation and found solutions, I want to finish as quickly as possible – just like the parties themselves, who are very tired – and before the parties change their minds.

Incurred risks – A premature closure has multiple causes and consequences. Certain points of agreement perhaps lack clarity and allow for divergent interpretations, which will lead to a clumsy implementation of the agreement. On forgotten or neglected points, I missed opportunities for value creation. The conflict could also flare up again. Possibly, I did not envision the question of ratification by the principals, which risks their later refusal. I also neglected to organize a follow-up that would have been desired or desirable. In doing so, due to my last-minute negligence, the parties' future looks bleak.

Recommendations – I make sure that the agreement does not leave any aspect unresolved, that it respects the mandate of each party. I document, in writing, the obligations of each side with precision. I ask the parties to verify the adequacy of the agreements with whomever they find it useful. I consider an action plan and a potential follow-up.

Expected outcome – I maximize the chances of contributing to the quality of the agreement and of its implementation.

Letting Discouragement Get the Better of Me

Instinctive behavior – I express my disappointment, even my discontent, vis-à-vis the parties.

Probable causes – The parties have neither come up with their own solutions nor built on those I may have suggested. I feel that the parties have not invested the necessary efforts or goodwill into the mediation. This is why they did not reach an agreement. I resent this failure and take it personally.

Incurred risks – The expression of my feelings does not take into account the efforts of the parties (nor my own) nor a certain number of agreed-upon points that contradict my pessimistic vision. I also prejudge unfavorably the potential capacity of the parties to find an agreement *in extremis* or in the next session. My negative attitude could infect the parties, adding to their disappointment and discouragement. I become a liability.

Recommendations – Without a doubt here, where the parties' freedom and responsibility are privileged, I need to learn, in all humility, to be satisfied with doing my best even if the parties do not come to an agreement. Maybe I need to explain more and in a better way? What seems obvious to me as a mediator is not necessarily so clear for the parties. It is my responsibility to shed light on how such ideas could satisfy the parties. I do not achieve anything by repeating the same argument. I inquire, study the motivations of the parties in depth, and find other ways to explain. In particular, I keep my regrets to myself, and I maintain distance, patience, and perseverance. It serves nobody to adopt a posture that the parties would find accusatory or that would discourage them. Why should I nurture regrets? The others are different from me, and it is not unnatural that they do not wish to follow a solution that I believe is ideal. I only have one obligation: all through the mediation process, *I do the best I can*. My conscience is at peace.

Expected outcome – I remain optimistic and accumulate results that a responsible approach to mediation maximizes. I demonstrate rock-solid patience and do not add my problems to those of the parties, who feel supported, even in the midst of apparent failure.

Following this section that focused on the problems resulting from the *mediator's* initiatives, who wants to do the right thing but risks getting results at odds with their expectations, the second part of the chapter will focus on the behaviors of the *parties*, which sometimes also lead to adverse effects, even unwelcome responses on the part of the mediator, who needs to overcome critical moments. Finally, whether an initiative comes from the mediator or the parties, this last chapter illustrates the necessity of permanently working on their *interaction*.

The Parties' Initiatives: Facing up to Critical Moments

The previous section dealt with certain pitfalls potentially generated by the mediator. But the parties' behaviors can pose as many problems. Most often, these obstacles are created neither with bad intentions nor with an understanding of their risks. As in the beginning of the chapter, the examination of these critical moments will also highlight the group of principles and tools suggested up to now.

Let us examine a dozen situations involving the parties' behaviors, as well as different possible response strategies that the mediator might implement.

Dealing with Bad Faith

When signs of manipulation, lies, and concealment appear, the mediation itself is in peril, along with any agreement that would result from it. Bad faith undermines trust and hinders the work of the mediator. But bad faith is difficult to establish. In this regard, it is important to clarify some distinctions:

- *Bad faith … in good faith:* A party prefers to lie in order to not bother the other side, all the while protecting themselves. Fearing the other side's reaction, they do not admit that they do not have the financial means to settle a debt, that they drink too much, etc.

- *Bad faith … in bad faith:* A party believes that it is better to lie, first to protect themselves, and second without any scruples toward the other side. They do not necessarily realize the consequences of the lie for the other party.

Likewise, the mediator may face either:

- *"Imagined" good faith:* It seems as if the parties are acting in good faith, but it is unclear. The mediator remains particularly vigilant, questions and probes, without calling into question a party, even if the latter cannot back up what they are saying with solid facts.

Or

- *"Established" bad faith:* Conversely, concrete elements bring to light the bad faith of one party. For example, they announce numbers that are proven to be 30% less than what was mentioned during a previous meeting; one party deliberately hides an element, while the other party brings the proof of its existence to a later meeting – even having divulged it to mediators in a private meeting.

In the case of established bad faith, three strategies may be useful:

- *Strategy 1: Make good faith a preventative rule* – Some mediators introduce the principle of good faith among the rules (Chapter 5) from the very beginning: "*I ask you to accept a common rule of good faith: to be sincere when sharing your vision of the reality to the other. If by any chance it so happens that either of you express words that do not match your actual actions, I would be forced to stop the mediation because we would have difficulty building a lasting solution in this case.*" If necessary, the mediator will recall this rule and discuss with the parties whether or not to continue the mediation.

- *Strategy 2: Explore bad faith* – The mediator who notes bad faith and can prove it (falsification of documents, lie, willful and grave omission) proposes a private meeting *with each* party. To the party exhibiting presumed bad faith, the mediator calmly hands over a mirror, exhibits the case, without accusing but asking them to note the facts. Then the mediator asks a key question: *"Can I ask what made you do this?"* More often than we think, the mediator obtains a response that expresses the fear of not satisfying an essential need. Equipped with this information, the mediator thus invites a modification of behavior and proposes *a contract of good faith*. If the party accepts it, the mediator resumes mediation. Instead of reproaching the party for bad faith, accompanied with the threat of interrupting mediation, or not doing anything at all, the mediator explores what is hidden *behind the act of bad faith* to know what is truly motivating it and to get the party to stop this unhelpful tactic.

- *Strategy 3: Stop the mediation* – If the established bad faith continues, the mediator warns the parties that they are about to interrupt the mediation. The mediator invites both sides to consider, one last time, the remaining options. If the parties refuse to explicitly commit to good faith, the mediator needs not to hesitate to purely and simply stop the mediation.

Disagreement of the Parties on the Facts

Can mediation proceed when the parties disagree on the facts? This classic, difficult situation reverts to the previous question concerning bad faith, where two cases are to be distinguished.

- *Bad faith:* Each party maintains a version that is convenient to them without having access to information that separates the two sides. It is one side's word against that of the other.

Dialogue in criminal mediation: Battle on the landing

Party A: You arrived on the fourth floor. You rang the bell. We opened our door to you. And you, family B, you attacked us, and then entered our apartment.

Party B: We, family B, peacefully went up the stairs. And it is you, A, who waited for us at the top of the stairs and attacked us upon our arrival on the fourth floor.

- *Good faith:* The parties are in disagreement based on their memory of the events. No one really has access to the facts, but instead only to what their memory wants to retain. Two narratives of the "same facts" coexist.

Instinctive Strategy: Investigating to Objectively Establish Facts

The mediator looks for documented evidence that will come closer to the facts, as in a legal discovery approach. However, it so happens that despite the supply of documents and of "proof," the parties persist in their respective narratives.

Contradictory versions

"It is you who hit first" versus *"No, it is you who hit first, and we defended ourselves."*

"There were three of you" versus *"No, I was alone."*

"She clearly specified these rules ..." versus *"No, she did not."*

These contradictory versions can be claimed:

- *In bad faith:* A party presents, often especially to the mediator, a version that puts themselves in a position of strength or, on the contrary, makes themselves look like a victim;

- *In good faith:* Each side's memory reconstructs the reality of facts, selects a part thereof, and genuinely forgets and modifies other parts.

With the aid of documents, testimony, and clues, we can approximate the facts. As the legal expression goes, we sometimes obtain some "*prima facie* evidence.*" But the problem remains. Even in the case of photos or of video recordings, as sometimes occurs in criminal mediation, the facts are not presented in context nor in their totality but according to a restricted scope and timeline. In addition, the facts are colored by affects and emotions. Finally, in order to avoid losing face, a party guilty of bad faith will have difficulty changing their version: they have put themselves in a hole and continue digging – and the mediation is at an impasse.

Whereas the lawyer will look for the facts to link them to the law, the mediator explores the *facts* as well as its *effects* on the *impacted* party. It is this causal interaction that might have escalated the conflict. This is the logic underlying the following three other strategic approaches.

Three Other Reflective Strategies to Break the Impasse

Deep down, it is of little importance whether the parties *know* the truth or the reality concerning the facts, or whether they *refuse to tell* the truth in front of the mediator: mediators are not judges and do not have to demand this transparency. If there is a lasting deadlock on the facts, whether or not the parties are of good or bad faith, one option is to skip over the facts. Here, the mediator ends the impasse: "*You yourselves know what happened …*" or "*Each of you has a different memory of the facts,*" which avoids offending the sensitivity of each party. To still succeed, the mediator can leverage three strategies:

- *Strategy 1: Ask each side to speak, not on the facts but on "what the events did to you"* – It means exploring experienced feelings, scorned values, revealed needs … and make each side listen to the *subjective perceptions* of the other side. Here, the parties no longer need to agree on an *objective reality*. Each party will only have to state that they heard the other party. Here again, we recall the important concept of mutual understanding without agreement (Chapter 6).

- *Strategy 2: Re-focus on the future* – The skipping over facts does not prevent the mediator from inviting the parties to express precise wishes regarding their future relationship. The mediator resumes their questioning: "*In your future relations, what would you like the other party to say or do, not say or not do? Could you start by saying: 'In my future relations with A, I would like ...' Go ahead.*" In general, at this stage, when needs have been well identified, then explored in depth (Chapter 6), even if there is disagreement on certain facts, the parties shift their attention to the desired future.

- *Strategy 3: Establish different scenarios according to different facts* – When each party insists on their version of facts, the mediator proposes moving forward while keeping both scenarios. "*To explore your needs and reflect them in the future, let us imagine many scenarios. Let us imagine first the facts as Mr. A recalls them. What does that imply for your future relations? ... Now, let us imagine the facts as Mr. B recalls them. What does that imply for your future relations?*" In doing so, we can discover shared values and desired behaviors.

Too Few or Too Many Words

We make a distinction between silence, the flood of words, and pointless repetition.

Silence

What to do when a party is reticent to speak? Understand the reason, first of all. The explanation could be as much from fear – the result of feeling uncomfortable, intimidated, or threatened – as from a voluntary strategy or from simple habit. The mediator thus first needs to *know that they do not know* and must beware of jumping to a hasty conclusion.

- *Strategy 1: Accept the silence as indicative of reflection after being asked a question* – More often than not, the mediator will allow this silence, even if they perceive a slight pause or uneasiness. Maybe it is necessary to simply give the party time to feel safe, find their place and rhythm in the exchange. Contentious situations are often difficult for the parties; family, business, or national representatives assume responsibility for the destiny of an entire group, including their own. By speaking, they might put themselves at risk. The mediator needs to remain patient and allow time for risk-taking. Another reason for the silence may be that the party simply did not understand the question and dared not admit it!

- *Strategy 2: Explore the causes of this silence* – The questioning focuses on the inner dialogue of the silent party. Abandoning the in-depth questions for a while, the mediator concentrates on what is causing the difficulty to communicate: "*It is difficult … There might be a part of you that hesitates to speak. What makes it so difficult to say it out loud?*" Depending on the responses, the mediator will be able to locate the difficulty and remedy it, or accept that the party does not want to speak at this stage if they so choose. Maybe this moment will come later on.

- *Strategy 3: Propose a private meeting with each of the parties* – Most often, when in a one-on-one meeting, the parties will explain themselves more easily. It may be a good idea to remind the party of the confidentiality of the meeting, unless they authorize the mediator to speak to the other party "on their behalf." In this case, the mediator remains vigilant to relay only what they have been authorized to transmit. Sometimes, a party's silence is not only caused by the other party's presence, but also by that of the mediator, or by the situation itself. The mediator will reassure the party and explain or modify some of their behaviors that may have been bothersome and will encourage the party to develop, in front of the other side, a theme that seems pertinent.

- *Strategy 4: Remind the parties the mediation can only focus on what is shared* – In order to invite the parties to open up, the mediator reiterates that if each side reserves the right to say only what they want, we will only be able to deal with what is said – and not the unsaid, the partially said, or hardly said.

The Flood of Words

Certain mediators are so committed to the non-interruption rule that they allow each party to speak as long as they like. But if a party appears so loquacious that no one can any longer follow what they are saying, or if the other party feels deprived of speaking, it is better to interrupt the party than let them continue.

- *Strategy 1: Interrupting in order to reformulate understanding at this stage* – After having verified their understanding of what has been said, the mediator invites the party to continue. The mediator reserves the right to interrupt, not to prevent speaking but to assure understanding.

- *Strategy 2: Interrupting in order to allow everyone the time to speak* – The flood of thoughts from one party prevents the other side from expressing themselves. The mediator interrupts, suggesting that they will be able to resume shortly, after having heard the other party for the same amount of time. Thus, the mediator interrupts not to prevent the party from speaking but to allow everyone the chance to speak.

- *Strategy 3: Asking both parties to limit their interventions to a time frame* – Faced with an ongoing asymmetry between two parties, one speaking a lot and the other much less, at some point the mediator might need to suggest that all the parties speak, for example, for a maximum of two minutes, check that they agree on the time frame, and try to stick to this time-bound approach as the dialogue progresses. Here, the mediator intervenes not to prevent speaking but to balance the conversation among the parties.

Pointless Repetition

Some mediators fear cornering themselves with the rule of non-interruption. However, faced with a party who does not stop repeating themselves, the right to interrupt is also justified, in order to avoid pointless waste of time or to prevent the other party from becoming irritated.

- *Facing a talkative party*, who mentions tangential things that vaguely concern the subject matter of the mediation. *Strategy:* Ask them to specify how what they are saying relates to the mediation. Either the party becomes aware that their chatter is off topic, making them return to the subject of the mediation, or they explain the link between what they are talking about and the subject of the mediation. For example, in a mediation at the office around management control methods, one of the parties talks at length about their various vacations. After being asked about the relevance of this point, the party reveals that the conflict was created as a result of incompatible agenda constraints *when one of the colleagues was on vacation*. Thus, any solutions to be found needed to focus on modifying management control methods as much as the vacation leave system.

- *Facing a party who continually repeats themselves*, fearing not having been understood. *Strategy:* Engage in active listening, which includes a complete and precise reformulation. Here, the mediator is attentive, proving that they heard the remarks well, then asking: "*Would you like to add anything else?*" In general, when someone is reassured that they have been well understood, they usually no longer repeat themselves – or do so a lot less. The mediator can make their reformulation shorter if a party repeats themselves.

Constant Interruption and Cacophony

Many strategies exist for mediators.

- *Strategy 1: Let the parties vent* – A moment of cacophony invites the release of emotions and internal tensions, as in a catharsis. The parties uncover for one another (and the mediator) what lies at the roots of the conflict. Sometimes it is preferable to respect this time of venting with the idea that the parties will tire themselves out and will themselves return to mutual listening.

Thirty minutes of tension … as a pattern

During the first mediation session, a couple starts by engaging in violent exchanges. The co-mediators explore all the paths that they know to moderate them and engage in an alternating dialogue where each side can hear the other side. Wasted effort. The couple continues to yell at one another. At the end of half an hour, things calm down, and the mediators can start the exchanges. At the following meeting, to the surprise of the mediators, persuaded that the dialogue would resume where it left off, the phenomenon is reproduced: 30 minutes of yelling, then calm. It continues like this for every session, as if this exchange, simultaneously emotional and violent, marked a necessary ritual, each side only agreeing to listen to the other side after having vented.

- *Strategy 2: Make a diversion while leaving the parties to their cacophony* – After a few minutes, the mediator gets up, looks around the room, and even looks out the window. Without saying a word, but unambiguously, they make known their disinterest in the parties' behavior. After some time, the parties will take notice, worry about it, and turn toward the mediator, who will be able to resume the course of mediation. The message has been received. This approach requires composure and self-mastery.

- *Strategy 3: Propose a break* – To mitigate tensions, proposing a break is a classic strategy, especially if the immediate environment offers the possibility of taking a walk or getting a breath of fresh air. In 1996, during the Oslo process, by which the Norwegians facilitated secret meetings between the Israelis and the Palestinians, the Norwegian secret service rented manors around the capital of Norway with gardens where both delegations could get some air when tensions mounted, before going back to talks.

- *Strategy 4: Resolutely intervene among the parties,* by making a concise reformulation proving that each side has been heard – *"You didn't receive the merchandise (look at one). And you, following a strike, you couldn't have sent it (look at the other side). Well, how do you envision the next steps?"* In general, the mediator gets the parties' attention and then invites them to resume their alternating dialogue.

- *Strategy 5: Remind the parties of the rule of non-interruption* – The mediator recalls the agreement given by each side on this rule during the introduction. They ask parties to renew their commitment to the rule.

- *Strategy 6: Get up and physically step in between parties* – In the (rare) cases where there is so much negative or violent energy, none of the previous strategies may succeed. This sixth one is radical: the physical gesture of the mediator – done calmly and with determination – imposes a time-out on the parties. The discussion is stopped for a moment. The mediator takes advantage of the calm and implements strategies 3 to 5 in order to restart a balanced exchange. If this approach proves to be impossible, the only solution may be to suspend or stop the session, and sometimes the mediation altogether.

Unyielding Parties

Despite the agreed-upon rules and process, despite the mediator's efforts, the parties stick to their initial positions. Deep down, each party is ready to be open. But faced with the other side, each one succumbs to the spirit of one-upmanship and prefers to remain in the world of excessive anchoring, "*asking too much to earn more,*" which already caused the initial, direct negotiations to fail. When the mediator is confronted with this power struggle, they need to explore the motivations in-depth.

- *Strategy 1: Let it ripen* – There is an inevitable amount of time necessary for the conflict to mature so that it may be resolved. Some parties sometimes will not budge from their positions in order to demonstrate how much they "stuck to their guns." The moment will come when another dynamic will prevail, and the parties will be more open to conflict resolution. The mediator knows how to wait for this time to come.

- *Strategy 2: Explore the reasons for impasse* – The mediator asks any blocking party probing questions (Chapter 6): "*Why would you like that and not something else? Why is it so important for you? What justification determines your choice?*" Chapter 7 reiterates that faced with a similar need (being recognized, obtaining financial means, benefiting from compensation), various solutions exist: it doesn't help to get stuck on one solution only, when many other potential options exist.

- *Strategy 3: Reflect the impasse back to the parties and remind them of their responsibilities* – The mediator serenely declares that if each party continues like this, the mediation will not succeed. Reminding them of their responsibilities, the mediator asks: *"What do you propose to get out of this impasse?"*

- *Strategy 4: Invite the parties to reflect on the consequences of mediation failure* – The mediator is patient with the parties up to a point, where they might need to ask a tough question: *"What will happen for each of you if this mediation doesn't succeed?"* In this way, they invite parties to lucidly evaluate their solution away from the mediation table. In general, parties engage in mediation precisely because their alternatives to mediation are not satisfying – pursuing war, conflict, strike, disputes, waiting many years for a court decision, losing control in an arbitration, etc. This absence of a promising perspective offers the mediator a powerful argument to get the parties back on track. Certainly, they reserve the right to not follow through with the mediation, but with an understanding of the real-world consequences. This is why at some point the mediator needs to be explicit about the risks of no agreement, if necessary, by inviting parties to speak with their lawyers, consultants, experts, family, and friends about the prospects outside mediation.

Personal Attacks among Parties

Personal attacks are frequent. The conflict demonizes the other side, who is viewed as guilty, irresponsible, unfair, etc. It is for this very reason that the parties find themselves in mediation. Imagine one party attributing full blame to the other and launching insults and all forms of personal attacks, including on the other's identity, culture, organization, affiliations, etc. (*"You are all …"*). Some people will not react to these attacks: they know that, in the heat of the conflict, it proves to be a form of release. On the contrary, for others, these attacks leave a deep mark and accentuate the conflict: *"See how they talk to me. They should apologize."* The difficulty is all the more significant when the attack is not subtly formulated (*"On this invoice, there was an accounting problem, right?"*), but generalized (*"You are all liars!"*), making the other lose face in front of everyone. Even if a party may say nothing on the spot, they may carry with them a lot of resentment, which will not help the mediation that follows.

Some strategies anticipate and immediately deal with these types of attacks:

- *Strategy 1: Remind the parties of their agreement on the rule of mutual respect, or this rule's redefinition* – The mediator reminds the parties that they agreed to the principle that everyone can say everything that is on their mind – with the caveat of being respectful. If necessary, with the parties' help, the mediator defines more precisely what respect looks like in the current situation.

- *Strategy 2: Question the use of certain terms by refocusing on the problem* – As soon as a party finishes their sentence, the mediator highlights the precise word employed. Instead of reproaching the party, the mediator asks: *"You used the term 'dishonest.' What events impelled you to use this particular word?"* By inviting the party to explain their motivation in using this term, sometimes a past upsetting action emerges that explains the insult. The mediator tries to clarify it: *"If I understand you well, according to you, contrary to the contract signed a year ago, the fact of discovering an unforeseen 20% increase on the invoice for the purchase of 145 tons of ..., is considered as inadmissible."* If the mediator restates the complaint well (reframing a personal attack as an inquiry about the underlying problem), the party will confirm it: *"That's right."* The mediator then gets an acknowledgment of this explanation: *"Thus, the problem is about discovering an increase of 20% that seems unacceptable to you, and not that Mr. X would be dishonest. Is that right?"* The "accusing" party, satisfied that the mediator has understood the cause of their past sentiment, will often confirm that the present word used was due to irritation about a particular fact. The work thus resumes deep down with the other side, who is no longer *"dishonest"* and stigmatized as such, but someone who *"had increased the prices without warning."*

- *Strategy 3: Use the "I" message* – Either during the introduction or at a critical moment during the mediation, the mediator invites each side to start their sentences with "I" or "we," rather than "you" (Chapters 5 and 6). Expressing one's motivations and perceptions in this way reduces blame on the other party. The messages become more audible for the other side; the most difficult things to hear remain articulated, but without accusatory language.

Personal Blame on the Mediator's Performance

The attacks sometimes turn against the mediator, who is seen as "incompetent," "partial," "neglecting my problem," "listening to the other side more than me," "looking to impose their solution," etc. Yet, the mediator thinks that they are doing just fine. Well intended, they feel that they are applying their methods and principles, with impartiality and neutrality. They have been attentive to, and have avoided, as much as possible, the pitfalls of the instinctive behaviors mentioned above. Still, there is a difference in perceptions between how the mediator evaluates their performance and how it is viewed by one or both of the parties.

Faced with a personal attack of this type, the pitfall to avoid, as we recalled, is … to defend oneself: *"No, I haven't been partial. You are mistaken, I didn't cut you short. I looked at you and listened to you as much as to the other side."* With this retort, the mediator loses some of their standing and risks alienating themselves from the parties even further. Here are six strategies the mediator can follow to get themselves out of this uncomfortable situation:

- *Strategy 1: Question in order to understand* – Faced with an accusation, it is more valuable to respond with an inquiry: *"Could you please say more about what makes you say that?"* One or two questions allow for understanding the party's perception. Knowing the source of the attack, the mediator is able to better respond by using the following strategies.

- *Strategy 2: Recognize the behavior in question* – If the reasons for the attack originate in a specific event or in particular remarks by the mediator, nothing is served by denying it. It is more valuable to recognize it, invoke their good faith, and apologize. If, on the other hand, the reality perceived by the mediator is different, the following strategies are available:

- *Strategy 3: Say that you don't have any memory of that, but it is possible the party could have observed it or perceived it that way.*

- *Strategy 4: Recall that it wasn't your intention to …* (take sides, etc.).

- *Strategy 5: Ensure that in the following mediation you will be particularly attentive to …*

- *Strategy 6: Ask the parties, if they ever have this feeling again, to immediately let you know.*

Bound thereby with genuine sincerity, these strategies contribute to reestablishing trust between the mediator and the parties.

A Party Threatens to Leave

How should the mediator react when one of the parties announces that they are going to leave the mediation table, or even starts to act on it, collecting their belongings, and gets up to leave the room?

- *Strategy 1: Question in order to understand* – Inquire: *"You wish to leave. Why?"*

- *Strategy 2: Let them leave* – Certain mediators do it, because a party's self-determination is a fundamental principle (Chapter 3). But this approach leads to further difficulties: we don't know why the person left, nor if they will come back, or when. Other strategies affirm this freedom while facilitating, if possible, the continuation of interactions.

- *Strategy 3: Include a preventative rule in the introduction* – The mediator can be explicit about the possibility of leaving the mediation from the get-go: *"Each side can leave mediation at any moment, provided they explain why they wish to leave."*

- *Strategy 4: Invite the party to explain why they wish to leave,* even if they are already in the hallway. This approach works in front of the party or, better, in private with the mediator (in the hallway, for example). If the party is reassured, they may come back. Upon returning to the room, the mediator asks them to describe their perception to the other party or does so themselves if the party has requested it. Finally, it is possible that the party announces a need that the mediator cannot significantly address (other urgency, tiredness, …). In this case, the best course of action is to convene a new meeting, with the other party's agreement.

- *Strategy 5: Commit as a mediator and/or make the parties commit to respecting a party's requests to avoid stopping the mediation* – For example, even if a party wishes to leave, they may agree to stay and to continue the exchanges if there is a mutual commitment of respect, if the parties speed up the process to get to solutions, and/or if the other party brings their boss to the mediation table, etc. Let's also note that threatening to leave the room is sometimes just a negotiation tactic to put pressure on the other side.

- *Strategy 6: Allow the party to explain themselves in a private meeting* – In a head-to-head meeting, the mediator can more easily deal with the question, either to understand the party's legitimate concern (and get back to strategy 5), or to explain to the party who wants to leave that this type of behavior cannot be indulged and might lead to the end of the mediation itself.

Strong Emotions

How to deal with an explosion of anger, sadness, or despair? When one of the parties bursts into tears? Some mediators find it difficult to manage strong emotions. For example, some lawyers have told us that mediation should not leave room for emotions; other corporate mediators have stated that in business, "there are no feelings." We beg to differ. In mediation, emotions count in many ways:

- Emotions can be *sincere* and need recognition by the mediator and the parties.

- Emotions can be *overwhelming* and sincere, engulfing the mediator as well as the parties in the gravity of the moment.

- Emotions can also be *fake* and/or deliberately amplified: parties play with them to inspire pity, seduce, manipulate, dramatize, and try to get what they want.

Two strategies can be helpful.

- *Strategy 1: Welcome the emotions and prudently name them* – The mediator invites a party to confirm their perception: *"I have the impression of a deep sadness after the factory's closure. It seems painful for you. The damage caused has created a lot of anger. Is that right?"* This rephrasing, reflection on perceived feelings, and their acknowledgment help the party to progressively deal with them. But it doesn't suffice to simply name them. The mediator needs to accompany the party as the next strategy suggests.

- *Strategy 2: Allow for time to let emotions flow before initiating problem-solving* – Experience teaches us that in the majority of cases, emotions can only be managed once they have been welcomed and expressed. A human being is not a machine and emotions need to be expressed, which takes some time. Only when a party feels calmer is it possible to resume problem-solving.

Stalling Tactics

A party looks to gain time rather than find a solution. They manipulate both the mediator and the other party to strengthen their position, prepare for a departure abroad, organize their insolvency, etc. Here again, the mediator needs to test their suspicions rather than making assumptions.

- *Strategy 1: Recall the commitments made during the introduction* – The principle of self-determination includes the willingness to give a fair chance to mediation. In a joint session, a mediator can remind both parties of their commitment, without targeting either one of them. This reminder serves as an indirect warning. If it doesn't suffice, strategy 2 can be tried.

- *Strategy 2: Use a private meeting to communicate* – The mediator can gently bring up some facts they have noticed and ask a party to elaborate on them. According to the party's response, the mediator will take note of the misunderstanding, propose changes in behaviors, or put an end to the mediation. In any case, the party who tries to stall now knows that the mediator is aware of the issue and may bring it up again, if necessary.

A Party in Conflict with Themselves

How to proceed when a party, oscillating between contradictory needs, cannot reach a decision? Some people experience a form of inner conflict that prevents them from taking a stand. In family mediation, for example, just at the moment when exchanges are ripe for closure to settle the divorce terms, comes an inner voice that murmurs: *"No, can't we still try again to be together?"* The mediation is then reoriented on prolonging a shared life. And, at the moment of success, comes the other side's inner voice: *"It is too late. That will not work … We must stop."* What prolongs mediation is no longer so much the conflict between parties, but the parties' *inner conflicts.* They are torn internally. This situation also happens within an organization, or in a group, that is composed of sub-groups, in which case *internal* mediation may also be required before they can agree with the other side. In this spirit, three strategies are possible.

- *Strategy 1: Suspend the mediation until the mandates are clarified* – The mediator gives the party time to arrive at an internal decision. For example, they may need to consult their principal, so that their mandate and constraints are clear. The objective is that both the parties and their principals recommit to mediation until an agreement is reached, without the party questioning whether or not they have the capacity to agree.

- *Strategy 2: Invite the person, group, or organization to a private meeting* – The mediator proposes that the parties reach an internal agreement on the choice of options first before exchanging views with the other party.

- *Strategy 3: The same as above, with the mediator playing the role of internal mediator for the party* – With everyone's agreement, the mediator helps extract preferential choices and build the concerned party's inner consensus. The mediator extends their mission and applies the same methods of questioning, of motivation search, and problem-solving with each party internally.

An Absent Party or Stakeholder

Two scenarios are prevalent. *One, a specialist is absent from mediation:* a lawyer, insurance company representative, expert, or technician. Parties exploit the absence of the expert's opinion to impose their own solutions on the other.

- *Strategy 1: Adjourn to invite the absentee* to a mediation session or obtain a written opinion.

- *Strategy 2: Invite the parties to think of safe solutions* that reduce the risks as much as possible for both parties. Parties can try to come up with many different scenarios, in anticipation of the expert's opinion. If necessary, the mediator can plan for extra meetings with the experts, once they become available again, to evaluate the situation.

Defective machines or incompetent local technicians?

Some machine tools, imported in a significant quantity from abroad, do not work with the expected output (at only 75% performance). The manufacturer attributes the blame to the buyer: the local technicians are not competent enough to use them correctly. The buyer attributes the defect to the manufacturer: his technicians were competent, but the machines were defective. An independent expert's assessment could have been considered but would involve stopping the manufacturing process and add the costs of travel and a hotel for a team of experts, not to mention contingency fees or the uncertainty as to who will be deemed responsible for the defects. After mediation, the parties agreed to a two-week test:

- A seller's technician would stay in the buyer's country where the machines are installed, in order to observe and assist the local technicians in the use of machine tools, all the while confirming the output.

- If, at the end of two weeks, the machine tools maintained with at least a 95% performance, the technician would leave, and the buyer would pay the remaining amount for the tools.

- If not, the manufacturer agrees to take the machine tools back to its country of export and replace them.

In the second scenario, the parties represent principals – members of an association, union ("the base"), a group of young people in conflict with another, an administrative board – and it often happens that the authorized representatives find themselves trapped by the fact that the principals – who are not directly involved in the mediation process – reject the possible agreement. This rejection by the real decision-makers also backfires on the mediator. To anticipate this problem, the mediator has many additional strategies:

- *Strategy 3: During the pre-mediation stage, make sure it is clear who decides* – In their preparation, the mediator establishes the cartography of the real decision-makers. Who are they? How will they decide? By majority? Unanimously?

- *Strategy 4: Before or during mediation, the mediator obtains agreement from the principals to attend* – When necessary, for example, as the mediation comes close to a successful end, the final decision-makers are invited to participate in the mediation sessions.

- *Strategy 5: Invite parties to keep their principals in the loop* – To facilitate this phase of reporting back, it is important to let parties provide principals with information on a regular basis throughout the process. To do so, the mediator invites the parties to take advantage of pauses and adjournments to reach out to their principals and keep them in the loop.

- *Strategy 6: The mediator stays in direct contact with the principals* – With the parties' agreement, and by getting an exemption from the confidentiality clause, the mediator contacts the principals to report, in a balanced and exact manner, on how the discussions are progressing.

- *Strategy 7: Use the one-text procedure to report to principals* – After one or many sessions, the mediator produces a single text with the help of the representatives in order to inform their respective principals.

Lack or Absence of Dialogue among the Parties

We distinguish between absence at a physical meeting and the lasting absence of direct dialogue even during a meeting.

The Parties Refuse to Physically Meet One Another

The motives for not wanting to see each other are diverse: a political ban to not meet "the enemy," impossibility of meeting because of internal pressure, lack of recognition or illegality of one of the parties, or physical barriers, such as geographic distance, for example. De facto, the dialogue only exists through the mediator, who is authorized to transmit information between parties. In this shuttle diplomacy, the mediator leverages several possible strategies.

- *Strategy 1: Shuttle between the parties until the end of mediation* – The mediator cancels joint meetings, because the parties no longer want to attend them and probably do not want a relationship. The mediator travels back and forth between the parties until an agreement on the problem is found – or not.

- *Strategy 2: Shuttle until a return to direct relations* – The mediator works on the relationship and on mutual perceptions, until each side again accepts to meet the other and discuss with them. In addition, by also focusing on the problem, the mediator makes positive moves, which can yield some limited but unexpected results, and thus help renew direct contact in the mediator's presence.

- *Strategy 3: Invite the parties to an informal meeting* – When an official meeting, centered on the problem, is impossible, informal contact is sometimes possible. A cocktail, meal, colloquium, seminar, ceremony, or even a festive occasion can offer a variety of opportunities for impromptu meetings, during which the relationship resumes, preparing the field for later, in-depth work on the problem.

The CEO and the union leader at a restaurant

During a prolonged strike in France, the appointed and accepted mediator noted that the CEO and the leader of the majority trade union had never met one another face to face. He proposed to them – for the first meeting – to have dinner in a little-known restaurant in a remote neighborhood, where journalists would be avoided. At the end of the meal, each side shared with the other something like *"I had never met you before, but what I learned today persuaded me that maybe we can work with each other toward an agreement."* Mediation was pursued and an agreement found.

- *Strategy 4: Organize a secret meeting* – Sometimes, parties refuse to meet one another because they don't want anyone to know that they have been in contact with each other, notably their respective constituencies or the general public, etc. However, they will often agree to meet secretly – like in the aforementioned Oslo process between Israelis and Palestinians.

The Parties Ignore One Another during the Mediation Sessions

Even if the parties are brought together in the same room, it can be difficult for them to reestablish a working relationship. For example, after a few hours of sessions, the parties are still neither talking to, nor looking at, one another. They address only the mediator. This situation is all the more problematic in cases where the parties (families, neighbors, colleagues, associates, housemates or co-owners, leaders, neighboring countries) need to continue the relationship. As a preventative measure, the mediator can adjust the space so that each side can easily address the other as much as the mediator (Chapter 4).

- *Strategy 1: Invite the parties to turn toward one another* – After each side has been heard, the mediator invites the parties to speak to each other, ask questions, and respond to the other's questions. *"Without a doubt, you have some questions to ask one another. Feel free to do so and respond to them."* The mediator then backs away, becoming a witness to the resumption of dialogue, while continuing to ensure the ground rules of listening and respect.

- *Strategy 2: Invite the parties to address only each other* – Once both parties can explain themselves well and be understood, the mediator, if they sense that the moment is ripe, can invite one party (and then the other) to speak to the other side directly: *"Could you tell Mrs. H …?"* Adding: *"by looking at her, rather than me …"* Sometimes one of the parties will do it halfway by using the third person: *"I told* him *that* he *could accept these works of restoration if we postponed them for some months, no?"* The mediator can invite more direct remarks: *"Could you say it to him directly? 'You could agree to …'"* Of course, inviting does not mean obliging. The mediator will not insist but knows that the more the parties are able to directly address each other, the more they are ready to resolve their conflict.

- *Strategy 3: Invite the parties to remind themselves of the past when they got along with the other and truly appreciated each other* – Conflict is such that we tend to only see what we do not like in the other. We omit the positive attributes of the person to focus only on the negative ones, which does not contribute to establishing a relationship, or even maintaining an exchange. Yet, in reality, when there is a past, most likely, there have been good moments or qualities that we enjoyed. Recalling these moments introduces much-needed warmth into the present relationship. Suddenly, the face of the other opens up, their gaze spontaneously changes direction, and looks toward the other. The mediator can then gently come back to the conflict at hand by asking parties to keep these memories alive during the discussions.

*

The group of pitfalls mentioned here led to some antidotes, which are certainly not foolproof, but can heighten both the mediator's expertise and their human qualities. The mediator is a human being just like the rest of us; they are an "other," just like one party is an "other" to the other party. In this interaction among "others," the mediator calls upon the similarity of each "other" in order to resolve the disagreement. The mediator also accepts their own limitations, without claiming to be all-powerful. They are not. Indeed, this is where their strength lies, and which explains why the parties agree to trust them.

These diverse pitfalls and the strategies to surmount them can feed the reflection of both the parties and the mediator. In any difficulty, the mediator, an artisan of human relationships, employs their art and technique of mediation. But there isn't only one way of proceeding. Any party can, during any moment of the process, suggest to the mediator a different, more preferable approach and thus contribute to the mediation's success. After all, a mediation process is co-created by the mediator and the parties. That everyone fully participates in the mediation can only favor each side's contribution to this endeavor of joint problem-solving.

Finally, if a particular obstacle proves to be insurmountable, and the mediation doesn't succeed: is it a failure? For the parties? For the mediator? For everyone? We believe not, neither for one side nor for the other. For the parties, a mediation that doesn't lead to an agreement is not without any results. Indeed, there may have been many positive elements, including information exchange, mutual listening, disagreement analysis, examination of possibilities, and the resumption of a relationship. They are all positive aspects that can be used to prepare the ground for the success of a fresh attempt at mediation or perhaps even at a direct negotiation. Hence, the importance of the mediator's concluding comments, during which the "micro-agreements" can be mentioned. The single most important thing is that the mediator and – when possible – the parties should be able say to themselves: *"We did everything we could."*

CONCLUSION: AN ETHICAL PERSPECTIVE AND QUESTIONING

Packed with methods and practical guidelines, our book is intended as a daily companion for anyone involved in mediation. But mediation cannot be reduced to technical practices, however effective they may be, at the risk of losing sight of its purpose. What should we think of the mediator who, concerned about technically *doing well*, forgets the fundamental aims of mediation – including those that contribute to *doing good*? Even if we favored a methodological approach, the reader will have discerned a philosophy of responsibility underlying the methods. It is founded on human values and ethics, and it is important for us to consider them one last time.

This conclusion thus takes philosophical questioning seriously. A first initial questioning is about people and relationships; it lays the foundation for a second level of questioning, on the problems to be solved in the dispute. By the relevance and perspicacity of their questioning and its correlate, listening, the mediator reveals their own ethics, embodied in their actions and in what they bring to the parties. This questioning constitutes an attempt to establish the *mediator as an ethical model* (Lempereur 2003c, 2014b).

Questioning: The Philosophical Foundation of the Mediator's Actions

Let us explore the various forms of questioning and its power as the foundation of the mediator's actions.

The Mediator and the Power of Self-Questioning

Socrates sets the first recommendation: "Know thyself." While seeking the purpose of their actions, the mediator needs to question their art, and to never stop listening to their inner voice. Acting otherwise would be risky. Asking questions about yourself as a mediator is a way to favor a reflective approach to practices: "I doubt, therefore *I am* a mediator." This Cartesian doubt helps to keep at bay a blind trust in personal instincts and routines; ongoing questioning promotes critical thinking and seeks more relevant answers. One is not born a mediator; one becomes one through such lively self-questioning. Of course, some of us have natural predispositions to help bring peace between parties in conflict, but even the best of us make mistakes at times; hence the importance of introspection, looking for more adequate ideas of practice thanks to questioning.

The question of self is illuminated by *the other*. Which other? *First,* there is the other within oneself: the mediator engages in a dialogue with their inner voice; they never stop wondering how to do a better job. They become aware that perhaps a particular approach that they have been trying for a while without the anticipated results needs a tweak: "*This does not seem to work. What if I tried something else?*" Mediators need to heighten their awareness and their questioning if they feel they become agitated internally, or lose their cool. They can only be effective as peacemakers if they are at peace with themselves and remain a calm eye in the storm (Lempereur and Willer 2016; Lempereur 2019).

Second, there are the concrete others in front of the mediators, the most important ones, i.e. the parties, who guide the mediators in their questioning endeavor. A mediator learns to silence their inner voice in order to be fully available to listen to the parties. They take in what they sense and hear; they know how to balance the dialogue, step back, and question their own inner impressions and biases, which at times disturb their attention. For if the mediator listens to themselves too much, they will lose the focus on this party here and now. No one can be a responsible mediator without inviting the parties to stimulate questioning in themselves; the parties contribute significantly to encouraging such questioning. Through their engagement with the parties, mediators end up reviewing in their heads what works in their practice and what does not. The parties and the context surrounding them engage them in a methodical triage. All the self-questioning that is going on within the mediator and that often is not even noticeable by the parties serves the mediation process. For a time, in session, these parties in conflict are "a little part of the mediator" and thus of the mediator's questioning. On the one hand, these parties trust the mediator and allow themselves to be guided, which reduces the mediator's self-doubts. On the other hand, the parties have doubts themselves about whether mediation is working and therefore lead the mediator to doubt themselves too. There are moments when the parties have confidence in the mediator and other times when they feel discouraged and wonder if this "neutral other" is going to help them resolve their conflict or not. Mediators often feel and share the parties' doubts, which by contagion may be so overwhelming that it could lead to some unhelpful questioning. This is where trusting the power of methods becomes so important, because it can help overcome both the parties' and the mediator's confusion and doubts, and re-channel a questioning that proves self-defeating. Methods are used to question the questioning itself, to counter it in order to seek answers, and to move forward.

Third, mediators have another group of questioners, their peers, *the other mediators*. For example, in co-mediation, each neutral sees the other practicing, and vice versa. Once the session ends, the mediators debrief what happened, share their mutual observations, raise new questions on why certain methods were used and not others, how they worked or not, and give each other advice. There is a mutual questioning at work that is directed toward a better performance next time.

Fourth, others who question mediators emanate from *professional organizations* – mediation associations and institutions – which set ethical or deontological guidelines, update promising practices, and dismiss problematic ones. Mediators and experts meet and – after discussions where everyone questions everyone else, reviews, criticizes, weighs, and refines – come up with consensual answers that future practice can put to the test. Colloquiums, seminars, courses, reports, works, and articles on mediation offer as many opportunities for mediators to engage in this broad mutual questioning, while helping to build, socialize, institutionalize, and professionalize a mediation community toward the common good.

The mediator is thus empowered by both self-questioning and a questioning that is activated by many others. This multifold questioning, by oneself and others, strengthens the mediator. In this way, the mediator builds up a diversity of approaches and of adaptable methods, always leaving the door open for more relevant methods of mediating.

The Mediator and the Power of Questioning the Other

Questioning is more than just a technique in mediation. It builds on a general philosophy (Meyer 1995) and on a philosophy of negotiation (Lempereur 1990, 1995, 2006, 2009a, 2011d). If the mediator becomes more effective through a deeper understanding of self by questioning, the same applies to the parties. The way the mediator questions the parties will impact them and, possibly, help them to see differently and more clearly the *question of themselves* and *of the other* (Lempereur 2009b).

If the mediator takes their time to analyze the past with the parties, it is because they need to *deeply question each party so that the parties question themselves and their views of the other party.* The more the mediator asks probing questions, the more the parties respond, and the more the mediator reformulates and questions again. As the parties provide more responses and feel they are getting a hearing, they also feel more in charge of their conflict and self-understanding, which in turn allows them to be able to handle even more questions, especially those on their deep motivations and needs.

A party in conflict has above all withdrawn into themselves, in their certainties and biases where questioning vanishes and is replaced by preconceived ideas and generalizations in which "the other" is labeled and underestimated, while the self tends to be overestimated (Lempereur 2004). In a bitter conflict, a party refuses to let the other ask them questions, because they perceive such questions not as simple inquiries but as a calling into question their identity. These ongoing perceptions of being wrongly challenged by the other as a human being are dominant; they become so unacceptable that one can no longer bear the other, to the point that the natural question/answer relationship between two human beings fades away and is set aside.

In this entangled forest, the clearing of mediation re-creates the possibility of real human exchanges and recomposition. We call on the mediator, who knows how to renew a cycle of mutual questioning. Through their intervention, the mediator keeps this questioning non-invasive and peaceful, because they are at peace with themselves (Lempereur 2019). Their questioning is reassuring, but also deep and life changing. Most parties often enter into mediation secretly hoping that the other party will change and question themselves: thanks to the mediator's intervention, each party believes that the other party will be shaken in their certainties and prejudices and admit their wrongdoings (Friedman 2017). Each party starts mediation with the feeling of being right, of having all the good reasons on their side, all the answers, including the solution to the problem. Each party thinks that mediation will leave them intact and that, as if by magic, the other party will recognize them for "having always been right" from the beginning. However, mediation allows another miracle: to find *oneself* first and then, maybe, to find *the other* again.

Finding oneself as a party is essential to overcome a conflict. This is because "I" believe the other party denies me and challenges me in an unbearable way. Rediscovering my humanity, through the benevolent gaze of a gentle other, the third party, is first of all finding a listening ear, a person who questions me not to judge or condemn me, but to try to understand what is important to me. And then a transformation often occurs. As soon as this someone else who is foreign to our conflict listens to me, I suddenly feel ready to listen to the other. In the same way I was comfortable as the mediator was asking me questions, I start relaxing as they put questions to the other party. I listen to all these questions (the ones the mediator asks me and the ones they ask the other side) and, through this dialectic, I hear those questions of my inner voice again. I am rediscovering the complexity that constitutes my inner being and that of the other. I hear myself saying, through my inner voice, that maybe things were more complicated than I thought. I admit to myself that all my actions were probably not free of errors either, that on a particular point I may have contributed to the escalation of the conflict.

I start understanding better and questioning myself deeply and my early views too. Strengthened by the mediator, my identity is able to move off-center: it accepts centrifugal forces without shaking or being overwhelmed by negative emotions. The mediator, who does not judge me but listens to me, makes sure I can make my own judgments, rediscover my ambivalent self. I am ready to analyze my actions without fear of losing myself, of losing face.

What I was saying to myself, in my head, just a few minutes ago, I heard myself saying to the mediator. Why am I being so candid? It is because I am no longer afraid because this space of "trialogue" has put me at ease. Taking risks is now possible. Certain points that I deemed important have been revealed, and our understanding of them has been deepened by the mediator's questioning. Beyond the superficial problems, "my" mediator has also helped me to voice my feelings, values, and needs; to externalize them. I feel validated, so much so that I am able to see the other in a new light. Once I come out of my shell, the other does the same; I am reassured, because what I hoped would happen is starting to take shape: the other is changing (and so am I). The other recognizes some of their errors and some of my reasons, and I start to feel a certain proximity to them. I am surprised to want to recognize something in them as well and, even if I am not sure what it is, the path is now before us. Their questions have become mine and mine theirs. We are listening to each other as if we found once again what linked us together. We are recomposing.

The challenge is to *find the other once again*, to find a place for the other party in myself. The mediator's questioning allows both of us to exchange questions and responses. The prudent and hesitant dynamic, which occurred at the start of mediation, has now accelerated, grown, and settled into a mutual recognition of identities and needs. Yes, I hear the other, and yes, I have the impression that the other hears me. Yes, I have a glimpse of what is happening and also of the conflict which happened. Finding the other is to *rejoice* in the desire to ask questions once again and resolve enigmas with the other, in their presence. I discover that the conflict is not simply about something but about someone; in fact, us. It is *relational* and not simply *transactional* (Lempereur 2018).

As long as there were no more links between us, it seemed impossible to come up with solutions to our problems. The mediation has revealed – surprisingly – that I am part of the problem and that the other is part of the solution: the main issue then is us. The mediator's patient questioning, in the phase "from the past to the present," builds the conditions for the *return of the other in me, and of me in the other*. Once the potential of a relationship is rediscovered, even if it is tenuous, the solution to the problems is facilitated. Here, the mediator employs all their energy to work on solving the problems.

The Mediator and the Power of Problem-Solving

It is undeniable that the mediator, through their questioning, helps the parties to rediscover *themselves* and *each other*. Nevertheless, this subjective finding is not enough. Détente does not mean agreement. It is also necessary to help the parties to find an objective way to address the problems they are confronted with, because behind the people in conflict are the objects of conflict. Demands are expressed on both sides, and both expect that future solutions will be optimal for them. This question of supply and demand is partly economic (Lempereur 2015b; Lempereur and Pekar 2017). For this negotiation, it is necessary to find the right balance in the exchange, but the mediator discovers that this question is both psychological and methodological. It is psychological to the extent that the parties, whenever challenged, tend to quickly return to conflictual forms of problem-solving, i.e. to positional bargaining where they are inflexible on their initial extreme requests (Lempereur 2003a). Each claims without questioning that "their" solution is the best, and that the other party has to accept it. At the same time, they tend to radically reject any proposal coming from the other party, questioning their relevance and legitimacy. We thus risk becoming bogged down in entrenched logic and returning to the starting point before mediation, where one party's only truth was to prevail over the other's, without questioning their own position.

Once again, reigniting questioning is the method used to overcome this positional dilemma. In the "present to future" phase, the mediator questions an instinctive approach to problem-solving, which would be satisfied with a mutually exclusive choice between two extreme solutions – take it or leave it – which would frustrate one or the other; or with a compromise "in the middle." In order not to lose the benefit of the mutual recognition of needs that took place, the mediator pursues the complex achievements of the first phase, and invites the parties, strengthened by a renewed relationship, to seek a solution that suits both parties. The mediator's questioning also aims at opening what is closed, at provoking flexibility and multiplicity where rigidity and uniqueness would otherwise prevail. "Thinking-out-of-the-box" techniques, inspiring creativity and value creation, such as brainstorming, contribute to it. Of course, some of the invented solutions will need to be questioned, i.e. evaluated, or excluded; and some potential pitfalls that question the overall mediation process will have to be overcome along the way, but from one questioning to the next, it is possible that an agreement will emerge. Whereas each party initially saw only their own solutions as the sole answer, together, with the mediator's help, because the parties question each other, try and fail, and assimilate, they still seek new solutions. They are more likely to find a shared solution, taking into account the other in the equation and responding to a diversity of variables. This is the greatness of mediation, to make the unlikely possible through an ongoing questioning that is now transferred to problem-solving.

As a consequence, through the power of questioning, the mediator often accomplishes two objectives: *the parties find each other* and *they find their own solution*. Sometimes a little less may be accomplished, but even here the mediation has not failed because the mediation process has been able to embed active questioning in the workings of the parties in order to relink people and things.

In a nutshell, the mediator has taken questions about themselves and others seriously. In order to be successful in their mission, they put in their best efforts to ensure that the parties engaged in questioning and problem-solving with the same level of dedication. Little by little, the mediator also revealed a powerful ethical model (Lempereur 2021).

The Mediator as a Powerful Ethical Model

To understand the ethics of mediation, it is useful to learn from the mediator's practical actions and steer clear of intellectual abstractions. Mediation ethics is the combination of both the mediator's and the parties' behaviors, but our hypothesis is that the parties' ethics can be shaped by the mediator's adequate actions rather than be already present prior to mediation. For this reason, we may need to highlight the possible foundations that the mediator uses to build their ethics.

The mediator seems to be driven by two ethical objectives. It matters to them that the parties, on the one hand, grasp the mediator's authentic ethical concern and, on the other hand, use it in return as a source of inspiration and a lever for their own actions. In sum, a successful neutrality would drive *an ethics of transfer* from the mediator toward the parties.

Ethics of Responsibility Toward Both Parties

At first glance, mediation is based on an *ethics of consequences*, i.e. what Weber (1919) calls an ethics of responsibility, because beyond intentions, however laudable they may be, the mediator needs to first of all be useful in their interventions from the standpoint of the future of the parties. They care less about their intentions than what they deliver. The Hippocratic oath that doctors take before practicing their profession may provide, by analogy, many necessary elements for the ethics of the mediator, a sort of "doctor of conflicts":

> The goal of medicine is to be useful to the patients or at least to not harm them. To achieve this goal, the doctor should have, in addition to innate qualities, a training initiated from childhood, which should be not only theoretical, but also practical. In addition to judgment and skills, the doctor must combine moral qualities: first self-sacrifice, ("the doctor, in the misfortunes of others, reaps for themselves the sorrows"), then refusal of vain glory through unnecessarily spectacular practices, and finally decent conduct and discretion about what they have heard and seen during their visits. [...] Doctors look for the collaboration of the patient and try to be pleasant to the extent that it isn't contrary to their interest (*Medicus gratiosus*). (Jouanna 1995, p. 448).

This quote is easily transposable to the mediator: mediation is conceived as a medicine to cure (often pathological) relations of misunderstanding between people. The mediator has to give relief to the parties as much as possible and heal a dispute that could not be resolved through direct negotiation.

In that respect, the mediator ultimately does not really care about an *ethics of intentions* based on questions such as: Are the mediator's intentions pure? Do they mean well? Rather, they look for satisfying answers to the following questions: Is the mediator perceived as ethical? Does the mediator succeed in appearing as such to both parties, in joint or private meetings? Does the mediator's intervention add value compared to the previous difficult direct negotiation between the parties? Do they not harm them ("do no harm" principle)? Is the situation worsened by the mediator's intervention? Beyond the two parties, can the mediator be considered as ethical by the "others," broadly defined?

That is, the parties become the best judges of the mediator's ethics, because the mediator only exists for them, through their profound selflessness. Do the parties see the mediator's concern at work? Do they perceive the meaning, the reconciliatory direction, oriented toward appeasement, a reunion of self with the other? No doubt the mediator doesn't succeed in every undertaking, but like the doctor or the lawyer, the mediator's *obligation of means* requires them to mobilize all the negotiation moves and methods to serve not a patient or a client, but both parties.

Beyond Impartiality and Neutrality

Multipartiality – rather than impartiality – is an ethical corollary for the mediator. Whenever they want to help both parties and solve their problems, the danger is that they become a permanent judge of what is just and unjust, adding their "part" to the already abundant partiality of the parties. In this sense, we would prefer to limit the requirements of the mediator to an *ambipartiality* – as in ambidexterity – focusing on the perspectives of the *two* parties without risking adding a *third*. But the mediator is the indirect trustee of the interests of others and not simply those of the parties. In a divorce mediation, for example, the mediator might invoke the children's interests. In criminal mediation, the interests of law and public order cannot be ignored. Hence, a broad *ambipartiality* imposes itself on the mediator.

In addition, the two parties often nurture two distinct visions of the world, of the facts, and thus of the solution they seek that will resolve their conflict (i.e. their positions). Here, the principle of *neutrality* with respect to the solution is essential, but sometimes impartiality will lead to nothing. Here, it is important to try to seek an optimal solution for the two parties, *an integrative solution* that incorporates both sides, that aims at "adjusting the interests" of all, as Callières (1716) suggested centuries ago.

The question of a multipartial or integrative approach is raised whenever an emerging solution seems to be unjust to one of the parties, who asks the mediator to adjudicate on its legitimacy. The same situation arises when a solution seems unethical to the mediator's inner sense of justice, of equity. This ethical dilemma, worse for the mediator in the latter case, remains the same: to say (at the risk of projecting their values of what is acceptable) or not to say (at the risk of seeming to endorse the unacceptable)? This dilemma challenges, at least in the mediator's inner questioning, the principles of impartiality and neutrality, which no longer appear as absolutes at that point.

Morality: Private Conception Versus Public Order

Even if the mediator strives to appear ethical and to show concern for a just solution, they are not supposed to adapt a moralizing stance. Notably, they avoid imposing their *private conception of morality*.

In any case, by being "with both parties," the mediator tries to place themselves behind a veil of ignorance (in the sense of Rawls [1971]) concerning their personal conception of justice. The mediator does not become the keeper of some higher morality to be enforced on others. At the very least, the mediator urges the parties to obey the law. This is the minimal standard, and the mediator cannot fail to invoke it. Just as a lawyer is obliged to prevent a client from committing a criminal offense, the mediator, in exceptional circumstances, does not invoke their personal morality, but a law of public order that cannot be ignored.

Fortunately, such cases are exceptional. The risk rather relates to a mediator's moralizing temptation that would be led by their private conscience. The trialogue process, involving the mediator, continuously serves a substantive dialogue between two parties, which leads the mediator to set aside their personal ethical conceptions as much as possible. Thus, let's imagine a financial agreement that suits both parties but is unbalanced according to the mediator's sense of justice. As long as the settlement is not violating the law, the mediator has to refrain from imposing their personal evaluation of the situation or their conception of justice. The mediator needs to only ensure that the parties have properly assessed the meaning of this agreement, compared it to their solutions away from mediation, or submitted it for review to their respective principals. Should the parties, after checking, remain in agreement on the agreement as it stands, the mediator's ethics, however well-founded, principled, and well-intentioned they may be, will give way.

Ethical Dilemmas for Three, Two, and One

Beyond compliance with the law, a mediator needs to solve ethical dilemmas in three types of situations: in the presence of both parties; with only one of them being present; and, finally, when negotiating with themselves.

In a *triangular relationship*, the mediator's ethics will express themselves through a continuous concern for both parties and their respective problems. The mediator expresses themselves directly on the ethics of a solution only at those rare moments when they aim to prevent a clear violation of the law.

However, mediators need to beware the temptations offered by *private meetings*, these moments when the mediator feels confident with one of the parties, when everything can be said to each other. Already Montaigne has warned us (Hampton 1995) about liars and dissimulators in *Essays*, that "whence it happens that of the same thing they tell one man that it is this, and another that it is that, giving it several colors" (36B). The mediator runs the risk of misrepresentation, by talking out of both sides of the mouth and thus "being situated both in the middle and on one side of the dialogue." Montaigne is very demanding: "I say nothing to one party that I may not, upon occasion, say to the other, with a slight change in emphasis" (794B), because "I have been very careful that they should neither be deceived in me nor deceive others by me" (791B). In sum, a mediator avoids getting close to one of the parties in such a way that they become their advocate, because then they lose all essential credibility, as well as neutrality and impartiality. Even in the absence of the other party, mediators need to keep the other party's concerns in mind, playing the devil's advocate if necessary, even in private conversations, to maintain their impartiality.

The mediator is left with a last ethical question. When the mediator is *alone*, literally (between sessions) or figuratively (with their conscience, in the presence of one or both parties), their inner voice can become louder and louder, deafeningly dissonant. Their questioning often indicates a major ethical dilemma, not of law, but within their inner self. If the parties consider a particular condition – borderline legal, for example – as essential to the agreement, while the mediator finds it unacceptable from the standpoint of their own views, can they proceed in their mission? The mediator may ask both parties to express their viewpoint on the matter. But what if the parties do not see any problems with such a solution and confirm their agreement? There's nothing for the mediator to do but to explicitly highlight their personal values, acknowledging the fact that they are acting outside what *they see* as the normal scope of a mediator's mandate. If, despite this final attempt, the parties persist in their willingness to implement that solution, the mediator often has only one way out: to withdraw, even if it means looking for a replacement. Fortunately, this case of *ethical withdrawal* is rare and extreme, but it cannot be excluded a priori from the toolkit of mediators.

On Ethics in Mediation

Therefore, the mediator is not so much the one who *states* the ethical rules or denounces their absence, as the one who *embodies* them and strives to empower the parties to do the same. The mediator doesn't lecture others. By their modest, patient, and constant virtue, the mediator inspires the parties to behave in an exemplary manner. The mediator spends little time, if any, pointing out mistakes, but, by using the Socratic method, they lead the parties to discover them by questioning. If errors are found, the mediator facilitates the parties' efforts to move beyond them, and to visualize another future. The mediator implicitly serves as a *model of ethics*.

Indeed, the ethics of mediation is not about prejudices, fixed ideologies, or preconceived conceptions of morality about who is right or wrong. It is first of all about questioning, assisted by listening, on understanding often irreconcilable visions of the world. It is embodied in a dynamic force of responses to be constructed by integrating the legitimate needs of all parties, overcoming the inherent injustice of a persistent conflict to seek a just and equitable solution.

This amounts to an *ethics of communication*. The mediator is meant to serve as a model, as a questioner and listener, because what has brought the parties into mediation, no matter who has initiated it, is often defective communication. The mediator, especially if they have explained the process well at the beginning, ensures responsible communication (Mnookin and Lempereur 2014). Listening isn't simply benevolent, but active. It is coupled with active speaking, where the mediator's words are chosen for their relevance to the questions that the parties are asking themselves (Lempereur and Colson 2004). By implementing this consummate art of communication with their techniques of rapprochement (Lempereur 2012b), the mediator hopes that the parties will do the same: listen and talk to each other better, start to respect each other as human beings, worthy of being heard in turn.

In mediation, successful communication leads to an *ethics of respect for the other*. To use a metaphor, the mediator builds these scaffolds in front of a building ready to collapse and that needs to be restored. Once the work has been successfully done, the building regains its former solidity and once the scaffolding is removed, everything holds together perfectly. *Ethical success is not to say, but to do.* It is not so much seen in the mediator who takes pride in it, as in the parties who magnify it in their actions. It translates into the *joy* of the parties, who could not have imagined beforehand they could ever look again at each other with kind eyes of mutual understanding.

BIBLIOGRAPHY

Allred, K. (2000). Accusations and anger: The role of attributions in conflict and negotiation. In: *The Handbook of Dispute Resolution* (ed. M. Deutsch). San Francisco: Jossey-Bass.

Arrow, K., Mnookin, R.H., Ross, L., Tversky, A., and Wilson, R. (eds.) (1995). *Barriers to Conflict Resolution*. New York: W.W. Norton & Company.

Baril, M. and Dickey, D. (2014). "MED-ARB: The Best of Both Worlds or Just a Limited ADR Option?" Mediate.com.

Baumann, B. (2004), "Écoute et parole actives dans un processus de concertation. Le cas de la Francilienne." *Revue Française de Gestion*, 30 (153), 157–172.

Benharda, I., Brett, J., and Lempereur, A. (2013). "Gender and role in conflict management: Female and male managers as third parties." *Negotiation and Conflict Management Research*, 6 (2), 67–81.

Bensimon, S. and Lempereur, A. (eds.) (2007). *La Médiation. Modes d'Emploi*. Paris: A2C.

Bercovitch, J. and Rubin, J.Z. (1992). *Mediation in International Relations: Multiple Approaches to Conflict Management*. New York: St. Martin's Press.

Bickerman, J. (2018). "Med-Arb: Maybe Not a Better Idea." American Bar Association, www.americanbar.org.

Bierstedt, R. (1954). The problem of authority. In: *Freedom and Control in Modern Society* (eds. M. Berger, T. Abel, and C. Page), 67–81. New York: Octagon Books.

Blohorn-Brenneur, B. (2006). *Justice et Médiation, un Juge du Travail Témoigne*. Paris: Le Cherche Midi.

Bonafé-Schmitt, J.-P. (1998). *La Médiation Pénale en France et aux Etats-Unis*. Paris: LGDJ.

Bonafé-Schmitt, J.-P., Dahan, J., Salzer, J., Souquet, M., and Vouche, J.-P. (1999). *Les Médiations, La Médiation*. Paris: Érès.

Boutros-Ghali, B. (1995). Interview. *Journal du Dimanche*, Jan 8.

Brown, C.J. (2002). "Facilitative Mediation: The Classic Approach Retains its Appeal." www.mediate.com.

Bush, R.A. and Folger, J.P. (2004). *The Promise of Mediation: The Transformative Approach to Conflict*. San Francisco: Jossey-Bass.

Callières, F. de (1716), *De la Manière de Négocier avec les Souverains* (ed. A. Lempereur). Paris: Michel Brunet (2002), Geneva: Droz.

Cardinet, A. (1997). *École et Médiation*. Paris: Érès.

Coleman, J. A. (1997). "Authority, power, leadership: Sociological understandings." *New Theology Review*, 10 (3), 31–44.

Colson, A. (2004). "Gérer la tension entre secret et transparence – Les cas analogues de la négociation et de l'entreprise." *Revue Française de Gestion*, 30 (153), 87–99.

Colson, A. (2007). Secret et transparence à l'égard de tiers en négociation. Contribution à une histoire de la négociation internationale, PhD dissertation. Canterbury: University of Kent Library.

Colson, A., Elgoibar, P., and Marchi, F. (2015). Employee representatives in France: Employers' perceptions and expectations towards improved industrial relations. In: *Promoting Social Dialogue in European Organizations* (ed. M. Euwema et al.), 67–78. London: Springer.

Colson, A. and Lempereur, A. (2011). A bridge to lasting peace: Post-conflict reconciliation and mediation in Burundi and the Democratic Republic of Congo. In: *Mediation in Political Conflicts. Soft Power or Counter Culture?* (ed. J. Faget), 153–169. Oxford: Hart Publishing.

Cooper, C.C. (2003). "Conceptualizing Mediation Use by Patrol Police Officers." San Francisco CA: Center on Juvenile and Criminal Justice, www.cjcj.org.

Curhan, J.R., Elfenbein, H.A., and Eisenkraft, N. (2010). "The objective value of subjective value: A multi-round negotiation study." *Journal of Applied Social Psychology*, 40 (3), 690–709.

De Carlo, L. (2005). "Accepting conflict and experiencing creativity: Teaching 'concertation' using La Francilienne," *Negotiation Journal*, 21(1), 85–103.

De Carlo, L. and Lempereur, A. (1998). *La Francilienne. Manuel du Formateur et CD Rom*. Cergy: ESSEC.

Drucker, P. (2006). *The Effective Executive*. New York: Collins.

Eberle, B. (2008). *SCAMPER: Creative Games and Activities for Imaginative Development*. Waco: Prufrock Press.

Euwema, M. (2019). *Mediation in Collective Labour Conflicts*. London: Springer.

Faget, J. (2010). *Médiations: Les Ateliers Silencieux de la Démocratie*. Paris: Érès.

Fisher, R., Ury, W., and Patton, Bruce (1991). *Getting to Yes: Negotiating Agreement Without Giving In* (2nd ed). New York: Houghton Mifflin.

Fiutak, T. (2009). *Le Médiateur dans l'Arène*. Paris: Érès, with a preface by Jacques Salzer.

French, J.R.P. Jr. and Raven, B.H. (1959). The bases of social power. In *Studies in Social Power* (ed. D. Cartwright), 150–167. Ann Arbor: University of Michigan, Institute for Social Research.

Friedman, G. (2015). *Inside Out: How Conflict Professionals Can Use Self-Reflection to Help Their Clients*. Chicago: American Bar Association.

Friedman, G. (2017). *En Soi vers l'Autre*. Paris: Médias & Médiations.

Friedman, G. and Himmelstein, J. (2009). *Challenging Conflict: Mediation Through Understanding*. Chicago: American Bar Association.

Fruchter, J. (2019). "When Does Evaluative Mediation Cross the Line from Neutral Analysis to Legal Advice ?" New York: Merge Mediation Group, www.jdsupra.com.

Gamson, W. (2000). *SIMSOC. Simulated Society. Participant's Manual*. New York: The Free Press.

Gino, F. (2016). "Antagonistic mediators can make resolving disputes easier." *Harvard Business Review*, online.

Girard, R. (1972). *La Violence et le Sacré*. Paris: Grasset.

Girard, R. (1982). *Le Bouc-Émissaire*. Paris: Grasset.

Goldberg, S.B. (2005). "The secrets of successful mediators." *Negotiation Journal*, 21 (3), 365–376.

Goldberg, S.B., Brett, J., and Blohorn-Brenneur, Béatrice, with Rogers, N.H. (2017). *How Mediation Works: Theory, Research and Practice.* Bingley: Emerald.

Goldberg, S.B., Sander, F., Rogers, N.H., and Cole, S.R. (2020). *Dispute Resolution: Negotiation, Mediation, Arbitration, and Other Processes.* New York: Wolters Kluwer.

Goldberg, S.B. and Shaw, M. (2007). "The secrets of successful (and unsuccessful) mediators continued: Studies two and three." *Negotiation Journal*, 23 (4), 393–418.

Hampton, T. (1995). Tendre négociateur': La Rhétorique diplomatique dans les Essais. In *Montaigne et la Rhétorique. Actes du Colloque de St Andrews* (eds. J. O'Brien, M. Quainton, and J. J. Supple). Paris: Honoré Champion.

Jenkins, A., Thuderoz, C., and Colson, A. (2019). Collective Labour Conflicts in France. In: *Mediation in Collective Labour Conflicts* (eds. M. Euwema et al.), 85–98. London: Springer.

Jouanna, J. (1995). "Hippocrate de Cos." *Encyclopedia Universalis*, Corpus 11, Paris, 448.

La Fontaine, J. de. (1668). *Fables* (ed. J. Michie) (1982). London: Penguin Classics.

Lasater, I. and Stiles, J. (2009). "What Is NVC Mediation? A Powerful Model for Healing and Reconciling Conflict," Mediate.com.

Lempereur, A. (1990). Problématologie du droit. In: *L'Homme et la Rhétorique* (ed. A. Lempereur), 213–232. Paris: Méridiens-Klincksieck.

Lempereur, A.(1995). Legal Questioning and Problem-Solving, SJD Dissertation, Cambridge: Harvard Law School.

Lempereur, A. (1998a). "La technique de conciliation: les six étapes du processus." *Gazette du Palais*, 277/279, 36–42.

Lempereur, A. (1998b). "Negotiation and mediation in France: The challenge of skill-based learning and interdisciplinary research in legal education." *Harvard Negotiation Law Review*, 3, 151–174.

Lempereur, A. (1998c). "Bilan du Dialogue national pour l'Europe. Essai sur l'identité européenne des Français." *L'Année européenne*, 254–260.

Lempereur, A. (ed.) (1999a). *Modèles de Médiateur et Médiateur-Modèle.* Paris-Cergy: ESSEC IRÉNÉ.

Lempereur, A. (1999b). "Structuration et rôle du processus dans les compétences de médiations: le cas du notaire-médiateur." *Droit et Patrimoine*, 77, 62–70.

Lempereur, A. (1999c). Mediation in Criminal Law. In: *The Philosophy of Law. An Encyclopedia* (ed. C.B. Gray), 541–543. New York: Garland Publishing.

Lempereur, A. (1999d). Existe-t-il des processus pour faciliter la médiation? In: *L'Avocat et le chef d'entreprise dans la pratique de la médiation commerciale*, 29–36. Paris: CMAP.

Lempereur, A. (2003a). "Les Limites de la négociation de positions." *Gestion 2000*, 4, 69–84.

Lempereur, A. (2003b). "Comment le négociateur peut-il gérer les comportements d'agression?" *Personnel*, 438, 62–65.

Lempereur, A. (2003c). "Le médiateur comme modèle éthique." *Médiations & Sociétés*, 3, 4–7.

Lempereur, A. (2003d). Contractualiser le processus en médiation. In *Art et Techniques de la Médiation* (eds. M. Bourry d'Antin, G. Pluyette, and S. Bensimon), 144–151. Paris: Litec, Juris-Classeur.

Lempereur, A. (2004). "Négociation: au-delà d'une vision déformante de l'autre et de soi." *Revue des Sciences de Gestion*, 39 (208–209), 41–48.

Lempereur, A. (2006). Pour une philosophie de la négociation. In: *La Négociation Post-moderne* (ed. C. Dupont). Paris: Publibook.

Lempereur, A. (2007). La médiation post-conflit. In: *La Médiation. Modes d'Emploi* (eds. by S. Bensimon and A. Lempereur), 153–173. Paris: A2C,.

Lempereur, A. (2009a). "Le questionnement comme philosophie fondatrice de la négociation." *Négociations*, 10, 69–80.

Lempereur, A. (2009b). La réconciliation entre ennemis est possible: voir, communiquer et agir autrement. In: *Introduction à la Psychologie Positive* (ed. J. Lecomte), 271–285. Paris: Dunod.

Lempereur, A. (2011a). Le droit est d'abord le droit des gens. In: *Médiation et Techniques de Négociation Intégrative* (eds. C. Smets-Gary and M. Becker), 9–18. Brussels: Larcier.

Lempereur, A. (2011b). "First things first for negotiators and organizations." *Journal of Decision Making and Negotiations*, online.

Lempereur, A. (2011c). "Faciliter une solution négociée aux conflits." *Revue française de Gestion*, 37 (210), 51–66.

Lempereur, A. (2011d). A la recherche du fondement en négociation: la philosophie du questionnement." In: *Entrer en Négociation. Mélanges en l'Honneur de Christophe Dupont* (ed. A. Colson), 62–77. Brussels: Larcier.

Lempereur, A. (2012a). "Responsible negotiation: Exploring the forest beyond the tree." *Journal of Global Responsibility*, 3 (2), 198–207.

Lempereur, A. (2012b). Le droit est Janus: dualité rhétorique entre conflit et coexistence. In: *Perelman. De la Nouvelle Rhétorique à la Logique Juridique* (eds. B. Frydman and M. Meyer), 99–129. Paris: Presses Universitaires de France.

Lempereur, A. (2014a). "When negative emotions take over negotiations: A responsible framework for analysis and action." *Human Capital Review*, online.

Lempereur, A. (2014b). "Ethique du médiateur." *L'Orient Le Jour*, Beirut, 21 Feb.

Lempereur, A. (2015a). "Médiation responsable." In: *Interdisciplinary Handbook of Conflict Resolution* (eds. P. Cecchi-Diméglio and B. Brenneur), 675–703. Paris: Larcier.

Lempereur, A. (2015b). "Le nœud gordien de la négociation: dénouer des demandes complexes et intenses." *Questions de Management*, 3 (11), 91–98.

Lempereur, A. (2015c). "For responsible negotiation meetings: Concocting a vaccine against Meetingitis," *Decision Making and Negotiations e-Journal*, 6 (12), SSRN.

Lempereur, A. (2016a). "Beyond Negocentrism: Questioning selves, relationships and contexts." *Negotiation Journal*, 32 (4), 335–343.

Lempereur, A. (2016b). "La Médiation responsable pour une équipe unie." *Gestion*, 98–101. HEC Montreal.

Lempereur, A. (2018). "Matrice de négociation: Questionnement pour une relation et une transaction responsables. In: *La Négociation. Techniques, Valeurs et Acteurs* (eds. P. Lardellier, Y. Enrègle, and R. Delaye), 39–64. Paris: L'Harmattan.

Lempereur, A. (2019). "Negotiating peace from inside out: Spinoza as a responsible trump." *Negotiation Journal*, 35 (1), 131–134.

Lempereur, A. (2021). *Puissance de la Médiation. Contre la Guerre Civile.* Paris: Descartes et Cie.

Lempereur, A. and Colson, A. (2004). *Méthode de Négociation.* Paris: Dunod.

Lempereur, A. and Colson, A. (with Pekar, M. ed.) (2010). *The First Move: A Negotiator's Companion.* Chichester: Wiley.

Lempereur, A. and Mnookin, R. (2015). Personnes, problèmes et processus sous tension en négociation et médiation. Gérer la communication, la résolution et la délégation. In: *Interdisciplinary Handbook of Conflict Resolution* (eds. P. Cecchi-Diméglio and B. Brenneur), 419–449. Paris: Larcier.

Lempereur, A. and Pekar, M. (2017). "The distributive knot: Negotiators' responsibility to untie complex demands." *Journal of Business & Industrial Marketing*, 32 (4), 535–540.

Lempereur, A., Pekar, M., and Cecchi-Dimeglio, P. (2015). La valse à trois temps de toute session de négociation ou de médiation: Commencer, continuer et conclure. In: *Interdisciplinary Handbook of Conflict Resolution* (eds. P. Cecchi-Diméglio and B. Brenneur), 387–399. Paris: Larcier.

Lempereur, A., Salzer, J., and Colson, A. (2007). *Méthode de Médiation.* Paris: Dunod.

Lempereur, A. and Scodellaro, M. (2003). "Conflits d'intérêts économiques entre avocats et clients: la question des honoraires." *Recueil Dalloz*, 21 (7118), 1380–1385.

Lempereur, A. and Willer, E. (2016). "The mediator as the eye in the storm: Active perceptions of emotions through the nonverbal." *International Association for Conflict Management*, NY, unpublished manuscript.

Martens, P. (2010). *Jean Carbonnier: Juriste, Sociologue, Historien, Moraliste et Poète.* Paris: Karthala.

Matsuura, M. and Schenk, T. (eds.) (2016). *Joint Fact-Finding in Urban Planning and Environmental Disputes.* New York: Routledge.

Meyer, M. (1995). *Of Problematology. Philosophy, Science and Language*, Chicago: University of Chicago Press.

Meynaud, J. and Schroeder, B. (1961). *La Médiation: Tendances de la Recherche et Bibliographie (1945–1959)*. Amsterdam: Comité International pour la documentation des Sciences Sociales avec l'appui de l'UNESCO.

Miles, E.W. (2013). "Developing strategies for asking questions in negotiation." *Negotiation Journal,* 29 (4), 383–412.

Mitchell, C.R. and Webb, K. (eds.) (1988). *New Approaches to International Mediation*. Westport, CT: Greenwood Press.

Mnookin, R. and Kornhauser, L. (1979). "Bargaining in the shadow of the law: The case of divorce." *Yale Law Journal,* 88, 950–997.

Mnookin, R. and Lempereur, A. (2014). "Pour une communication responsable en négociation: séquencer prises d'écoute et de parole." *Communication & Management,* 11 (2), 28–40.

Moore, C. (2014). *The Mediation Process: Practical Strategies for Resolving Conflict*. San Francisco CA: Jossey-Bass.

Natale, M. and Hantas, M. (1982). "Effect of temporary mood states on selective memory about the self." *Journal of Personality and Social Psychology,* 42 (5), 927–934.

Online Etymology Dictionary (2020). "Mediate." Online: etymonline.com.

Parkinson, L. (2014). *Family Mediation*. Bristol UK: Family Law.

Pequet, A. (1737). *Discours sur l'Art de Négocier* (ed. A. Lempereur). Paris: Nyon Fils; Paris-Cergy: ESSEC IRÉNÉ (2003).

Pohlmann, T. and Thomas, N.M. (2015). "Relearning the art of asking questions." *Harvard Business Review*. Online.

Rawls, J. (1971). *A Theory of Justice*. Cambridge MA: Belknap Press.

Rosenberg, M. (2003). *Nonviolent Communication* (2nd ed.). Encinitis, CA: Puddle Dance Press Book.

Ross, L. (1995). Reactive devaluation in negotiation and conflict resolution. In: *Barriers to Conflict Resolution* (eds. K. Arrow, R. Mnookin, L. Ross, A. Tversky, and R. Wilson). New York: W.W. Norton & Company.

Salzer, J. (2004). Pensez votre conflit en plusieurs dimensions. In: *Réglez vos Conflits* (ed. B. Bertrand Reynaud). Paris: Marabout.

Salzer, J. (2006). "La multi-analyse: entrer dans la complexité des conflits pour pouvoir en sortir." *Revue Génerale de Stratégie*, Agir, 24, 17–24.

Salzer, J. (2007). Pourquoi et comment les mêmes parties bloquées en négociation directe aboutissent à un accord en médiation? In: *Négociation et Transformations du monde* (ed. C. Dupont). Paris: Publibook.

Salzer, J. (2013). Médiation et générosité. In: *La Générosité* (eds. J. Deguise-Roy, E. Letonturier, S. Pflieger, and B. Valade). Paris: L'Harmattan.

Salzer, J. (2015). Sagesse des cultures et cultures en conflit. In: *Souffrances Familiales et Résilience* (eds. R. Coutanceau and R. Bennegadi). Paris: Dunod.

Salzer, J., Fefeu, M., and Saubesty, J.P. (2013). *Guide Pratique de l'Usager de la Médiation: Guerres et Paix dans l'Entreprise.* Paris: Médias et Médiations.

Salzer, J., Simonet, R., and Soudée, R. (2004). *Former à l'Écoute.* Paris: Editions Organisation.

Salzer, J. and Stimec, A. (2015). *La Boîte à Outils de Gestion des Conflits.* Paris: Dunod.

Sartre, J.-P. (1944). *Huis Clos,* suivi de *Les Mouches.* Paris: Gallimard, 2000.

Saunders, J. (2012). "Selective memory bias for self-threatening memories in trait anxiety." *Cognition and Emotion,* 27 (1), 21–36.

Schumpeter, J.A. (1975 [1942]). *Capitalism, Socialism and Democracy.* New York: Harper.

Sebenius, J.K. and Kogan, E.B. (2016). "Henry Kissinger's Negotiation Campaign to End the Vietnam War," *Harvard Busines School Working Papar,* No. 17-053.

Stone, D., Patton, B., and Heen, S. (1999). *Difficult Conversations: How To Discuss What Matters Most.* New York: Penguin.

Susskind, L. and Lempereur, A. (2017). "Chevaliers de la table ronde: Comment les responsables construisent le consensus par la concertation." In *Réinventer le Leadership* (ed. S. Frymousse), 52–69. Paris: Eyrolles.

Ury, W., Brett, J.M., and Goldberg, S.B. (1993). *Getting Disputes Resolved: Design Systems to Cut the Costs of Conflict.* Cambridge: PON Books.

Walker, S., Archbold, C., and Herbst, L. (2002). *Mediating Citizen Complaints Against Police Officers: A Guide For Police and Community Leaders.* U.S.

Department of Justice Office of Community Oriented Policing Services, Washington DC: Government Printing Office.

Watzlawick, P., Beavin Bavelas, J., and Jackson, D. (1967). *Pragmatics of Human Communication: A Study of Interactional Patterns, Pathologies and Paradoxes*. New York: Norton and Company, 2014.

Weber, M. (1919). Politics as a vocation. In: *From Max Weber: Essays in Sociology* (eds. H.H. Gerth and C.W. Mills), 1967. London: Routledge & Kegan Paul.

White, M. and Epston, D. (1992). *Experience, Contradiction, Narrative and Imagination*. Adelaide: Dulwich Centre.

Wilmot, W. and Yarbrough, E. (1996). *Artful Mediation, Constructive Conflict at Work*. Boulder: Cairns.

Winslade, J. and Monk, G.D. (2000). *Narrative Mediation: A New Approach to Conflict Resolution*. San Francisco: Jossey-Bass.

Wolpe, H., McDonald, S., Nindorera, E., McClintock, L., and Lempereur, A. (2004). "Rebuilding peace and state capacity in war-torn Burundi." *The Round Table*, 93 (375), 457–467.

ABOUT THE AUTHORS

Alain Lempereur is a mediator in conflicts and crises and has established responsible mediation and negotiation programs worldwide for over 25 years. He is the Alan B. Slifka Chair Professor and Director of the Conflict Resolution and Coexistence Program at Brandeis University. He is an affiliate faculty and executive committee member of the Program on Negotiation (PON) at Harvard Law School, where he edits the *PON Negotiation Briefings* and delivers the PON Global Seminar. He also teaches humanitarian negotiation and mediation as a core faculty of the Harvard Humanitarian Initiative. He has authored, co-authored, or edited over two dozen books and 150 articles, chapters, and reports in 15 languages. He has consulted in 70 countries for 35 international or nongovernmental organizations (EU, ICRC, MSF, OECD, UNITAR, WHO, WWF etc.), 23 governments, and 50 global corporations (Airbus, The BCG, Co-Dev, Faurecia, McKinsey, Sanofi-Pasteur etc.). He founded and, over 15 years, developed ESSEC IRENE, as well as *Negotiators of the World* to mediate among leaders in Burundi and the Democratic Republic of the Congo. As a member of the UN mediators' network, he facilitated stakeholders' meetings for the *International Dialogue on Peacebuilding and Statebuilding*, and among Israelis and Palestinians for *Forward Thinking* and the *Negotiation Strategies Institute*.

Jacques Salzer is a world expert in mediation. He has 35 years of research and experience in conflict management and has mediated over 80 conflicts. He is affiliated with the University of Paris-Dauphine and co-authored 14 books. He has co-created multiple mediation training programs in other universities and institutes in Africa, America, and Europe. For example, he trained mediators in Haiti and the Ivory Coast. He has been involved as a mediator or researcher in most conflict fields, promoting family, neighborhood, school, work, corporate, environmental, or political mediation. He has facilitated dialogues in many work places, but also between Israeli and Palestinian citizens. He prepared peace talks in Mali between the government and opposition groups from the north. Most recently, he has mediated post-war conflicts in various communities from Northern Iraq.

Aurélien Colson is Professor of political science at ESSEC Business School and has been the Director of the Institute for Research & Education on Negotiation (IRENE Paris, Singapore & Brussels) since 2008. His books have appeared in 15 languages. His research on international mediation and negotiation has been published in peer-reviewed journals. He has served as adviser to the French prime minister (1998–2002). He has run negotiation and mediation missions in over 40 countries, including for the European Union, the French Ministry of Foreign Affairs, and UN agencies. He has contributed to post-conflict mediation efforts, notably in Africa, and has been elected twice by leading NGOs to the steering committee of the European Peacebuilding Liaison Office. He served on the international advisory board of the European Institute of Peace. From 2012 until the present, the European Union asked him to lead the governance team of the Centres of Excellence for CBRN Risk Mitigation, a cooperation and security partnership bringing together 62 countries. He is regularly invited to share insights and best practices on mediation with a wide range of business leaders and senior public officials. Since 2014 he has been elected to a local city council, which involves a lot of hands-on mediation skills.

Michele Pekar is Associate Fellow at the Saïd Business School, University of Oxford, where she teaches negotiation preparation and facilitation on the Oxford Programme of Negotiation. She is Executive Director and Founding Partner of Co-Dev, Inc., a firm specializing in negotiation, mediation, facilitation, and leadership. She has 25 years of experience in negotiation and mediation as a practitioner, senior trainer, and coach in more than 20 countries and has delivered negotiation, mediation, and leadership training to corporate executives, diplomats at the United Nations (Geneva and Vienna), and business and engineering graduate students in Europe (College of Europe, ENPC, ESSEC, Kedge Business School, Mannheim

Business School, University of Corsica etc.). She has worked in fundraising at Harvard University. She has also negotiated worldwide strategic alliances and partnerships for top European business schools. She was involved in US politics for the State of Wisconsin. She is Editor of *The First Move: A Negotiator's Companion* (Wiley 2010) and in her spare time writes fiction and poetry.

Eugene B. Kogan is a negotiation strategist who enables senior executives globally to achieve outcomes in high-impact environments. He teaches about power dynamics and advanced negotiations at Harvard Division of Continuing Education's Professional Development Programs and conducts research on crisis leadership at Harvard Business School. He has served as the Research and Executive Director of Harvard's American Secretaries of State Project, which aimed to crystallize negotiation and leadership lessons from 50 years of diplomacy by all living US Secretaries of State since Henry Kissinger. He received the Howard Raiffa Award from the Program on Negotiation at Harvard Law School for his doctoral dissertation on nuclear negotiations, and has given guest lectures to business, public policy, and military leaders at Harvard Kennedy School, Harvard Graduate School of Education, Brandeis, Sciences Po Paris School of International Affairs, Vienna's Executive Academy, and Salzburg Business School.

DETAILED TABLE OF CONTENTS

INDEX